Virgil

BLACKWELL INTRODUCTIONS TO THE CLASSICAL WORLD

This series will provide concise introductions to classical culture in the broadest sense. Written by the most distinguished scholars in the field, these books survey key authors, periods and topics for students and scholars alike.

Published

Greek Tragedy
Nancy Sorkin Rabinowitz

Roman Satire
Daniel Hooley

Ancient History
Charles W. Hedrick, Jr.

Homer, second edition
Barry B. Powell

Classical Literature
Richard Rutherford

Ancient Rhetoric and Oratory
Thomas Habinek

Ancient Epic
Katherine Callen King

Catullus
Julia Haig Gaisser

Virgil
R. Alden Smith

Ovid
Katharina Volk

In Preparation

Roman Historiography
Andreas Mehl, translated by Hans-Friedrich Mueller

Virgil

R. Alden Smith

WILEY-BLACKWELL

A John Wiley & Sons, Ltd., Publication

This edition first published 2011
© 2011 R. Alden Smith

Blackwell Publishing was acquired by John Wiley & Sons in February 2007. Blackwell's publishing program has been merged with Wiley's global Scientific, Technical, and Medical business to form Wiley-Blackwell.

Registered Office
John Wiley & Sons Ltd, The Atrium, Southern Gate, Chichester, West Sussex, PO19 8SQ, United Kingdom

Editorial Offices
350 Main Street, Malden, MA 02148-5020, USA
9600 Garsington Road, Oxford, OX4 2DQ, UK
The Atrium, Southern Gate, Chichester, West Sussex, PO19 8SQ, UK

For details of our global editorial offices, for customer services, and for information about how to apply for permission to reuse the copyright material in this book please see our website at www.wiley.com/wiley-blackwell.

The right of R. Alden Smith to be identified as the author of this work has been asserted in accordance with the UK Copyright, Designs and Patents Act 1988.

Wiley also publishes its books in a variety of electronic formats. Some content that appears in print may not be available in electronic books.

Designations used by companies to distinguish their products are often claimed as trademarks. All brand names and product names used in this book are trade names, service marks, trademarks or registered trademarks of their respective owners. The publisher is not associated with any product or vendor mentioned in this book. This publication is designed to provide accurate and authoritative information in regard to the subject matter covered. It is sold on the understanding that the publisher is not engaged in rendering professional services. If professional advice or other expert assistance is required, the services of a competent professional should be sought.

Library of Congress Cataloging-in-Publication Data

Smith, Alden.
   Virgil / R. Alden Smith.
      p. cm. – (Blackwell introductions to the classical world)
   Includes bibliographical references and index.
   ISBN 978-1-4051-5949-4
   1. Virgil–Criticism and interpretation.   2. Virgil–Technique.   3. Virgil–Influence.
I. Title.
   PA6825.S633 2011
   871'.01–dc22
                              2010017708

A catalogue record for this book is available from the British Library.

Set in 10.5/13pt Galliard by Toppan Best-set Premedia Limited
Printed and bound in Malaysia by Vivar Printing Sdn Bhd

1   2011

unus liber tantis liberis
Katie, Harry, Ben, Rachel, Bayush, Sileshi, Tarikwa

Contents

Figures

Preface

Virgil is to ancient literature what Michelangelo is to Renaissance art; remove the adjectives, and the sentence may still be true. I am privileged to be one of those who study Virgil and to have come to know him, at least the Virgil who is his text.

For this project I owe a great measure of debt to my friends and colleagues. Many have read portions or all of this manuscript. I sincerely thank my colleague Julia Hejduk, who offered feedback, challenged ideas, checked translations—all of it *summa cum caritate*. To Jeff Hunt, whose comments were truly invaluable, I owe more that I can say. Jenny, his wife, also read much of the manuscript, improving it in both style and substance. Kenneth Jones and Richard Durán also offered welcome feedback on select chapters. I thank, too, Antony Augoustakis, Simon Burris, Susan Colón, Tommye Lou Davis, Jeff Fish, Brent Froberg, Daniel Hanchey, Tim Heckenlively, David Jeffrey, Steven Jones, Michael Sloan, and Amy Vail for their encouragement and informal exchange of ideas. I am also grateful to Darin Davis, for allowing me to present some of my ideas to Baylor's Crane Scholars. Thelma Mathews is deserving of my deepest gratitude for performing endless tasks on my behalf. I thank Paulette Edwards for extricating me from much administrative paperwork, and Doris Kelly for taming my schedule.

I received much aid from other colleagues and friends. Gareth Williams received me warmly at Columbia University, where much of this book was written, securing me access to Butler Library. I also thank Joe Farrell who assisted me logistically in Philadelphia when I researched in Penn's Van Pelt Library; there I met Dan Traister, Curator of Research Services in the Rare Book & Manuscript Library. I am grateful to him (and to my Baylor colleague, David White, who introduced us) for assistance in my research on manuscripts; Nico Knauer's advice on this topic was also valuable.

Professor Mario Geymonat (Venice) offered both welcome guidance on manuscripts and other topics. I thank Monsignor Piazzi of Verona's Biblioteca Capitolare for special assistance. For important aspects of my research in Italy I also thank *ex corde* Professor Gianni Profita and Dr Maurizio Fallace, Direttore Generale per i Beni Librari. Professors Peter Arzt-Grabner and Gerhard Petersmann were also very supportive, permitting me the opportunity to present some of my ideas at the University of Salzburg. I thank also Eleanor Stump of St. Louis University for library access and hospitality, and Karl Galinsky and David Armstrong for feedback on a lecture presented at the University of Texas.

For feedback on various parts of the manuscript, I am particularly grateful to Neil Coffee, Craig Kallendorf, Richard Thomas, and John Van Sickle. Sophia Papaiannou, too, offered many thoughtful comments. I cannot possibly mention all those who have been helpful with various bits of advice, but I must mention Giancarlo Abbamonte, Greg Daugherty, Patricia Johnston, Philip Lockhart, Michèle Lowrie, Piergiacomo Petrioli, Fabio Stock, and Katharina Volk; at Moody Library, Kenneth Carriveau and Janet Sheets. For a special matter in Chicago, I thank also Peter Knox and Ujival Vyas. As I began this project, it was an honor to serve as president of the Virgilian Society. I profited much from rich conversations with the late Sandy McKay. I thank, too, Vonnie Sullivan for her invaluable assistance and hospitality, and Bruce Jaffie and Lettie Teague for dinners in New York and various matters concerning wine.

My students at Baylor eagerly assisted with this project. I particularly thank my personal assistants T. J. McLemore, Kathleen Miller, Heather Outland, and Faith Wardlaw, as well as Anne Langhorne, Stephen Margheim, Joe Muller, Holly Murphy, and Anna Sitz. My 2008 Virgil class also offered insights: Jessie Carrothers, Sam and Ashely Cole, Ashley Crooks, Noelle Jacot, Gideon Jeffrey, Jason Milam, Clint Pechacek, William Priest, Harry Smith, and Mary Claire Russell, who deserves special mention, for skillfully rendering the illustrations.

I express my appreciation to the Baylor's sabbatical and research committees and, in particular, to Vice Provost Truell Hyde and his staff, as well as my supportive chair, John Thorburn. I owe much to my deans Tom Hibbs (Honors College) and Lee Nordt (Arts and Sciences), as well as Provost Elizabeth Davis and President David Garland.

At Wiley-Blackwell, I thank Sophie Gibson, Haze Humbert, Graeme Leonard, and Galen Smith, as well as anonymous reviewers who offered many useful criticisms. Finally, I wish to express deepest gratitude to my wife, Diane, for her boundless help and grace, and to my courageous children for patience and steadfastness. I dedicate this book them.

Note on Abbreviations

All abbreviations in this book are consonant with those of *L'Année Philologique*.

I

Generalizing about Virgil: Dialogue, Wisdom, Mission

And behold I hear a voice ... "pick it up and read it!"
Augustine (*Confessions* 8.12)

Literary code and genre dictate the nature of the tacit communication between the poet and the audience.
Charles Segal (from his introduction to Conte's
The Rhetoric of Imitation, 9)

Virgil wrote in code. The word "code," as it occurs in the citation above, refers to poetic style and to the method by which a poet conveys meaning. Poetry is encoded through certain generic associations and allusive connections. Though originally composed for a scroll, Virgil's poems have been preserved for us in the form of a book known as a "codex," the shape of a book that we still use today. The Latin word *codex* (i.e., *caudex*, originally "bark," later "book") is the origin of the English words code and codex. The epic code that the reader confronts when reading Virgil was itself recoded when it was transferred from the ancient scrolls to codex.

Virgil composed three major poetic works, each in dactylic hexameters under the generic term *epos* (Greek "word"). Virgil's works can thus be classified as three manifestations of epic code. Virgil's earliest work, the *Eclogues*, is bucolic, to all appearances concerning the world of herdsmen; his second, the *Georgics*, is didactic, ostensibly on farming; his grand narrative, the *Aeneid*, is heroic. These distinctions within the code belonging to *epos* represent the first signposts on our journey through Virgil's poetry.

Eclogue = Bucolic   Georgics = didactic

Of Codes and Codices

To decipher Virgil's code, the reader must begin by accessing the codex in its modern book form. The modern form is derived from ancient and medieval sources and such a history will be explored in the sixth chapter of this book. For the moment, however, let us consider one such manuscript as contributing to the history of Virgil's text.

In the sixteenth century, an important manuscript came into the hands of Francesco I de' Medici, and thus it came to be called Codex Mediceus. Francesco moved it from Rome to the seat of Medicean influence, Florence. Housed in the Biblioteca Medicea Laurenziana, this antique codex preserves emendations added in red ink by the fifteenth-century philologist Julius Pomponius Laetus (in Italian, Pomponio Leto).[1] Prior to Leto, however, an early owner and editor of the manuscript had added a subscription in a tiny font at the end of the *Eclogues*, just before the opening of the *Georgics* (Figure 1.1):

> Turcius Rufius Apronianus Asterius v(ir) c(larissimus) et inl(ustris)
>   ex comite domest(icorum) protect(orum) ex com(ite) priv(atarum)
>   largit(ionum)
> ex praef(ecto) urbi patricius et consul ordin(arius) legi et distincxi
>   codicem fratris Macharii v(iri) c(larissimi)
> non mei fiducia set eius cui si et ad omnia sum devotus arbitrio
>   XI Kal. Mai(as) Romae.[2]
> (I, Turcius Rufius Apronianus Asterius, right honorable former member of the protectors of the [imperial] house and former member of private distributors of wealth ‖ and former prefect of the city, patrician and duly elected consul, read and punctuated this codex of my right honorable brother [viz. "friend"] Macharius, ‖ not because of any confidence in myself but because of my confidence in him, to whomsoever [i.e., my future reader?] I have also in every respect been devoted with regard to my judgment [i.e., my job of editing]; [inscribed] on April 21 at Rome.)

This subscription provides an important dating marker known as a *terminus ante quem*.[3] Turcius Rufius Apronianus Asterius pored over the manuscript carefully, and his mysterious words – in the above translation the phrase "to whomsoever" is especially curious – offer tantalizing details. Like Leto years later, Apronianus would presumably have been doing his editing based on an earlier version that was one step closer to Virgil's autograph (original manuscript). Apronianus' encoding of the text is not simply the inclusion of this dedication but also his emendations and punctuation.

What is Apronianus trying to tell posterity in this subscription? First, he is attempting to say that, though he had earned the highest traditional

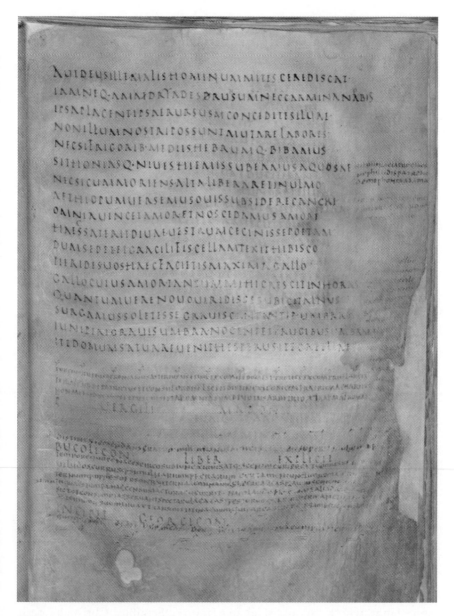

Figure 1.1. Virgil, Codex Mediceus (Ms. Plut. 39.1, cc. 8r, 9r). Used by permission of the Biblioteca Nazionale Centrale, Florence.

Roman office, he was not a mere politician but was one who had a deep appreciation for Virgil and has painstakingly emended the text. That he had done so during his consulship – Rome's high office instituted by Lucius Iunius Brutus in 509 BC – is obviously significant, as is the fact that he makes this subscription on April 21, the date of the annual Parilia festival, which was recognized as the birthday of Rome. The year AD 494 would have dated nearly one thousand years from the foundation of the Roman Republic. Thus, when Apronianus notes that he was a *consul ordinarius* (entering the office "on the appointed day" and thus, "duly elected"), he ties himself to the ancient, traditional office. The reference to the Parilia acknowledges Rome's pre-Christian past, as Pales was a pagan deity connected with pastures. This addendum fittingly comes after the *Eclogues* and before the *Georgics,* both of which treat flocks.[4] With this subscription, he accomplishes, then, a great deal, affirming the abiding value of ancient Rome's greatest poet.

To emphasize his connection with traditional Roman values, Apronianus further states that he was the sponsor of traditional pagan Roman games. Yet we also know him as an editor of Christian devotional poetry. His family had been, since the time of Constantine, connected to the ruling class. A certain L. Turcius Apronianus held an urban prefecture, and his son replicated this achievement in 362. The fourth-century historian Ammianus (23.1.4) tells us that one of these was also a senatorial legate in Antioch under the emperor Julian.

Material evidence enhances our understanding of the family: two statue bases, found in the Campus Martius, held representations of Apronianus and his wife; these images may have come from their home there. The other side of the family lived on the Esquiline. Possibly to protect their wealth from the Gothic invasion of 410, some family member hastily buried heirlooms near the house. This treasure, which includes objects that show pagan influence, certainly belonged to the same family as our manuscript inscriber. Cameron concludes that the family consisted of both pagan and Christian members; the Christian branch was likely to have intermarried with non-Christians.[5]

Such a reconstruction of this family's religious leanings suits our Apronianus, who both published an edition of Sedulius' Christian poetic work *Carmen Paschale* and at the same time was an *aficionado* of Virgil, punctuating the manuscript that he obtained from his "brother" Macharius.[6] When one is reading "Virgil," one is reading a collated text indebted to editors such as Apronianus.

↳ interesting understanding

The coexistence of his family's two cultural backgrounds – a family mosaic perhaps not so uncommon among contemporary aristocrats – suggests a workable interaction of pagan and Christian elements. Given his Christian affiliation, Apronianus' subscription is important to the Virgilian tradition because that tradition has now become a blend of two religious cultures and his subscription is literally a Christian addendum to a long pagan tradition. His dedication to Virgil's future readership shows his awareness of his transmission of Virgil in this codex, bearing witness to Apronianus not only as a significant editor but also as an important early reader of the text. Apronianus has thus encoded the text in such a way as to ensure that his manuscript of Virgil would be a part of the future, even if that should be a Christian future. In a sense, he buried in the pages of this manuscript an autobiographical nugget for posterity, as his forebear had buried the family treasure on the Esquiline.

Code of Readership

The reader who picks up a book and reads it opens a dialogue with the codex and, ultimately, with the code itself. Thus, the reader begins to interact with the text and its code; this interaction or negotiation with the text is "coded" because the reader is establishing his or her own code of readership while encountering Virgil's epic code. The notion of a code moves in both directions: what we are calling epic code moves from the text to the reader, while what we are calling the code of readership represents the reader's negotiation with the text. Such negotiation is assisted by the author, who "establishes the competence of the Model Reader, that is, the author constructs the addressee and motivates the text in order to do so. The text institutes strategic cooperation and regulates it."[7] The greater the appreciation that any reader has of the tradition, the closer he or she approximates the Model Reader and becomes equipped to negotiate the business of reading the text.

Though we shall never know fully what future reader Apronianus envisioned or what kind of reader Virgil had in mind, we can nevertheless establish a few characteristics for a Model Reader of any age. First, as any reader begins to approximate a Model Reader, he or she will increasingly acknowledge that a wider tradition informs Virgil's text and, to the extent that he or she is able, begin to embrace that tradition. For example, the more knowledgeable the reader is of Homer, the deeper that reader's understanding of the *Aeneid* will become. The Model Reader understands that the later author can best be understood in light of the earlier.

The second criterion for the Model Reader is some knowledge of the cultural milieu of Virgil's lifetime. While the attribution of a rigid political agenda to Virgil is unproductive, one cannot hide from the fact that Virgil was cognizant of his own relevance within the poetic tradition and was aware that the Roman world was in the midst of a major transition.

Thirdly, the Model Reader must have respect for the text's authorial voice. Apronianus seems to have shown such respect in dedicating his careful editorial work "in every respect" to his future reader or, possibly, God himself;[8] he recognizes the importance of his place within a tradition that preserves Virgil's authorial voice. All the discrepancies within the manuscripts notwithstanding – even those that may have been unwittingly introduced by Apronianus – the text known as "Virgil" still emerges, which the Model Reader seeks to understand in view of the tradition, in its historical context, and with respect for the integrity of the authorial voice. Conscientious readership does not preclude the reader's response but qualifies it: the Model Reader engages in honest negotiation with the text.

Poetic Craft

Long before Virgil began his literary production in the late 40s BC, versifying was a matter of poetic craftsmanship. The etymology of the Latin word *poeta*, descended from a Greek word meaning "make" (*poieo*), implies such fashioning. The other Latin word for poet, *uates*, means "seer" or "prophet," a metaphorical description that embodies poetic inspiration. Inspired by the Muses, the Roman poet opens a dialogue with his predecessors through allusion and cross-pollination of genres. This was especially true in Virgil's time: the skilled poet engaged his predecessors through a process of imitation, emulation, and interpretation.[9]

Virgilian allusion is generally consistent with the practice of poetic reference called Alexandrian, developed in the Hellenistic period (323–327 BC) and characterized by emulative playfulness.[10] Before that period, allusion had been, generally speaking, more imitative than emulative. The dictum that the plays of Aeschylus were "scraps from Homer's banquet" is an old one, attributed to Aeschylus himself by third-century author Athenaeus (*Deipnosophistae* 8.347e). Aeschylus does not so much emulate

✱Alexandrian Reference✱

Homer as avail himself of Homeric material, often expanding it. In the Hellenistic period something different begins to happen, as allusion effects a learned game, anticipating a reader with a code-breaking mentality. Alexandrian reference is not necessarily meant to be recognized immediately, for such allusive encoding is written for knowledgeable insiders or intended for discovery on a second or third reading.[11] Now, commentary becomes erudite, response somewhat cryptic, and allusion often opaque, intended for readers "in the know." To see where Virgil falls in this allusive spectrum, let us, before turning to his text, consider two examples outside his corpus. We shall see that Virgil's Alexandrian style encompasses the kind of allusion seen in Greek poets such as Pindar.

Nearly half a millennium before Virgil, Pindar, the eminent poet of Boeotian Thebes, composed *Olympian* 14 to celebrate the Olympic victory of Asopichos, son of a deceased Boeotian nobleman. This poem is addressed to the Graces, the chief goddesses of the Boeotian city Orchomenos:

> O Graces of Orchomenos, guardians of the ancient race of the Minyai, hear me when I pray. For through you all pleasant and sweet things are produced for mortals, if there is anyone wise, beautiful and famous. (14.4–7)

In a manner consistent with the classical form of allusion in his day, Pindar creates a communal mood for this poem by weaving into his text references to Hesiod, his Boeotian predecessor who had lived more than a century before him, specifically echoing Hesiod's description of the Graces (*Theogony* 63–74).

Pindar uses the poetic character Echo to report to Kleodamos in the Underworld the positive developments regarding Asopichos:

> In Lydian style of lays I have come, singing of Asopichos,
> for your sake Aglaia, who in the Minyan land is victorious in
>   Olympian games.
> Go, Echo, to the dark-walled abode of Persephone,
> Bringing to his father the fair announcement,
> so that when you see Kleodamos you may tell him of his son,
> how in the famous vale of Pisa he crowned his hair with
>   the glorious contests' garlands. (14.17–24)

Echo metaphorically embodies the allusion to Hesiod, for Pindar "echoes" Hesiod. Pindar's fame preserves Hesiod's memory, just as Asopichos' victory preserves his father's good name in Boeotia. The local flavor of this ode also helps to connect Asopichos and Kleodamos, his deceased father, with that of Pindar and his poetic father-figure, Hesiod. Though Pindar's allusion to Hesiod and his use of it could be said to anticipate Alexandrian practice, it is more general and, if somewhat intricate, not meant chiefly for readers in the know.[12]

A similar example can be seen in Euripides, who, about a third of the way through the *Medea*, refers to the celebrated bard Orpheus. Jason states that he would rather enjoy personal fame than great wealth or even "the capacity to sing songs sweeter than those of Orpheus" (543). Orpheus is the prototypical singer and *exemplum* of the faithful husband; his name in the mouth of Jason is thus incongruous and stinging, representative of Euripides' ironic method.[13]

Such early references, though adroit, are not as sophisticated as Alexandrian allusion. By the beginning of the Roman imperial period, the practice of allusion, having passed through the Alexandrian filter, surpasses even Jason's reference to Orpheus in Euripides' *Medea* or Pindar's expression of Boeotian loyalty to Hesiod in *Olympian* 14. Let us consider how it does so through two further examples.

The end of the first *Georgic* includes an interesting reference to the river Euphrates, which is based on a similar description of the Assyrian river in Callimachus:

> I was singing of these things ... while great Caesar thunders in war along the deep Euphrates and as victor gives laws throughout the willing nations and builds a road to Olympus. At that time sweet Parthenope was nursing me, Virgil, when I was flourishing in the pursuits of inglorious leisure. (1.559–64)

In this context, as Clauss has noted, the proximity of war (561) and peace (564) suggests that, after the battle of Actium, Virgil is stating that he "can avail himself of *ignobile otium*, the peace and leisure needed for non-military, georgic topics."[14] A few years earlier, Scodel and Thomas had noted that a reference to the Euphrates coming near the end of a book of Virgil is not a one-time occurrence, connecting the passages to Callimachus:

> Three times in his works Virgil mentions the Euphrates. At *Geo.* 1.509 the river threatens war; at *Geo.* 4.561 Octavian thunders there; at *Aen.* 8.726 the river, after Actium, is no longer threatening. Each of these references appears in the sixth line from the end of its respective book. This pattern is no coincidence: Virgil alludes to the Ἀσσυρίου ποταμοῖο μέγας ῥόος

[Assyrian River's great flood] of Callimachus Hymn 2.108 – the sixth line from the close. The Callimachean river is identified with the Euphrates by the scholiast, and the programmatic passage is a natural object for such delicate allusion.[15]

Several scholars have gone further, from Farrell's view that such an allusion symbolizes Virgil's allegiance to Callimachean principles to Jenkyns' reading it as chiefly a way of highlighting Octavian's ability to put aside the panic associated with problems in the east.[16]

As Scodel and Thomas note, Virgil also places a reference to the Euphrates precisely six lines from the end of *Aeneid* 8, where Aeneas' shield reveals the future glory of Rome. A reference to the Euphrates in such a context may suggest the extent of Augustus' military victories and the consequent political settlement; but it also evidences, via the allusion to Callimachus, Virgil's allegiance to Alexandrian poetic principles.[17] *"so delicate"*

Alexandrian allusion, so delicate that it takes into account precise verbal position, is also a feature of other Augustan poets. Ovid does something similar when, in the *Metamorphoses,* he cites *Aeneid* 10.475 in the exact same book at precisely the same verse number; both passages refer to the drawing of sword from a sheath. In the Ovidian context, the reference to the drawing of the sword acts as a symbol for the end of a perverse sexual liaison, whereas in the *Aeneid* it is a true martial reference. Ovid's allusion depends upon a reader who is erudite and attentive enough to notice – though not necessarily on a first reading – the striking precision of the citation. The reader must be sufficiently knowledgeable to recognize the playful way a heroic battlefield description is now applied in an unheroic moment.[18]

The two examples from Greek literature, cited above, come many years before Virgil; that of Ovid occurs only a quarter century after the *Aeneid.* Each can be seen as generally representative of the way allusion can function. The first two connect the new text with an earlier author or poetic corpus in a way that contextualizes the reference within the poetic tradition. The example from Virgil, however, demonstrates how an allusion can have a double function – referring both to political settlement and serving as a display of Alexandrian poetic principles – while that of Ovid shows how an author can playfully rival a predecessor, redeploying imagery and even citing text at precisely the same line number in a vastly different way.

★ double function ★

Two years after his and Scodel's brief but important contribution about the Euphrates, Thomas analyzed the various ways that Virgilian reference functions in the *Georgics*, establishing roughly seven categories of the poet's allusive capacity, from replication to highly complex double-author references. All such references represent the poet's conversing with a poetic forebear, whether imitating, correcting, conflating, or creating a window through one author to another.[19] Virgil's penchant for Alexandrian allusion does not preclude his capacity to engage in the more "classic" style of allusion seen in Pindar or Euripides. Virgil imitates in the classical style while also alluding in the Alexandrian manner. His signal contribution to Roman heroic epic is that he does so not merely for poetic showmanship but to engage universal human issues.[20]

Thematic Contours

Virgil employs this diversity of style to shape three major themes in his corpus. The first is that of dialogue, which manifests itself both externally in terms of allusion and internally through the balancing of differing points of view or dualistic ideas within the text, a feature that many years ago Adam Parry well characterized as Virgil's "two voices."[21]

The metaphor of competing voices is sometimes interpreted as "a touch of ambivalence."[22] This ambivalence might be better viewed as an aspect of Virgil's dualistic ebb and flow. In *Eclogue* 1, for example, Virgil presents two distinctly different points of view in his characters Meliboeus and Tityrus. A contrast between the soon-to-be-born child in *Eclogue* 4 and the recently deceased yet soon-to-be-deified Daphnis of *Eclogue* 5 closes the first half of Virgil's first poetry book. In the eighth *Eclogue*, the poet's persona wishes to but cannot write a tribute to his patron. The poetic landscape of the *Eclogues* is an amalgam of, and to some extent a dialogue between, east and west (Arcadia and Italy), city and countryside, hope and despair.

Such dualism is not confined to the *Eclogues*. The *labor improbus* (wicked work) of the farmer of the *Georgics* both contrasts with and complements *durus labor* (hard work) that produces the joy of the harvest: they are different experiences of the same world, not discursive constructs. In the *Aeneid*, Aeneas is both a (mostly) steadfast lover of his future country and a failed lover of Dido; he is devoted to his mission yet distracted from it; in book 11 he desires the peace requested by an embassy but in that same book he becomes the merciless avenger; at the *Aeneid*'s close he hesitates, but then kills furiously. The themes of Virgil's dualism relate to devotion, loyalty, courage, or love and by composing in this way, Virgil works through issues in his corpus by giving the impression of a dialogue.

Virgil's two voices are set in opposition, but rarely in such a way that coexistence is not possible. Such dualism moves beyond the pre-Socratic notion of Pythagorean opposites toward dialogue, with the ultimate goal being the communication of wisdom, not merely conflict. In this sense, Virgil is much more Socratic (and Platonic) than Pythagorean. Mediation of the opposites comes from the poetic persona's voice of wisdom.[23]

The second thematic contour of Virgil's poetic production is just such wisdom. All of his poems have a didactic function, and none is intended merely to be entertainment or simply to sustain literary tradition. Obviously dialogue, such as that of the *Eclogues*, is a means of communicating wisdom, as one can see in Platonic dialogues or the contrasting features of Pythagorean philosophy. Yet Virgil's wisdom book is not the *Eclogues* but the *Georgics*. While there are plenty of dialogic moments in the *Georgics* – for example, the pessimistic endings of books 1 and 3 over and against the more optimistic conclusions of 2 and 4 – Virgil conveys wisdom in the *Georgics* in a different way, infusing it through gnomic dictums and various familial and communal moments in the farmer's life. The wisdom of the *Georgics* encompasses every aspect of human existence; as is often noted, the *Georgics* is not so much about husbandry as about life.[24]

The third way that Virgil shapes his work thematically is by imbuing it with a sense of mission. One could argue that the mission of the *Eclogues* is to convey to a Roman audience through a new genre glimpses of human joy in the midst of political unrest; that of the *Georgics* is consideration of work, life, death, and regeneration. The *Aeneid*, however, embodies mission: its central character's destiny is the reestablishment of Troy as Rome. The *Aeneid* is thus not merely a well-told part of an epic cycle such as the *Iliad* or the *Odyssey*, or even a crafted tale of heroes and heroic deeds, like the *Argonautica*. It is a teleological epic, justifying and explaining a new nation's birth out of another's tragic collapse. In it Virgil creates a hero who, if less than perfect, nevertheless shows nobility and bravery.

Each of Virgil's works shares the themes discussed above: internal and external dialogue, soil-bound wisdom, and a sense of mission. While the *Eclogues* emphasize the first of these traits, the *Georgics* the second, and the *Aeneid* the third, each work also encompasses all three. To advance these major themes, Virgil inserts himself through deft allusions into a preexisting literary tradition, adapting and redefining the epic code. Let us look briefly at some of the figures who formed the literary tradition he inherited.

Poetic Models

The following abbreviated collection of sources is merely suggestive of Virgil's principal debts to a vast tradition, of which several names have already occurred in this book. While all were important allusive models, in the Alexandrian sense, some were far more important than others in the classic sense of allusion. Though the list is roughly chronological, coincidentally we begin with perhaps the most important figure.

The significance to Virgil of **Homer**, whose *floruit* was ca. 750 BC, is immeasurable. Both the *Iliad* and the *Odyssey* provided models of imitation for the *Aeneid*, in particular, and Homer was important to Virgil's other work. As Halperin has rightly observed about Virgil's use of traditional material, "allusions to the *Odyssey* … provide a source of thematic continuity within the genre of epos which help to define the literary genealogy of bucolic poetry."[25]

Hesiod (ca. 730–ca. 670 BC) also provided a source for Virgil. Hesiod's *Works and Days* (sometimes abbreviated by the first Greek word of its title as *Erga*) was a model for the *Georgics*, while his short epic *Theogony* also furnished Virgil with material for each of his works. Hesiod was the first to claim to have encountered the Muses on Mount Helicon (*Theogony* 22–35), where he portrays himself being commissioned by them, a scene important to Callimachus and one that also recurs in the *Eclogues* (6.69–73).

 The impact of **Greek tragedy** on Virgil is a topic that has only recently begun to be explored in a comprehensive way in Virgilian scholarship. We have already considered one example from Euripides, an influence that extends through Virgil's psychological portraiture of characters such as Dido. It would be remiss not to mention, too, the impact of Sophocles on Virgil's consideration of universal human issues or of Aeschylus vis-à-vis questions concerning suffering and divine purpose.

While Platonic dialogues may have had a general influence on Virgil's dialogic style, the chief source of inspiration for the *Eclogues* was certainly the poet **Theocritus** (ca. 300–ca. 260 BC), who hailed from Sicily. Theocritus wrote pastoral *Idylls*, mimes (short dramatic performances), hymns, epithalamia (wedding poems), and epyllia (short epics, of which

Eclogues = Theocritus

only fragments survive). Some of the *Idylls* are dialogues, while others are lyric monologues; others have elements of choral lyric, albeit in hexameters. Theocritus' form, style, imagery and characters unmistakably resonate with Virgil's own.

Just as Theocritus was an important source for Virgil's bucolic poems, so for Virgil's didactic work was **Nicander**, whose *floruit* was in the second century BC. Among Nicander's didactic works was his own *Georgika*, which provided Virgil with theme and title for his *Georgics*. While very little remains of Nicander's poem, Geymonat demonstrates the degree of Virgilian sophistication in an allusion to Nicander, for Virgil plays upon a phrase from Nicander at *Georgic* 1.178; beyond such a slender observation, however, we can only guess how Virgil drew on his work.[26]

More important, without doubt, was **Callimachus** (ca. 305–ca. 240 BC), who hailed from Cyrene but later moved to Alexandria where he compiled numerous scholarly works in that city's famous library, including *Pinakes*, a learned review of the library's holdings. Callimachus' best-known poem, the *Aetia* ("Causes"), offers an account of the origins of various mythological topics. In it Callimachus alludes to Hesiod by portraying himself as instructed by the Muses on Mount Helicon. In its prologue, Callimachus also states that he plans to respond to his detractors, whom he calls *telchines*. Their criticism was primarily directed at his anti-epic stance, which he shared with other learned Hellenistic poets who were attentive to Aristotelian poetic precepts outlined in the *Poetics* (23.1459a27).

Callimachus had a circle of students, including the polymaths Eratosthenes of Cyrene and Aristophanes of Byzantium. His most famous student was **Apollonius Rhodius** (ca. 270–ca. 180 BC), who became the head of the library at Alexandria. Many scholars presume him to have turned against his master, even becoming the chief of the inimical *telchines*. In any case, with the *Argonautica* Apollonius deviated significantly from Callimachus' dictum "a big book is the equivalent of a big evil" (fr. 465 Pf.). The *Argonautica* was an important model for Virgil's *Aeneid*. Another Alexandrian poet important to Virgil was **Aratus** of Soli (ca. 300–ca. 240 BC), whose *Phaenomena* is a short epic on the constellations in the didactic tradition stemming from Hesiod.

Among the authors whom Virgil would have grown up reading, Naevius (*fl.* 235 BC) and Ennius (239–169 BC) figure prominently. **Naevius** was born in Capua and served in the First Punic War (which ended in 241 BC). While some fragments of his tragedies survive, Naevius is best known for his comedies, of which some twenty-eight titles and a few fragments have been preserved. He also wrote an epic entitled *The Punic War* in which there may have been an account of Aeneas' encounter with Dido in Carthage.[27] Homer was rendered into Latin Saturnian verse by **Livius Andronicus**, a third-century poet with whom Virgil was also familiar.

Quintus **Ennius**, too, is a vastly important Virgilian model, particularly for the *Aeneid*. In 204 BC Ennius came from Calabria with Cato the Elder to Rome. His production was diverse, including drama (primarily tragedies), satires, panegyric (a poem of praise, in this case honoring Scipio), didactic (*Hedyphagetica* on gastronomy), and epos. In this last category Ennius distinguished himself with the *Annales*, the definitive Roman epic before the *Aeneid*. In its opening, Ennius claims that Homer revealed him to be a reincarnation of the Greek poet. Aeneas is a character in Ennius' *Annales*, though the focus is not, as Skutsch demonstrates in the opening note of his commentary, the central focus. Rather, Ennius merely includes Aeneas' wanderings and exploits in Italy. Even from the comparatively few fragments of Ennius that remain (e.g., Skutsch xvii, *Est locus Hesperiam quam mortales perhibebant*, "there is a place which mortals were calling Hesperia"; cf. *Aen*. 1.530 and 3.163) one can see how indebted Virgil was to his epic forebear.

Closer to Virgil's own time, a group of poets dubbed *neoteroi* ("new poets" or "neoterics") by Cicero (*Ad Atticum* 7.2.1) developed into an influential literary movement in Rome. One such poet was Gaius Valerius **Catullus** (ca. 85–late 50s BC). Roughly in the middle of Catullus' collection, which may not have been assembled by him, lies an epyllion (a small epic poem) that treats the marriage of Peleus and Thetis, a sea goddess, the parents of the epic hero Achilles. Within that narrative Catullus places a vignette describing Theseus and Ariadne, a love story that would provide an important impulse for *Aeneid* 4. One cannot overstate the importance of Catullus and other neoterics to all of Virgil's poetic production. In particular, Virgil embraced the neoteric penchant for Alexandrian allusion, often alluding to Catullus.

Virgil was conversant with other neoteric poets as well. Gaius Licinius **Calvus** (*fl.* 50s BC) wrote an *Io* to which Virgil alludes in the *Eclogues*. This poem, of which only fragments remain, can be viewed as representative of neoteric epyllion, characterized by a delicate and highly allusive style. Though that style characterizes all of Virgil's work, the tone and content of the *Io* would have been far removed from the *Aeneid*, comparable in tone and form to Catullus' Peleus and Thetis narrative (c. 64), discussed above, or the Aristaeus epyllion of the fourth *Georgic*. Another poem in this vein would have been the *Dictynna* of Publius **Valerius Cato**, a leader among the neoterics. Helvius **Cinna** (ca. 90–44 BC), alluded to in Catullus 95 and in Virgil's ninth *Eclogue*, wrote a mythological epyllion entitled *Zmyrna*. Others include those who wrote invectives; Quintus **Cornificius** was also known to Virgil, though we know him only from a reference in Catullus 38. The coterie around Valerius Cato, if he really was a leader among those poets, was likely substantial.

We know but little about the life of Titus **Lucretius** Carus, a contemporary of Catullus, though we are fortunate to have his magnum opus, the *De Rerum Natura*, a lengthy didactic poem in which Lucretius puts forth in dactylic hexameters the natural law of the universe in the tradition of Greek philosophers who wrote "on nature" (*peri physeos*). In this work he vigorously espouses the tenets of Epicurean philosophy. To say that Lucretius had a profound impact on Virgil would barely scratch the surface. Though Virgil reveals his most obvious debt to Lucretius in the *Georgics,* Lucretius' influence is nevertheless also important for the *Aeneid,* as the studies of Hardie, Dyson, and Kronenberg have amply demonstrated.

While some of Virgil's characters reveal that he was interested in Epicurean notions, Virgil is not likely to have embraced Epicurean philosophy wholeheartedly. Nevertheless, Virgil was not infrequently in the company of Epicurean friends such as **Philodemus** of Gadara (ca. 110–ca. 40 BC), at whose villa in Campania he spent a good deal of time. If Virgil was in Rome between 49 and 46 BC, he also may have come to know the Pythagorean philosopher **Nigidius Figulus** (ca. 98–45 BC). Though Virgil does not seem to have subscribed to Epicurean or Pythagorean beliefs, his poetry does show some debt to both.

Finally, let us consider one other poet important to Virgil. Writing after the height of the neoteric movement to which he was indebted, Cornelius **Gallus** (b. 70 BC), one of Virgil's closest poetic colleagues, was Rome's first elegist. Like Calvus, Gallus was both a poet and a military commander. Octavian commissioned him to settle affairs in Egypt. Having contravened Augustus' sovereignty, however, he was recalled to Rome and tried for treason. A senate decree condemned him to loss of property. Convicted, he committed suicide in 26 BC, an event that undoubtedly moved Virgil deeply.

These poets, along with other prose writers not discussed above, such as Theophrastus, Varro, Cicero, and Cato the Elder, are among the rich field of literary sources that Virgil engaged through poetic allusion.

Virgil's Allusive (and Imitative) Style

In the case of the classical manner of reference discussed above, a poet such as Pindar binds his work to that of his predecessor to establish his own place in the poetic tradition. The Alexandrian style of allusion can have a similar effect but does so in a self-conscious and learned way. This type of allusion invites the reader to play the role of insider, who can appreciate the author's manipulation of the poetic code.

We saw earlier that Virgilian allusion, though consistent with Alexandrian practice, also has "classical" features. The opening line of the *Aeneid*, which begins with the famous *arma uirumque cano* ("Arms and the man I sing," 1.1), alludes to the opening lines of the two Homeric poems, with *arma* approximating the theme of "wrath" with which the *Iliad* begins and *uirum* actually translating the introductory word of Homer's *Odyssey*. Richard Lansing has recently suggested that the forty-eight words of Virgil's prologue (*Aen.* 1.1–7) correspond to the number of books of both Homeric epics, while also doubling precisely the length of Apollonius' prologue.

Yet Virgil's allusions are sometimes not so obvious. In *Georgic* 1, Virgil picks up a thread from one of his poetic forerunners Aratus, mentioned in the previous section. When alluding to Hesiod in the second line of his *Phaenomena*, Aratus employs the adjective *arreton* (unspoken) in an apparent paronomasia on his own name. Later in that poem Aratus fashions an acrostic, beginning with a code word for refined poetry, *lepte* ("slender," *Phaenomena* 783); the first word of each of the four subsequent lines begins with a letter from that adjective, a word that aptly characterizes Aratus' style not only in this passage (783–7) but throughout the *Phaenomena*.[28]

Virgil does something similar in *Georgic* 1 when he describes certain astral phenomena. I cite here the most relevant section of the Latin text (1.429–33), which is translated more extensively and somewhat freely to preserve the acrostic, below:

> *ma*ximus agricolis pelagoque parabitur imber;
> at si uirgineum suffuderit ore ruborem,
> *ue*ntus erit: uento semper rubet aurea Phoebe.
> sin ortu quarto (namque is certissimus auctor)
> *pu*ra neque obtunsis per caelum cornibus ibit.
>
> (But if you will look back upon the swift sun and
>   moons that follow in order,
> never will the morrow's time deceive you,

nor will you be captured by the calm night's treachery.
As soon as the moon collects her *back-turning* fires,
if she shall enclose the black sky within her darkling horn,)
MAssive rain will be furnished to farmers and those on the sea.
˂ Yet if she shall spread a *maidenly* blush over her face,
there will be
VEhement wind; Golden Phoebe always blushes at the wind.
But if at the fourth rising – for that is *the most certain author* –
PUre she will pass, with horns not obscured, through the sky …
(The sun, too, both when it rises and when it buries itself in the waves,
will give signs; *the most certain signs* will follow the sun.)

(1.424–33, 438–9)

Virgil's description of the sun, moon, and constellations immediately identifies this text with that of Aratus. The second half of Aratus' poem is known as the *Prognoseis dia semeion*, of which the final word is the Greek equivalent of the Latin word *signa*, which is itself a plausible rendering of the Greek title *Phaenomena*. To reveal to the attentive reader that he refers to Aratus *qua* author, Virgil puns not only on the title of the work but also on the author, who is represented here by the moon's fourth rising as the "most certain author" (i.e., indicator), the same adjective that will describe the "most certain signs" (*signa*, i.e., *phaenomena*), in the lines that follow.

In lines 393–423 that precede this section, Virgil had employed an interesting rhyming pattern, first noticed by Ewald, to alert the reader to look for something special. Virgil conflates the self-identification of the *Phaenomena*'s opening and the acrostic pattern that Aratus had employed with the first letters of *lepte*. In a reverse acrostic, indicated by the capital letters at the beginning of lines 429, 431, and 433, Virgil alludes to a retrograde abbreviation of his own name, Publius Vergilius Maro.[29]

Though it is difficult to say why Virgil does this in a retrograde fashion – as other Hellenistic poets, such as Nicander, had more obvious self-identifying acrostics (e.g., *Theriaca* 345–53) – there are hints, such as the phrases, "if you will look back" (425) and "back turning/returning fires." Furthermore, Virgil places in his text the word "pure" in the same position as the word of that meaning (*kathare*) in Aratus' text (*Ph.* 783). We read in the ancient biography of Virgil (VSD 36–7) that his Neapolitan nickname was "Maiden" (*Parthenias*), which in Latin is *uirgineus* ("maidenly," 430), fittingly associated with purity.

I began this chapter by stating that Virgil wrote in code. That code is steeped in the Hellenistic tradition that before the Augustan period had

Alexandria as its intellectual seat. As we saw in the case of the citation of book and verse by Ovid, such allusion presupposes a reader able to interpret the code. Still, Virgil's allusions can function on more than one level at once, which Karl Galinsky has dubbed "polysemous," a term that Thomas extends further in his *Harvard Studies* article (2000). However far one pushes the tone, it is clear that Virgil has great range in his depth of allusion. Such intertextual repartee will not be discovered by every reader but it has a special richness for the one who recognizes it.

Yet it is also important to note that such cleverness is adornment to the universal human issues that Virgil seeks to address in his texts. These issues align themselves with the major themes of dialogue, wisdom, and mission outlined in this chapter, and it is through his organization of these themes and adornment of them via Alexandrian erudition that Virgil establishes his niche within the epic tradition. Thus, the *Aeneid* is also quite different from the works of Virgil's Roman epic predecessors, as seen in neoteric poetry such as Catullus' sixty-fourth poem or didactic epic such as Lucretius' *De Rerum Natura*. In the *Aeneid*, Virgil encompasses aspects of each of these, especially in terms of diction and style, but he does not fully adopt the neoteric epyllion format of Catullus or the didactic format of Lucretius. Nor does he write in a year-by-year (annalistic) format, as had the third-century prose author Quintus Fabius Pictor, who composed in Greek, or the great Latin epicist, Ennius. Indeed, Catullus' playful reference to the *Annales* of a certain Volusius as "fecal folios" may indicate that the old annalistic genre, unless done well, could be less than popular in the middle to late first century BC.

Instead, Virgil looks back to Homer as no one else had. Though Ennius may fancy himself as Homer reincarnated, Virgil's relationship to Homer might more aptly be so described. Accordingly, although thoroughly Alexandrian, Virgil is different from poets like Calvus, Cinna, or Valerius Cato, whose epyllia seem to have been more along the lines of Catullus 64 and of the style encapsulated briefly in Virgil's sixth eclogue, which alludes to such poetry but is obviously not an epyllion in and of itself. Even Virgil's Aristaeus epyllion in *Georgic* 4 anticipates Ovid's *Metamorphoses* more than it heralds Virgil's own *Aeneid*. The *Aeneid*, though not flatly irregular, represents a somewhat surprising development within the epic genre; remove the *Aeneid*, and the road to Ovid, passing through the brief cosmological poem of Silenus in *Eclogue* 6 and the Aristaeus epyllion of *Georgic* 4, is in some ways more easily paved.

To sum up thus far: Virgil practices both classical reference and Alexandrian allusion. In the *Aeneid*, in particular, he imitates Homer, not merely to show debt but also to reinvigorate the tradition that stems from Homer as the first and greatest epic poet. Virgil's imitative, "classical" references comprise a new text based on Homer. But he goes beyond this with Alexandrian reference, the more sophisticated form of textual connection that enjoys a polysemous quality. Thus, while Alexandrian learnedness need not suggest such fanciful connections or secret messages in the text as Brown's *The Da Vinci Code* purports that the "Last Supper" contains, Alexandrian allusion does function similar to Giovanni Pala's interpretation of that same painting: in *La Musica Celata* (2007), Pala claims to detect a musical scale encoded in the arrangement and size of the disciples as they are seated around the table with Christ. Should Pala's theory be correct, his analysis would offer an artistic parallel to the Alexandrian learnedness to which Virgil adheres.

Telling Themes: Virgil and Story

In his articulation of universal human issues Virgil employs Alexandrian allusion to accentuate the central themes that stay with the reader well after he or she has finished reading. We have seen that the notions of dialogue, wisdom and mission are the three principal themes through which the poet connects his text with those of his predecessors and his subthemes also support these principal features. One often finds the dialogic juxtaposition of good and evil, joy and sorrow, mercy and brutality. His poetry is marked by wistful glances back to a lost golden age; a struggle for control when chaos abounds; the discovery of community and peace in the midst of discord and strife; duty to country and family over personal gain; the value of history balanced with future hope; and a sense of purpose and destiny in the face of harsh adversity. Such dualism may be indebted to the Pythagorean proportion of opposites. Yet Virgil is not "Pythagorean" per se but rather merely generally indebted to this kind of thought, as can be seen especially in his *Eclogues.*

Let us take a single example of Virgil's technique as a storyteller to illustrate this point. In *Eclogue* 1, the goatherd Tityrus, whose property was to be confiscated for military compensation, speaks of his trip to Rome, where he appealed that ruling. Given his low social status, his holdings should naturally be meager. Nevertheless, Tityrus speaks to Meliboeus, another displaced goatherd, about the result of his journey to the city where he had encountered a "god":

> It was not possible for me to … recognize elsewhere the gods that were so present there. Meliboeus, I saw there that young man for whom our altars smoke twelve days every year; there when I asked him he first gave me an answer: "Lads, feed your oxen as you did before, put your bulls under the heifers." (40–5)

Free from foreign contagions, Tityrus will have real pastureland by the rivers he has known (51). Though Meliboeus notes that Tityrus will enjoy the beauty of rustic life where gardeners sing (56), Meliboeus reveals a bleaker destiny for himself and other displaced goatherds who will have to go as far away as Africa, Scythia, or Britain. He emotively predicts his own homecoming, when he will see his "realm" that a callous soldier, a foreigner (71), will then possess. "Behold," Meliboeus cries, "to what end discord has driven wretched citizens" (72). He then sarcastically enjoins himself to put his vineyard in order, bidding his goats move on; no longer will he sing (77).

Tityrus responds, inviting Meliboeus to share his table, which is as humble as that of the *Georgics*' Tarentine rustic, whom we shall consider shortly. Tityrus does not share in the imagined vision of barbarian confiscation but has hope for community, suggested in the poem's final vista: "the high roof peaks of villas smoke, and greater shadows cascade from lofty mountains" (82–3). There is, in short, a distinct ebb and flow reflected in the banter and fortunes of the poem's two principal characters. Such dualism and dialogue will characterize this collection.

Virgil's second body of poetry, the *Georgics*, is characterized by wisdom derived from the earth's goodness. Such uncomplicated wisdom can be seen in a somewhat mysterious character who appears near the beginning of *Georgic* 4. After a lengthy description of civil strife in the community of bees, Virgil moves the locus to warmer climes than even Paestum, coming suddenly to Tarentum, a southern Italian city. The narrator states that he saw there an old man who possessed an impoverished parcel of land:

> And I recall now that beneath the turrets of the Oebalian citadel where the dark Galaesus moistens the golden farmland, I saw an old man from Corycia, who had but a few acres of an abandoned farm, its land neither fit for cattle nor suited to flocks nor good for the vine. (125–9)

It is unclear why Virgil describes this man as Corycian, a label that could possibly indicate his origin from Corycia in Cilicia or serve as a reference to a cave of nymphs on Mt. Parnassus. Whatever his background, the aged fellow regards his humble circumstances as worthy of kingly wealth (132), near a city and yet a world away. Every evening he returns home and loads his table with homegrown produce (134–5); he was the first to plant according to seasons, first to abound in bees, and first to squeeze honey from combs. His elms are separated into proper rows (144), his pears planted, and his thornbushes grafted with plums (146). His mode of living is wise and simple.

The fact that he is unnamed gives the reader pause. The detail about his beekeeping is strange, for Aristaeus, the character that will figure prominently later in the fourth *Georgic*, is the beekeeper par excellence.[30] Other details add to the aura of mystery about him, suggesting he is not a single individual but an amalgamation of several characters associated with wisdom. Though not a philosopher per se, he shows that he has a contemplative outlook on life, for he lives humbly and tends to everything in due season.

For this sage figure, life is not merely about labor for its own sake, nor is it about political connections and the vain striving of the city. Rather, his *joie de vivre* and inner satisfaction are found in mere satiety; he experiences contentment rather than greed. Informed by the character of Cato as portrayed, for example, in Cicero's *De senectute*, and within that treatise by the southern Italian philosopher Archytas, Virgil's farmer stakes his own claim in the southern Italian soil: his wisdom and contentment are simple and earthy. An important aspect of Virgil's mission in the *Georgics* is to convey such wisdom.

Let us turn now to Virgil's magnum opus, which, though it is thoroughly mission-charged, also has the characteristics of dualism and wisdom that we see in the *Eclogues* and the *Georgics*. In *Aeneid* 1, after a sea storm has scattered the Trojan fleet, Aeneas spends time in Carthage with Dido, who falls in love with him. In his fourth book, Virgil recounts that Jupiter sends Mercury to redirect the hero to his journey. The messenger god recites Jupiter's questions: why is Aeneas, playing the role of a husband, building another city's walls? He addresses Aeneas' lack of memory of his mission ("alas, you who are forgetful of your own realm …," 4.267), charging him to have regard for the destiny owed to his son Ascanius. Aeneas' subsequent hesitation results in a second appearance of Mercury. As he sleeps on the deck of his ship, Aeneas has a vision of the god, who urges quick departure (562, 569) and warns him that Dido is resolved to die (564). Aeneas now responds swiftly, explaining the vision to his men (574).

Both appearances of Mercury are charged with a sense of mission. Though Aeneas may need to be admonished, it is nevertheless also clear that he is cognizant of his mission, for Virgil describes him as "resolved to leave" (554) even before the god's second epiphany. Mercury's words, which repeat Jupiter's own wise Olympian counsel, admonish Aeneas not to be uxorious toward Dido and to recall his mission. We see also an internal dialogue in which Aeneas engages after the first epiphany of Mercury, when Aeneas debates in his own mind the best course of action (283).

This internal dialogue gives rise to the possibility that the other of Virgil's "two voices" might question the premises of Aeneas' mission. Such gloominess is consistent with the point of view that Virgil attributes to Meliboeus, who loses his property in *Eclogue* 1, and with the psychological effect of the devastating plague that closes the third *Georgic*. Such "dark readings" are sometimes credited to the so called Harvard school of Virgilian criticism. A "positive" view of Virgilian criticism is known as the European school, so-called because it tends to be predominant among continental scholars.

Mercury's instruction reveals the text's complex nature: Aeneas' true calling is set in opposition with his personal desire to remain in Carthage. The passage thus features dialogue, wisdom and mission: as he confronts his own internal conflict, Aeneas must rely on wisdom to extricate himself from his diversion from his mission. The mission of Virgil's Model Reader – the reader who wishes to pick up and read the codex and begin to crack its code – is not to settle the tension between the European and Harvard schools, but to accept that tension as an important contour in the Virgilian landscape, valuing the ebb and flow that characterizes Virgil's text.

Just as the emphasis of each of Virgil's works is different, so are his principal goals. We shall never know how Virgil came to these goals or to what extent his own experience of the world shaped his work. Nevertheless, it is worthwhile to consider what we can know of that experience, one that encompassed the dualism of republic and empire, required wisdom to understand the dramatic changes of late republican times, and found itself in the midst of mission-driven imperial Rome. Let us now turn to that world and the events that shaped Virgil's worldview, for though we have few particulars of Virgil's life, we know a good deal about the world in which he lived.

Notes

1 Cf. Giancarlo Abbamonte and Fabio Stok, "Intuizioni esegetiche di Pomponio Leto nel suo commento alle *georgiche* e all' *Eneide* di Virgilio," in Carlo Santini and Fabio Stok (eds.), *Esegesi dimenticate di autori classici* (2008), 135–210, esp. 176–201. Cf. also M. Geymonat, "The Transmission of Virgil's Works in Antiquity and the Middle Ages," in

Nicolas Horsfall (ed.), *A Companion to the Study of Virgil* (Leiden, 2nd edn., 2000), 305.

2   My transcription agrees with that of Alexander Riese, *Anthologia Latina siue Poesis Latinae Supplementum, Pars Prior: Carmina in Codicum Scripta* (Leipzig, 1869); see also notes in F. Schoell, *Histoire abrégée de la littérature romaine* (Paris, 1815) and A. H. M. Jones, J. R. Martindale, and J. Morris, *The Prosopography of the Later Roman Empire*, vol. 2 (Cambridge, 1980), 173; Ralph W. Mathisen, *People, Personal Expression, and Social Relations in Late Antiquity: Selected Latin Texts from Gaul and Western Europe* (Ann Arbor, MI, 2003), 18–21; on Turcius Apronianus, cf. Michele Renee Salzman, *The Making of a Christian Aristocracy: Social and Religious Change in the Western Empire* (Cambridge, MA, 2002), 74–81; for the Latin *fratris*, "(of my) brother," see Jones et al. (1980), 173. On the spelling of *sed* (but), cf. W. M. Lindsay, "The Lost 'Codex Optimus' of Nonius Marcellus," *CR* 10 (1896), 16, n. 2. This translation, and all translations in this book, are my own unless otherwise indicated.

3   I.e., the manuscript was copied before April 21, AD 494. Cf. M. Geymonat, "Codici," in *Virgilio: Enciclopedia Virgiliana* (Rome, 1984), 832; Carolus Zagemeister and Guilemus Wattenbach, *Exempla Codicum Latinorum Litteris Maiusculis Scriptorum* (Heidelberg, 1876), 3. Cf. also H. R. Fairclough, "Observations on Sabbadini's Variorum Edition of Virgil," *TAPA* 63 (1932), 223.

4   See James L. Butrica, "Propertius on the Parilia (4.4.73–8)," *CQ* 50 (2000), 473, n. 4. See also A. T. Grafton and N. M. Swerdlow, "The Horoscope of the Foundation of Rome," *CP* 81 (1986), 148–53.

5   K. J. Shelton, "The Esquiline Treasure: The Nature of the Evidence," *AJA* 89 (1985), 148–51; Alan Cameron, "The Date and the Owners of the Esquiline Treasure," *AJA* 89 (1985), 144.

6   Does "brother" indicate a fellow Christian or merely a close friend and admirer of Virgil? Cf. L. D. Reynolds and N. G. Wilson, *Scribes and Scholars: A Guide to the Transmission of Greek and Latin Literature* (Oxford, 1968; 3rd edn., 1991), 41.

7   Gian Biagio Conte, *The Rhetoric of Imitation: Genre and Poetic Memory in Virgil and Other Latin Poets*, ed. Charles P. Segal (Ithaca, NY, 1986), 30.

8   So Mathisen (2003), 20.

9   J. K. Newman, *The Concept of Vates in Augustan Poetry* (Brussels, 1967); see Stephen Harrison, *Generic Enrichment in Vergil and Horace* (Oxford, 2007), 22–33; Niklas Holzberg, *Vergil: Der Dichter und Sein Werk* (Munich, 2006), 24f. See also Wilhelm Kroll, *Studien zum Verständnis der romischen Literatur* (1924), 202–24. On imitation, cf. Arno Reiff, "*Interpretatio, imitatio, aemulatio*. Begriff und Vorstellung literarischer Abhängigkeit bei den Römern," Diss. Köln, 1959.

10   Seminal works on allusion include Conte (1986) and Richard Thomas, "Virgil's *Georgics* and the Art of Reference," *HSCP* 90 (1986), 171–98.

Cf., earlier, Rudolf Pfeiffer, "The Future of Studies in the Field of Hellenistic Poetry," *JHS* 75 (1955), 69.

11   Cf. Peter Bing, "A Pun on Aratus' Name in Verse 2 of the *Phainomena?*" *HSCP* 93 (1990), 281; for a similar playful allusion, cf. Mario Geymonat, "Spigolature Nicandree," *Acme* 23 (1970), 137–43.

12   R. A. Smith, "Pindar's *Olympian* 14: A Literal and Literary Homecoming," *Hermes* 127 (1999), 261–2.

13   M. R. Mezzabotta, "Jason and Orpheus: Euripides *Medea* 543," *AJP* 115 (1994), 48; also, Philip Vellacott, *Ironic Drama: A Study of Euripides' Method and Meaning* (Cambridge, 1975), 23–52 and 106–13.

14   James J. Clauss, "Vergil and the Euphrates Revisited," *AJP* 109 (1988), 309–20.

15   Ruth S. Scodel and Richard F. Thomas, "Virgil and the Euphrates," *AJP* 105 (1984), 339.

16   Joseph Farrell, *Vergil's* Georgics *and the Traditions of Ancient Epic: The Art of Allusion in Literary History* (Oxford, 1991), 165–6; see also Thomas, Georgics, vol. 1, ad 509; cf. also Richard Jenkyns, "Virgil and the Euphrates," *AJP* 114 (1993), 115–21.

17   On the tension between the Hellenistic style of Apollonius vis-à-vis Callimachus, see Damien Nelis, *Vergil's* Aeneid *and the Argonautica of Apollonius Rhodius* (Leeds, 2001), 393–5; also see Philip Hardie, *Virgil's* Aeneid: Cosmos and Imperium (Oxford, 1986), 50.

18   R. A. Smith, "Ov. *Met.* 10.475: An Instance of 'Meta-allusion,' " *Gymnasium* 97 (1990), 458–60; see also Stephen M. Wheeler, "Ovid's Use of Lucretius in *Metamorphoses* 1.67–8," *CQ* 45 (1995), 200–3; Reinhold F. Glei, "Der interepische poetologische Diskurs: Zum Verhältnis von *Metamorphosen* und *Aeneis*," in Hildegard L. C. Tristram (ed.), *New Methods in the Research of Epic: Neue Methoden der Epenforschung* (Tübingen, 1998), 89; Llewelyn Morgan, *Patterns of Redemption in Virgil's* Georgics (Cambridge, 1999), 226, n. 17; Smith (1997), 71–4.

19   Thomas (1986), 171–98.

20   Cf. Reiff (1959), *passim*; also Conte (1986), 34.

21   Adam Parry, "The Two Voices of Virgil's *Aeneid*," *Arion* 2 (1963), 66–80.

22   R. O. A. M. Lyne, "*Scilicet et tempus ueniet*: ... Vergil *G.* 1.463–514," in his *Collected Papers on Latin Poetry* (Oxford, 2007), 58; cf. Karl Galinsky, rev. of M. C. J. Putnam, *Virgil's Poem of the Earth: Studies in the* Georgics, *CP* 76 (1981), 329.

23   I thank Sophia Papaiaonnou for fruitful discussion of this point.

24   E.g., Michael von Albrecht, *Vergil: Bucolica, Georgica, Aeneis, Eine Einführung* (Heidelberg, 2006), 86.

25   D. M. Halperin, *Before Pastoral: Theocritus and the Ancient Tradition of Bucolic Poetry* (New Haven, CT, 1983), 227. Halperin distinguishes

between Virgil's use of Hesiod and Homer, regarding Virgil's debt to Hesiod as being largely due to epic inversion, allusion by which epic themes are made quasi-comical: "Hesiod seemed to have anticipated Alexandrian aesthetic ideals" (246).

26   Geymonat (1970), 137–43, esp. 139f.; Brown (1963), 111.

27   Gordon Williams (*OCD*, 2nd edn., 1970), 720, discusses the possibility that fr. 23 of Morel, *Fragmenta poetarum Latinorum epicorum et lyricorum praeter Ennium et Lucilium* (Leipzig, 1927) reflects such content. See the lengthy discussion by A. S. Pease, *Publi Vergili Maronis Aeneidos Liber Quartus* (Cambridge, MA, 1935), 18–23. Cf. Gian Biagio Conte, *Latin Literature: A History*, tr. Joseph Solodow (Baltimore, MD, 1994), 45.

28   Bing (1990), 281–85; Kathryn Gutzwiller (Malden, MA, 2007), 42f. The word λεπτός is rendered in Latin as *tenuis*; cf. David O. Ross, *Backgrounds to Augustan Poetry: Gallus, Elegy and Rome* (Cambridge, 1975), 26f., 76. J.-M. Jacques, "Sur un acrostiche d'Aratos," *REA* 62 (1960), 48–61; cf. Farrell (1991), 81–3. D. C. Feeney and D. Nelis, "Two Vergilian Acrostics: Certissima Signa?" *CQ* 55 (2005), 644–6, take this phrase to be a self-reference rather than an allusion to Aratus. See the intelligent discussion of Thomas, ad loc. For a more skeptical view, see M. Hendry, "A Martial Acronym in Ennius?" *LCM* 19 (1994), 7f.

29   Cf. 393–423; cf. Owen M. Ewald, "Virgilian End Rhymes (*Geo.* 1.393–423)," *HSCP* 93 (1990), 311–13; see Alexei Grishin, "*Ludus in undis*: An Acrostic in *Eclogue* 9," *HCSP* 104 (2008), 237–40, for similarly clever acrostic. Further, see Edwin L. Brown, *Numeri Vergiliani. Studies in "Eclogues" and "Georgics,"* Coll. Latomus 631 (Brussels, 1963), 102–3; cf. R. F. Thomas, *Virgil:* Georgics *1* (Cambridge, 1988), ad 1.427–37; more recently, Feeney and Nelis (2005), esp. 645, n. 8.

30   Cf. Eva Crane, *The World History of Beekeeping and Honey Hunting* (London, 1999), 204.

2

Publius Vergilius Maro: A Preamble

Mantua me genuit, Calabri
rapuere, tenet nunc
Parthenope; cecini pascua rura duces.

(Mantua gave me birth, among the Calabrians
I died; now Parthenope holds me.
Of pastures, farms and leaders I sang.)
Virgil's Epitaph (VSD 36)

We know very little about the historical Virgil. A largely unhistorical version of him is described by the second-century biographer Suetonius in a work later redacted in the fourth century by the scholar Aelius Donatus, using the name of both authors entitled, Vita Suetonii Donati (VSD). Critics such as Horsfall have shown the VSD to be a compendium of inferences derived from Virgil's poetry and thus to be regarded with circumspection.

Two of Donatus' students were St Jerome, biblical scholar and translator, and Servius, the fourth-century Virgilian scholar whose vast commentary (*Expositio*) includes further particulars about Virgil's life, also likely derived from the poetry. The *Expositio*, normally referred to among Anglophone scholars as "Servius" or "Servius' commentary," was later expanded by Tiberius Claudius Donatus, who, despite the similarity of his name, is unrelated to Servius' mentor, Aelius Donatus. Various versions of Servius were in circulation for over a millennium until, early in the seventeenth century, the scholar Pierre Daniel published a definitive version consisting of the entire commentary of Servius along with Tiberius Claudius Donatus' scholarly notes. This commentary is known as the Servius Auctus ("Augmented Servius") or Servius Danielis ("Daniel's Servius").

In light of the general unreliability of the sources, this chapter will not consider Virgil's life per se but rather will offer, as a preamble for his life, a brief consideration of the social and political climate in which he was born and lived. To this end, it will be useful first to distinguish between two "Virgils." First, there is the Virgil who *is* the text; thus one says, "in Virgil, the notions of dialogue, wisdom, and mission are pervasive," or "in Virgil, the presence of human pathos is virtually ubiquitous." In such sentences, Virgil is envisioned as his text. The second Virgil, the historical one, is largely lost to us. Tacitly accepting the Servian model, many critics have overinterpreted the words of Virgilian characters such as Tityrus, Meliboeus, or Moeris, fruitlessly attempting to construct a historical Virgil.

The Proto-Augustan Milieu

A few days before the biggest challenge of Cicero's consulship (63 BC), Virgil turned seven. At that moment, the consuls Cicero and Antonius had to contend with a conspiracy launched by a failed Roman aristocrat named Catiline. Catiline had assembled an army of fugitive slaves and brigands and had stationed them in the rural setting of "the jaws of Etruria" between Mantua and Rome. Assuming Cicero, as a political newcomer (*novus homo*), to be inexperienced, Catiline decided to launch a *coup d'état*. Cicero foiled the attempt and became a national hero, as patriotism ran high in the city and throughout Italy.

Rome had long before evolved into the seat of power for the Italic peninsula. As a result of the first Punic War, Sicily became Rome's first province (241 BC), followed by Corsica and Sardinia; in the next century Spain was added, followed by Macedon, Africa, and Pergamum. Of the last of these, Plutarch (*Tiberius Gracchus*, 14.1–2) and Livy (*Periochae* 58) record the irregularity of the acquisition, for King Attalus III bequeathed that kingdom to Rome (133 BC). That bequest played an important role in the transformation of Rome from republic to empire, a transition well under way at the time of Virgil's birth.

In the year of Attalus' bequest, Tiberius Gracchus – holder of the highest elected plebeian office, tribune – sought to redistribute to Rome's urban poor the large farms (*latifundia*) of the Roman elite. Gracchus was opposed and ultimately killed by senatorial conservatives. In 122 BC Gracchus' brother Gaius, also a tribune, would suffer the same fate for attempting further reforms having to do with agrarian laws and the constitution of juries. The fallout from half-century-old anti-*latifundia* legislation (such as that of the Gracchi brothers) and the redefinition of the Italian populace (e.g., by Sulla, who as dictator facilitated the extension of voting rights) was settled before Virgil's birth; the memory, however, was fresh.

In the second *Georgic*, Virgil reveals that such memory obtains into the 30s, for he alludes to *latifundia* by using a variation on the word, split through *tmesis* ("cutting") into *latis ... fundis*:

> But here are repose without care, and guileless life, rich in different kinds of wealth, and even leisure for the *wide farmland*, and there are caves, and living waters, and chilly valleys, and the lowing of cows and delicate slumbers under a tree. (2.467–71)

Though Virgil describes a farmer who lives in a state of security, the leisure proposed here would have existed only for the wealthy owners of these estates and not for the farmers who worked the land. Despite legislation against such ranches, they were plentiful when Virgil composed the *Georgics*. Though we know little of Virgil's family background, it is probably safe to say that Virgil is unlikely himself to have owned such an estate, though his father may have been a property holder of some kind. We do know that Virgil hailed from Mantua in northern Italy. When Virgil was born, Pompey, then thirty-four years old and a swiftly rising star, was consul for the first time. Virgil's birthday was October 15, 70 BC.

By 59 BC Pompey, with Caesar and Crassus, formed an alliance, known by a misnomer as the "first triumvirate"; this unofficial sharing of leadership would not dissolve until the death of Crassus in 53. Although Julius Caesar was this trio's leader, he was often the subject of jokes and poems. For example, in the mid-50s Catullus wrote the following epigram vividly translated by Frank O. Copley:

> Julius Caesar, you're a snot,
> I don't care if you like it or not.
> Maybe you're good luck, maybe you're bad.
> I don't care, now go on and be mad. (Catullus 93)

Catullus shows that he is perhaps a bit wary of Caesar's rise to power and political machinations. And Virgil would have known well Catullus' poetry and outlook.

After Crassus' death, Pompey failed to silence Caesar's enemies, who were calling for Caesar to be replaced in Gaul. Pompey's ineffectiveness in this regard provoked a rift between himself and Caesar, exacerbated by a dispute as to which of the two of them had legitimate claim to a certain legion of soldiers. As a result of that dispute, Caesar crossed the Rubicon, a river approximately 150 kilometers southeast of Mantua. At that time (49 BC), the twenty-year-old Virgil may have been studying in Milan or Cremona, where he may have first received news of the opening of civil war.

The war resulted in Pompey's death (48 BC) and ultimately Caesar's as well, albeit four years later. For Virgil writing his *Georgics* in the 30s, the wounds of that battle were still fresh. When the news of Pompey's defeat at Pharsalus reached Rome, Virgil would have been nearly twenty-three years old; he had spent his early childhood and, in particular, his young adulthood in an Italy marred by civil strife.

At the close of the first book of the *Georgics*, Virgil treats the death of Caesar and the civil strife among the Romans, describing in some detail portents that include epic themes of speaking animals and sweating statues (*G.* 1.471–80; cf. *Il.* 19.404–24). Virgil heightens the pathos when he depicts a future when farmers will discover in the fields the unburied bones of their countrymen:

> The farmer, working earth with his bent plough, will discover spears eaten away by destructive rust or, with his heavy rakes, will strike upon helmets useless now; he will marvel at the bones that loom large in tombs he has disturbed. (494–7)

By the time Virgil came to Rome in the mid-40s, he would have often pondered the heavy price of war, which – especially the civil war just mentioned – profoundly affected Virgil's worldview.

When Caesar was assassinated in 44, Virgil recognized the end of an era in Roman government. Yet another young man, who came to Rome shortly after Caesar's death, changed the political landscape for the remainder of Virgil's lifetime. Octavian, to whom Virgil would obliquely dedicate much of his poetry, cultivated a friendly, if at first indirect, relationship with Virgil. Cicero knew Octavian and considered him a vastly better hope for Rome than the alternative, Marcus Antonius, who had been a high-ranking tribune and chief confidant of Caesar. Cicero's aspiration for Octavian to eclipse Antony would ultimately materialize, though perhaps not as he envisioned it.

In 43 BC the *lex Titia* ("Titian law") formalized an alliance between Lepidus, Caesar's last master of the horse, and Caesar's two named heirs, Marc Antony and Octavian, the latter of whom received three-quarters of his great uncle's estate and arranged for Cicero's murder. Reeling from both Caesar's assassination and Cicero's execution, the Senate bestowed upon Lepidus, Antony, and Octavian the official title of *triumviri rei publicae constituendae* ("three men designated to restore the republic"). From 42 until the pact of Tarentum in 37, which would renew the triumvirate for another five years, Octavian secured his own authority within the remnants of republican institutions, maintaining all the while a teetering three-way balance of power with his colleagues. Virgil wrote his *Eclogues* in the midst of such political volatility.

The Augustan Context

Several analyses have attempted to establish by internal references the dates of certain *Eclogues*. Most of the poems are believed to have been composed later than 43 BC, though a prototypical version of some of the *Eclogues* may have circulated earlier, as an anecdote in Servius suggests: astonished upon hearing a public recitation of *Eclogue* 6, Cicero stated that in Virgil there was "another hope for great Rome" (ad 6.11).[1] If not entirely apocryphal, this account may imply that such recitations included prototypes of some eclogues (or at least this one eclogue) released before Cicero's death on December 7, 43.

The *Eclogues* in their current form were certainly written later. Octavian did not commence with the confiscations of property in northern Italy until 41 BC, which gives us a *terminus post quem* for the poems touching on that theme. Whether or not Virgil's family was personally subject to the confiscations, he clearly was deeply moved by the farmers' displacement, devoting two poems to this important topic. Accordingly, even if *Eclogue* 1 does not have an autobiographical element, the reality of the harsh outcome of the confiscations provides a context for this poem.

Octavian's avenging of Caesar's murder was accomplished specifically at the battle of Philippi in October of 42 BC. The proclamation on the first day of that same year that Julius Caesar had been deified made Octavian the son of a god (*filius diui*), a distinction more politically than religiously significant. In accordance with a vow associated with this victory, Octavian and other nobles executed a plan to rebuild the city.

Asinius Pollio, for example, having refurbished the Atrium Libertatis, transformed it into Rome's first public library. That building was but one of many rebuilt in a period that would see Rome as a whole move from brick to marble.[2] The completion of Pollio's library coincided with signs of political stability and with the flowering of a fresh and vibrant generation of poets, who may well have frequented that library to compose their learned poetry.

Yet the post-Philippi stability would be short-lived. In 40 Antony married Octavian's sister, Octavia. Though three years later the triumvirates renewed their alliance, by the early 30s Antony drifted apart, having become romantically involved with the Egyptian queen Cleopatra, who suited Antony's sensual and political tastes. Both Antony and Cleopatra provided prototypes for characters in the *Aeneid*: Antony served as a model of Aeneas in Carthage and of the inferior but formidable foe, such as *Georgic* 4's "king" bee or Turnus in the *Aeneid;* Cleopatra served as a model for Queen Dido.

Conflict between Antony and Octavian arose precisely when Virgil was composing the *Georgics,* his second major body of poetry, completed by 29 BC. That poem is characterized by a movement between optimistic and pessimistic tones suggestive of the mood at Rome prior to Actium. One such instance comes at the close of the first book, where Virgil offers a memorable picture of an ungovernable chariot:

> Impious Mars is ruthless in the entire world, as when chariots have poured forth from the starting gates and give space; fruitlessly holding onto the reins, the charioteer is carried along by the horses, and the chariot takes no heed of the reins. (*G.* 1.511–14)

This image could be seen as a metaphor for the difficulty of guiding affairs of state. Such volatility is reflected in the character and composition of the *Georgics.*

Throughout the 30s Antony's affections for Cleopatra were pronounced, while in Rome she was regarded as a starkly negative influence upon the triumvir. In 35 BC, when Octavian sent his sister along with two thousand troops to Antony for deployment in the east, Antony received the legions but sent Octavia back, proclaiming himself Cleopatra's consort. As the second triumvirate was drawing to a close, the writing was on the wall for Antony, much of it in his own hand.

Once reviled by Cicero in his famous *Philippic* orations for his debauched behavior, Antony did nothing in the 30s to alter that negative image. Indeed, he even wrote a treatise entitled "On His Drunkenness," describing how overindulging in Bacchus had its own virtues. One need not regard Virgil a prude to believe him whelmed by Antony's adolescent comportment.

The negative perception of Antony is clearly not forgotten some years later when Virgil casts Antony in an unfavorable light in *Aeneid* 8:

> From here with barbaric strength and various weapons, Antony, the victor from the peoples of the sunrise and the red horizon, brings Egypt with him and the East's power, and furthest Bactra, too; and her evilness, his Egyptian consort, follows him. All have rushed together and the whole sea foams, dashed by the oars drawn back and ship beaks that have three prongs. (685–90)

Virgil's portrayal includes savage details, such as Antony's "barbaric" power derived from a non-Roman source. His foreignness is enhanced because he is attended by an "Egyptian wife." The negative perception of Cleopatra is also apparent in Horace's first book of *Odes* (1.37), where that poet celebrates her death after the battle of Actium in 31 BC.

That battle, between Antony and Octavian, was the pivotal conflict of Virgil's adulthood. Defeated, Antony and Cleopatra returned to Egypt, pursued by Octavian and Marcus Agrippa, Octavian's chief military strategist. Near Alexandria Antony was hemmed in by Octavian's forces. In a desperate measure, Antony challenged Octavian to single combat. Octavian's terse response is recorded in Plutarch: "there are many ways for Antony to die." Antony and Cleopatra committed suicide, according to Plutarch in dramatic fashion (*Antony*, 75–8).

After Antony's death, Octavian reorganized the east before returning to Italy in 29 BC. Having encountered Virgil en route, Octavian soon celebrated in Rome his famous triple triumph over Illyricum, Actium, and Egypt, a description of which Virgil included in an ecphrasis (extended description) of the shield in *Aeneid* 8:

> But Caesar, having been transported within the walls of Rome in triple triumph, was consecrating three hundred supremely grand shrines through the entire city, his everlasting vow to Italian gods. The streets were brimming with joy in games and applause; there was a chorus of matrons in all the temples, altars in all of them; in front of the altars slain bullocks covered the ground. He himself, sitting on the snow-white threshold of shining Phoebus, reviews the gifts of the peoples and places them on the haughty doorposts. Conquered nations process in a long line, as varied in

their languages as in their manner of dress and their weapons. (*Aen.* 8.714–23)

After this celebration, which established clearly his claim to power, Octavian would begin to develop a coherent philosophy of his role as Rome's chief regent. To do so, he surrounded himself with a coterie of bright and insightful advisers, including Statilius Taurus, his nephew Claudius Marcellus, Marcus Agrippa, and Gaius Maecenas, his liaison to the literary community and the official dedicatee of the *Georgics*, which appeared in 29, the year in which Octavian held his seventh consulship.

The *Res Gestae Divi Augusti*, an autobiographical inscription that celebrates Octavian/Augustus' accomplishments, states that during his sixth and seventh consulships Octavian transferred the republic from his own power to "the discretion of the Senate and people of Rome" (*Res Gestae* 34). Regardless of the sincerity of Octavian's proposal, its results are clear: the Senate conferred more power upon him, granting him in 27 BC supreme power over the Roman army for a period of ten years. In that same year, the name (*cognomen*) Augustus was added to Octavian's own. By another decree, the month of Sextilis was called "Augustus" in his honor. As Heinze noted many years ago and more recently Galinsky expanded upon, the adjective *augustus* ("august," "influential") is derived from the Latin verb *augere* ("to make to grow"); its nominal form *auctoritas* ("authority") suggested the extent of Augustus' political sway. The *pax augusta* ("Augustan peace") was inaugurated in 30 BC when Octavian closed the gates of the temple of Janus after the battle of Actium; this moment allowed for a flowering of the arts on a par with that of Periclean Athens.[3]

In the final years of Virgil's composition of the *Aeneid*, the foundations of a new order of government were established. While Augustus continued to lay his powers aside – he gave up the consulship beginning in 23, taking instead the lesser post of curatorship of the grain supply while retaining his ex-tribune status (granted in 36) and that of ex-consul (granted in 27) – it could not have been lost on many Romans that in exchange for political stability little by little the center of government lay not with the Senate or people but with the emperor. Whatever Virgil's private thoughts about these developments may have been, his poetic depictions of or allusions to the emperor are far from negative, possibly because he recognized that Augustan Rome at the very least provided an environment in which the arts could flourish. That environment was established and maintained, in part, through patronage.

Patronage: Pollio, Maecenas, and Augustus

We know very little about the Virgil who arrived in Rome in the mid-40s. According to the VSD, he tried, as a young lawyer, to plead a case but had difficulty speaking fluidly. However apocryphal the VSD's story may be, it is clear that, when Virgil arrived in Rome, he shied away from a career in law, the prize typical of Roman young men.

We do not know precisely when Virgil began his poetic career. Scholars are divided on the genuineness of the poems of the so-called *Appendix Vergiliana*, variously attributed to a youthful Virgil. Among these works the *Culex*, the *Ciris*, and the *Aetna* show the best poetic craftsmanship. If any of them do belong to Virgil, they would have been but early experimental pieces. Inasmuch as there exists no consensus in the scholarly community as to their authenticity or date, they will not be included in this study.

We do know, however, that by the late 40s Virgil was well engaged in the production of the *Eclogues*. There is no single patron or dedicatee of the collection, though three figures stand out. The sixth *Eclogue* is dedicated to Alfenus Varus, a jurist who in 39 BC served as suffect consul (an official who took over the duties of the elected consul). Varus was, in some measure, responsible for land confiscations during the second triumvirate. A second clear dedicatee is Pollio, consul in 40, who may have been Virgil's patron when Virgil first came to Rome. Pollio is named in both the third and fourth *Eclogues*. Some scholars follow a lead from the VSD, which claims Pollio urged Virgil to write bucolic poetry (19.25), and posit an original "Pollio group" of *Eclogues*. *Eclogue* 8 may also be devoted to Pollio, as a reference to the composition of tragedy in that poem could possibly indicate. The other candidate for the dedication of this poem is Octavian, though no specific dedicatee is named.[4]

As noted earlier, Maecenas provided a liaison between the literary community and Octavian. In his fifth satire (*Sermones* 1.5), Horace describes a trip that he, Virgil, and Maecenas, among others, took to Brundisium. In that poem, Maecenas and Virgil both join Horace's party en route, enjoying each other's company along the way. While one need not extrapolate precise historical details from a poem of this nature, one can infer a camaraderie emblematic of the learned coterie of which Virgil and Maecenas were members.

Peter White has demonstrated that poets encountered notables of Roman *haut culture* through what he calls the "society of the great house." While figures such as Asinius Pollio and Messalla Corvinus, who would later be the patron of Tibullus and Ovid, have an easily ascertainable niche within such society, the emergence of Maecenas is more mysterious. The notion of a "circle" of poets around the figure of Maecenas is a misleading metaphor, for there is no evidence that Maecenas precisely directed the projects of his poet friends. Given the vast array of styles of poetry dedicated to Maecenas, it is unlikely that he pressed his friends to produce poetry of a certain genre, theme, or tone. Rather, as Horace suggests (*Serm.* 1.5), this society consisted of a bond of friendship affirmed by mutual poetic interests and respect.[5]

We have no way of knowing how Virgil, in particular, came into association with Maecenas or Octavian. Inferences from the *Eclogues* engender speculation that Virgil's personal experience is symbolized by the herdsman Tityrus' visit to Rome, where he encountered the youth (Octavian) who restored his confiscated property; yet this cannot be proved. Another possibility might be inferred from a single detail presented in the VSD. There one reads that Virgil had a home very near the gardens of Maecenas on the Esquiline:

> Because of his friends' liberalities [Virgil] possessed almost 10,000,000 sesterces and had a house in Rome on the Esquiline next to the gardens of Maecenas, although he also enjoyed his privacy a good deal in Campania and Sicily. (2.13)

Though no chronology is offered and, as we have seen, it would be unwise to rely too much on any detail of the VSD, the possibility that Virgil did reside in proximity to a landholding of Maecenas merits consideration. The detail of Virgil's house is, at any rate, not widely disputed in modern scholarly discourse. However Virgil may have acquired the property, the location near Maecenas dovetails nicely with a "society" based on *amicitia* or friendship. Such proximity would have allowed Virgil, Maecenas, and others frequent social interaction.

In any case, Maecenas is the sole dedicatee of the *Georgics*, though Octavian appears there as a character and occasional addressee.[6] Such invocation does not appear to be a matter of reciprocity and White's "society" seems reasonable in light of the internal evidence of Virgil's and Horace's poetry. That evidence would suggest that a relationship between Maecenas and Virgil began to develop at some point in the early 30s. In his first book of *Epistles*, published nearly two decades later, Horace recalls for the emperor his own introduction into this group:

Indeed, it was not mere luck that brought you to me: there was a point at which the brilliant one, Virgil, and after him, Varius, told you what I was. (1.6.54–5)

Amicitia between poets and their patrons relied on introduction and presentation. While we do not know precisely how Virgil was introduced to Maecenas, White's description of the inner workings of this group of cultured *literati* offers a tenable model.

Over the course of time, however, it may be that not all was well within this group. Maecenas is never mentioned in Virgil's poetry after the fourth *Georgic*. Speculation for Maecenas' waning influence centers upon an incident involving his brother-in-law, Terentius Varro Murena, and Fannius Caepio. Having achieved a hard-fought victory over the Alpine tribe of the Salassi three years previously, Murena held the consulship jointly with Augustus in 23 BC. Dio Cassius (54.4) and Suetonius (*Augustus* 19) speak of Murena hatching a plot against the emperor, with a court case spoken against the conspirators successfully by the future emperor Tiberius.

Admittedly the details are jumbled, for the dates in Dio are off by a year from those recorded in consular records (*fasti*), and in the same sources the first name (*praenomen*) of Murena is inconsistent. Moreover, Suetonius offers only a passing reference to Augustus' displeasure with Maecenas, who is supposed to have given information to his wife Terentia, Murena's sister:[7]

> Though I shall not cite too many examples, sometimes in fact [Augustus] even found deficiency in Marcus Agrippa's patience and Maecenas' discretion; Agrippa, from a mild suspicion of coolness toward himself and because Marcellus was being promoted over him, dropped everything and took off for Mytilene, while the other, as soon as he had discovered it, divulged to his wife, Terentia, the secret about the conspiracy of Murena. (*Divus Augustus* 66.3)

The argument for Maecenas' incurring political disfavor, laid out by Ronald Syme in *Roman Revolution* (1939), held sway for a season. Syme's broad thesis lay in his assumption that there was a serious power struggle within the Augustan cabinet between Agrippa and Maecenas. Gordon Williams downplays the conspiracy and shifts the date for Maecenas' movement out of the inner circle to 20 BC, positing a decline in Maecenas' influence. Counterarguments have been advanced by White, who questions the accuracy and importance of the Murena conspiracy.

Yet even if Maecenas did not fall entirely from favor – and some evidence in Seneca does suggest Maecenas' abiding influence (*Suas.* 1.12, 3.5) – the possibility of a conspiracy touching upon Maecenas at least tangentially cannot be entirely dismissed.

A more important fall that occurred in the 20s was that of Virgil's friend and contemporary poet, Gallus. Dio Cassius suggests that lack of discretion on Gallus' part contributed to his loss of Augustus' favor. A rather boastful stele may suggest that there may have been legitimate cause for Octavian's concern about Gallus' loyalty:[8]

> Cornelius Gallus ... first Prefect of Alexandria and Egypt ... overcame the enemy, was twice victorious in conflict, and was sacker of five cities, Boresos, Coptus, Ceramice, Diospolis Magna, and Ophieum, with their leaders of their rebellions caught by his army once it had crossed the Nile's cataracts into a place where arms had never hitherto been brought. (*ILS* 8995)

Dio adds that in Egypt Gallus had also placed many statues of himself and recorded his accomplishments on pyramids, an act that Gibson aptly connects with Horace's *sphragis* (poetic seal on his poetic collection, *Carm.* 3.30). As a result of consternation among the senators in Rome in 26 BC, Gallus was tried *in absentia* and convicted of unspecified charges associated with apparent *hybris*; he responded to the sentence by committing suicide.[9]

Thus, within one year of Octavian having adopted the name Augustus, one of Rome's finest poets suffered *damnatio memoriae* ("condemnation of the memory"), i.e., the official deletion of his name from public monuments and the destruction of his written works. As we saw in the discussion of Virgil's models in the previous chapter, Cornelius Gallus was not only an important poetic influence with regard to Virgil's style but was also a close friend. Servius (ad *G.* 4.1) speaks to the depth of this friendship, suggesting that the fourth *Georgic* originally featured "praises of Gallus" instead of the tale of Orpheus. Even if the fanciful notion of Virgil rewriting an episode of the *Georgics* (but not rewriting *Eclogue* 10, which also deals with Gallus' poetic accomplishment) seems unlikely, Gallus' death certainly had a profound effect on Virgil.

The death of Gallus in 26 had to have muted the joy associated with the new political order and, three years later, a conspiracy involving a friend such as Maecenas could not have simply passed unnoticed as Virgil was nearing completion of the *Aeneid* between 23 and 19. Before his death, Virgil had, for the most part, finished the epic, a mission-charged poem that reflects and balances the positive and the negative of the human experience. The *Aeneid* conveys wisdom derived from that sense of mission, while it also weighs the cost of human suffering.

Virgil's untimely death came on September 21, 19 BC in Brundisium, as he was returning from a trip to Greece. His *Aeneid* still lacked the final editorial touch, as numerous half-lines attest. The often repeated story drawn from the VSD (39f.) about his deathbed request that the *Aeneid* be burnt is likely to be entirely apocryphal. The poem was lightly edited by the poets Plotius and Tucca after Virgil's death.

The contacts of Virgil and Horace with Maecenas were not, strictly speaking, political; "taken one by one, they show less influence of political imperatives than of long-established tendencies which anchored literary activity in aristocratic social life," revealing "no sign of an overall strategy" for patronage on the part of Maecenas or Augustus.[10] Yet Virgil clearly had his own poetic strategy. In the chapters that follow, we shall see that Virgil was concerned with his principal themes of mission, which dominates the *Aeneid*; wisdom, which generally characterizes the *Georgics*; and dialogue, which is prominent in the *Eclogues*. Let us now turn to the last of these to begin our fuller consideration of the Virgil who is his text.

Notes

1   Servius states that Virgil adopted Cicero's phrase to describe Ascanius at *Aeneid* 12.168. See also Stephen Hinds, "Petrarch, Cicero, Virgil: Virtual Community in *Familiares* 24.4," *MD* 52 (2004), 168–9; R. A. Smith, *The Primacy of Vision in Virgil's* Aeneid (Austin, TX, 2005), 105f.; M. L. Clarke, "Rhetorical Influences in the *Aeneid*," *G&R* 18 (1949), 14–27. If no prototypical eclogues were in circulation, the anecdote is highly problematic.

2   S.v. "Atrium Libertatis," in Larry Richardson Jr., *A New Topographical Dictionary of Ancient Rome* (Baltimore, MD, 1992), 41; J. C. Anderson Jr., *The Historical Topography of the Imperial Fora*, Collection Latomus 182 (Brussels, 1984), 21–6; F. Castaglioni, "Atrium Libertatis," *RendLinc* 8 (1946), 276–91; M. Bonnefond-Coudry, "Le Senat republicaine dans l'atrium Libertatis?" *MEFRA* 91 (1979), 601–22; A. Barchiesi, *The Poet and the Prince: Ovid and Augustan Discourse* (Berkeley, CA, 1997), 87–9. On Augustus' diction, cf. Suetonius, *Divus Augustus*, 28.3. See Karl Galinsky, *Augustan Culture: An Interpretive Introduction* (Princeton, NJ, 1996), 141–224.

3 Richard Heinze, "Auctoritas," *Hermes* 60 (1925), 349–50; Galinsky (1996), 15–17, 204. See also Paul Zanker, *The Power of Images in the Age of Augustus*, tr. Alan Shapiro (Ann Arbor, MI, 1988), 98–100; Richardson (1992), s.v. *Ianus Geminus*, 207–8.

4 Coleman, ad *Ecl.* 6.7. Horsfall (2000), 29–30; see also John Van Sickle, "A Reader Challenged Theoretically Wonders, 'Where's the Book?' A Review of Brian W. Breed, *Pastoral Inscriptions: Reading and Writing Virgil's Eclogues*," *Vergilius* 53 (2007), 154; Wendell Clausen, *Virgil:* Eclogues (Oxford, 1994), 233–6. Though Clausen regards *Ecl.* 8 as dedicated to Octavian, most accept Pollio as the addressee. Elaine Fantham, *Roman Literary Culture: From Cicero to Apuleius* (Baltimore, MD, 1996), 70, hints that both could be intended.

5 Peter White, *Promised Verse: Poets and the Society of Augustan Rome* (Cambridge, 1993), 35–9.

6 Octavian is invoked at *G.* 1.25 and 503; *G.* 2.170.

7 Michael Swan, "The Consular Fasti of 23 BC and the Conspiracy of Varro Murena," *HSCP* 71 (1966), 235–47; Sir Ronald Syme, *The Roman Revolution* (Oxford, 1939), 333–43; Gordon Williams, "Did Maecenas 'Fall from Favor'? Augustan Literary Patronage," in Kurt Raaflaub and Mark Toher (eds.), *Between Republic and Empire* (Berkeley and Los Angeles, CA, 1990) is also a proponent of the conspiracy argument.

8 Hermann Dessau, *Inscriptiones Latinae Selectae* (rpt. Chicago, 1979), III.2.8995 [= *CIL* III.14147, 5]. Cf. J.-P. Boucher, *Caius Cornelius Gallus* (Paris, 1966), 45, who views the stele as a declaration of Octavian's political agenda. Bruce Gibson, "Horace: *Carm.* 3.30.1–6," *CQ* 47 (1997), 313.

9 Erich S. Gruen, "The Expansion of the Empire under Augustus," in Alan K. Bowman, Edward Champlin, and Andrew Lintott (eds.), *Cambridge Ancient History X: The Augustan Empire 43 BC–69 AD* (Cambridge, 1996), 148.

10 White (1993), 139.

3

Eclogue Dialogues

The natural property of Number is ten.
Pythagoras (DK 58 B 15)

On the top of the first page of the oldest extant Virgilian manuscript appears the title *Liber Bucolicon*. A blend of Greek and Roman, the Latin word *liber* means "book," while the transliteration of the Greek word *boukolikon* means "of cowherd songs." In light of the fact that Theocritus' collection, written just over two centuries earlier, was ultimately given this very name (though not necessarily by Theocritus), Virgil's use of this title is highly significant.[1] Virgil's later allusion to the collection in his *Georgics* ("I sang the songs of shepherds," 4.565) may suggest this title referred to the entire collection. The alternate title *Eclogae*, traditionally preferred by Anglophone scholars, is first seen in the VSD; the Greek word, *ecloga* (selection), corresponds to the Callimachean principle of "a small drop from a sacred fount" (*Hymn* 2.112) that emphasized each poem's individuality. Martindale observes that "the title was in all probability given by later editors 'Selections' (sc. *Eclogues*) serves to suggest that … [it was] composed as it were of chips from the writer's block."[2] Yet there remains a question as to whether these selections were excised from an already complete "block" or were the pieces assembled to form it.

From one point of view, it seems that they were assembled and later edited to form the collection. Recently, Brian Breed has suggested that these poems are likely to have been both literary and intended for performance. The VSD mentions that Virgil had enjoyed success in his own presentation of various *Eclogues*, while a slender piece of papyrological evidence for *Eclogue* 8 also suggests other sorts of individual "pastoral" performances.[3] Yet the nature of any such performances and of pastoral itself remains in question.

Scholars have spent much time addressing this issue, and clearly one aspect of the answer pertains to the content, for these poems include characters and themes that suggest a rustic atmosphere. That said, one must keep in mind that Virgil's pastoral poems are all written in dactylic hexameter, the "epic" meter that goes back to Homer. The Sicilian poet Theocritus refined this branch of epic to such an extent that he created a subcategory of that genre.

Dactylic hexameter consists of a series of six "feet" (or measures) with two basic beats within each foot. Each beat can be a long vowel sound, though the second beat can be resolved into two short vowel sounds (*viz.* in musical terms the way two quarter notes correspond to a half note). The first beat in the foot is always long. When the first sound is combined with a second long vowel sound, the resultant measure is called a spondee; a long vowel sound followed by two short vowels forms a dactyl. Before Virgil, this metrical pattern had been used by Ennius for the *Annales* and by Lucretius for his *De Rerum Natura*, the composition of which preceded the *Eclogues* by just over a decade. This is the only meter that Virgil used.

Theocritus most often employed dactylic hexameter for his bucolic poems. Writing near the beginning of the Hellenistic period (third century BC), Theocritus refined several genres to form pastoral, including the "low" genre of mime, which consisted of short comical skits. Theocritus would have known this genre through the work of the fifth-century mimographer Sophron of Syracuse. He also adapted certain aspects of the higher genres of Homeric epos and Hesiodic didactic. It is not surprising, therefore, that the direct line of descent to Virgil's *Eclogues* comes through Theocritus. Virgil's debt is much broader than merely his use of some of the names of Theocritus' characters or his invocation of Sicilian Muses.

In his distinctive adaptation of the genre, Virgil regularly engages issues connected to Rome. *Eclogue* 1 begins with a dialogue between the herdsmen Tityrus and Meliboeus about the matter of redistribution of land under Octavian; *Eclogue* 10 closes the collection with a poem that celebrates Virgil's contemporary poet Gallus, whose lover Lycoris is described as having followed a rival lover on his circuit of military service. Poetry and politics are thus connected to sophisticated subjects.

Readers, ancient and modern, have traditionally approached these poems in the order in which they come. Zetzel, among others, has made a strong case for reading them in this way, as Virgil is very likely to have so arranged them. Much work also has been done to establish the chronology of and to determine the design of the *Eclogues*, for which Van Sickle's thorough study remains seminal.[4] He calls attention to the poems' careful structural patterns, while at the same time deemphasizing the significance of the mystical aspect of numerology that scholars such as Maury have emphasized, particularly Virgil's use of numbers derived from Pythagorean ideas. Others, such as Heinze, who suggested Stoic influence, stressed different philosophical impulses for the collection. Virgil's work also shows signs of Epicurean influence, as he was associated with the Epicurean circle of Philodemus in Herculaneum. In short, one can find traces of many philosophical systems in the Virgilian corpus.

A century ago, Warde Fowler suggested the first-century philosopher Nigidius Figulus as a source for Virgil's use of Pythagorean ideas. The most important Pythagorean number was unquestionably ten, the outworking of a principle known as the *tetraktys*, the summation of the sequence of one plus two plus three plus four. Of this sequence, the numbers one, four, and ten hold places of prominence, since number one begins the sequence and number four is the building block of the formula that will arrive at ten.[5] The *tetraktys*, then, may be behind Virgil's choice to present his collection in ten poems and may put some added emphasis upon *Eclogues* 1, 4, and 10, which arguably are judiciously placed. *Eclogue* 4 stands in the critical position for the collection, vital for understanding the relationship of the theme of dialogue between future and past, city and country, politics and life, which this poem and the entire collection encompass.

Eclogue 4 also holds the promise of a new political order, with its focus upon the figure that will bring peace. *Eclogue* 10 is not simply a masterful tag to this collection but, rather, is the culmination of the bucolic tradition, justifying both its own place in the tradition and flirting with the notion that Gallus might have had a place within it. Virgil's tenth *Eclogue* extols Gallus as the successor of Orpheus and Hesiod.

Of greater significance to the *Eclogues* than numbers, however, is the notion of dualism – a concept by no means exclusive to Pythagoreans, but one that was important in their community – for Virgil frequently presents ideas along dualistic lines. The *Eclogues* particularly reveal such dualistic thought, for they are paired in reciprocal arrangement, often presenting two contrasting points of view.

If one compares Virgil's technique to that of Theocritus, it is clear that though Theocritus presents amoebean (dialogic) banter, he does not contrast experiences of political reality in the way that Virgil does. Virgil's

Tityrus and Meliboeus (*Ecl.* 1), engage such issues, as do his Moeris and Lycidas (*Ecl.* 9), for these characters compare their individual perceptions of the world. Dialogue derived from dualism clearly characterizes this collection.

Such dualism not only emerges from reading the poems closely but can also be seen in the fact that they are regularly considered in pairs. Even certain titles or subtitles of articles that treat these poems indicate inherent dualism and dichotomies: "Freedom and Ownership," "Nature and Art," "Dueling Contests," "Thrust and Counter-Thrust," "Easterners and Westerners," "Science and Myth," "Divine and Earthly Competition," "Goat Myth and Goat Song," and "Remembering and Forgetting." The last of these may serve as an example. Though its author ostensibly sets out to discuss Virgil's pronouncement about the demise of pastoral, he actually focuses on Virgil's dualistic tendencies, counting no less than five such instances.

Although the possibility of Pythagorean influence is by no means essential for the collection's structural or thematic elements, Pythagorean dualism may help to explain why these poems seem to function in pairs, also why Virgil's collection consists of ten poems and why Virgil emphasizes the reciprocal give-and-take of the amoebean banter inherited from Theocritus. Virgil goes further than his forebear, creating a world both Arcadian and Italian, rural and urban, carefree and yet fraught with *Realpolitik*. While the *Eclogues* are connected to each other in a variety of ways, each individual poem would seem to have a complementary piece.

The first pair I will consider is that of *Eclogues* 1 and 9, a grouping all scholars recognize. The second pair, *Eclogues* 2 and 8, is a set of poems meant to unite lovers, for *Eclogue* 2 beckons love while *Eclogue* 8 deals with songs to recover those whom the herdsmen's personae have lost. The third pair (3 and 7) consists of contests, typical of the bucolic genre. I will argue that the enigmatic and forward-looking *Eclogue* 4 is juxtaposed to the poem with which it is to be contrasted, *Eclogue* 5. The latter poem has been, since the time of Servius, regarded as metaphorical for the death and apotheosis of Julius Caesar, and commentators agree that there are good reasons to view Daphnis as symbolizing Caesar. This reading may shed light on the identity of the child of *Eclogue* 4, but this will be discussed later in more detail. *Eclogue* 6, a poem in the mouth of a poet (Silenus) within the poem, corresponds with *Eclogue* 10, which also contains a poet within the poem. These two poems frame the second half of the collection.

Virgil's dualism involves the transference of the Greek bucolic genre into the world of Roman poetry. With his Arcadia, a real Greek landscape located in the northern Peloponnese now transformed into a new bucolic world, Virgil does not portray mere rural escapism. His fresh approach to this genre shows that he has changed it; having taken hold of the Arcadian landscape, he places it firmly in his Italy.

L'arte allusiva: Virgil's Imitative Style

In the third *Eclogue*, two herdsmen, Damoetas and Menalcas, discuss possible prizes for their proposed competition. Damoetas declines Menalcas' suggestion of a prize from the flock, suggesting instead cups of beech-wood, embossed by Alcimedon:

> on these cups a slow-growing vine, added with a delicate twist, covers the spreading clusters with pale ivy. In the middle are two emblems, one of Conon, the other – who was the other, who demarcated all the cosmos for humankind with a rod, explaining what seasons the reaper and what seasons the stooping plowman should have? (3.38–42)

These cups, described in an ecphrasis, are even more desirable prizes than animals. Yet Virgil's characters are not merely shepherds; they are poets, whose pastoral genre is inspired not by a literal meadow or hillside but by the poetic tradition itself. Art is a better prize for learned poets who will comprehend the cups' astrological images.

In mentioning Conon by name, Damoetas reveals knowledge of mathematicians and their scholarly contribution. His knowledge extends to his mentioning an unnamed "other," perhaps the third-century BC mathematician/astronomer Archimedes, the author of several works on spheres, who also may have constructed a planetarium.[6] Further possibilities for this figure include Eratosthenes or Archytus' student Eudoxus, who was among the first to employ mathematics to determine the course of the planets. While the Verona scholiast suggests four others, only the names of Archimedes and Eratosthenes do not conform to the metrical pattern of dactylic hexameter. Whichever it is, Virgil here alludes to learned studies, which to proper herdsmen would have been entirely inaccessible. Virgil's flock-attending poets, however, "know" such studies well.

The precise identity of the second astronomer is less important than the fact that mention of him involves an allusion to Catullus. In one poem of his collection, written roughly fifteen years before the *Eclogues*,

Catullus had adapted Callimachus' "Lock of Berenice," a poem written to describe Conon's astronomical discovery of Queen Berenice's severed lock. Berenice had dedicated her lock for the safe return of her husband, Ptolemy III, from his Syrian campaign (66.1–7). Virgil's citation of Conon ties his portrait on this cup to Catullus' making a constellation (known as a catasterism) out of Berenice's lock. This cup is, therefore, Alexandrian in two senses: it evokes the Alexandrian tradition of the advancement of knowledge in mathematics and the sciences while revealing also a political savvy conveyed through poetry. Likewise, Callimachus' poem refers to the queen putting her lock in the stars, which also anticipates the way that Daphnis ascends on high in *Eclogue* 5.

Far from simple herdsmen's prizes, then, these cups also broadly evoke the pastoral tradition. For example, Theocritus mentions a prize cup on which a woman is portrayed:

> Next to her two men, handsome with their long-coiffed hair, contend in alternating words with one another. But such things do not touch her heart. Rather, laughing, she looks on this one, yet then again she casts her attention toward that man. But they, with their eyes swollen because of their love, strive fruitlessly. And next after them an old fisherman is carved … (45) A small way above the sea-beaten old man there is a fair threshing floor, laden with reddening clusters, which a certain little boy keeps watch over. (*Idyll* 1.33–47)

While clearly indebted to Theocritus, Virgil's treatment is distinct. In what Jeffrey Wills calls an allusive variation, Virgil has made two cups the prize: doubling the prize may suggest *aemulatio* (rivalry) with his predecessor.[7] Theocritus' cup resonates with Homer's description of the shield of Achilles, where the imagined viewer sees two cities:

> And on it he made two fine cities of mortal men. In one are weddings and wedding feasts, where young women are led out of their bowers around the city by torchlight. A great wedding hymn arises: young men, dancers, writhe about, and among them flutes and lyres make a great sound. And the women, each standing at her house door, are astounded. The people gather in the market where a quarrel breaks out – two men arguing about the death settlement of a slain man. One proclaims publicly that he has rendered full compensation, the other denies having received anything. (*Il.* 18.490–500)

This description consists of sights, sounds, and life in one of the two cities described. While in Homer two men argue over the morbid subject of compensation for the death of a kinsman, in Theocritus the dispute has been transformed: two men quarrel over their love for one woman. Theocritus thus has taken "the topos of the stopped moment"[8] and modified it to fit this new context. The shield's portrait of two cities and the debate within one of them has now been recast in a more personal manner, focused on the individual rather than the state; further, it is depicted not on a shield, a weapon of war, but on a goblet, a symbol of peace.

By his allusion to Homer, Theocritus has evoked the epic tradition, only to adapt it to this new bucolic context. Virgil, however, evokes Theocritus, the father of the bucolic tradition, overlaying his adaptation with the "new poet" (or neoteric) Catullus, who is himself an heir to Callimachus in the Alexandrian tradition. Thus, Virgil creates his place in the tradition while also forging a three-way communication among reader, text, and original context. In the case of Virgil's allusion to the cups, there is even a further dialogue going back to Homer, as well as a reference to contemporary works of art of similar design.

Let us return to the passage in question. Damoetas responds to Menalcas by wagering two cups that he also received from Alcimedon, which feature in their ecphrasis the story of Orpheus and the trees that follow him:

> For me, that same Alcimedon made two cups and he covered the handles with soft acanthus, and in the middle he placed Orpheus and the trees that followed him. Nor yet have I put my lips to them but I keep them put aside. If you look to the calf, there is no reason for you to praise the cups.
>
> M: Today you will never get away; I will go wherever you call. (*Ecl.* 3.44–9)

While the first of these lines contains yet another reference to the fabrication of cups in Theocritus (*Id.* 1.55), where acanthus is also a feature, the final allusion is less direct. To Damoetas' counterproposal of his own cups, Menalcas states that Damoetas will never get away. Clausen notes (ad 49) that this particular pattern of words harks back to a line from the *Trojan Horse*, a play of Naevius (third-century BC). Naevius' "today you will never get away but that you die by my right hand" would be imitated by Virgil in his version of the same story in the second book of the *Aeneid* (2.670). Yet what might an imitation of Naevius in the third *Eclogue* mean?

Clausen notes that the tone of this line was, by Virgil's time, colloquial, something that in the context of shepherds' banter would be entirely appropriate. Furthermore, Menalcas' suggestion of such relentless pursuit is clearly hyperbolic. For Naevius the stakes are martial engagement and death itself, but in Menalcas' mouth, relentless pursuit in a literary contest. This allusion then contrasts the Naevian with the new context, showing that Menalcas will demonstrate the value of the cups and the importance of the dialogue and poetic rivalry between these two friends. That dialogue is paralleled in Virgil's own dialogue with Naevius and other models.

All of these examples of allusion occur in just a few lines of the third *Eclogue* (38–49), revealing in a short space both the depth and breadth of Virgilian allusion. Virgil uses a number of models in the *Eclogues*, principally Theocritus. But one can go further. Homer, Callimachus, and Catullus are also vital pieces of the complicated puzzle of source material.

Let this short analysis serve two purposes: it reveals the diverse way that the poetic tradition resonates in and beyond Virgil's poetry and suggests that understanding the function of an allusion is important for proper appreciation of Virgil's literary craftsmanship.

Poetic Pairing

Allusion denotes indebtedness to tradition that is invoked not merely for poetic showmanship but as the frame within which Virgil will engage universal human issues. Thus, not surprisingly Virgil is indebted to a wider tradition than poetry alone. For the *Eclogues*, dualism characterizes the universal issues and is reflected in the thematic pairing of the poems. Many have noted that poems 1 and 9, 3 and 7, or 2 and 8 can be so viewed. Such dualism is not confined merely to structure. As we now consider the *Eclogues* in pairs, we shall see that dualism is important for content as well.

Eclogues I and 9

Eclogue 1 is a poem of paradoxes. This can be seen in the contrast between its two characters: Meliboeus, a landholder who has faced confiscation of property without recourse, now plans for departure from his beloved farm. He speaks first, addressing Tityrus, an aging slave, who paradoxically has *not* lost his land. This slave has obtained freedom (*libertas*) through the intervention of a "god." Syme long ago noted that *libertas* was a politically charged watchword that Octavian used in attempts to overcome Antonius after Caesar's death. Yet ironically *libertas* is the condition that the slave Tityrus says he now enjoys.

Central to this poem is a tension between the desire for rural freedom and the characters' grappling with the political realities attendant upon urban life. Emphasizing this dichotomy, Putnam notes that, even in the way Virgil describes trees in the first *Eclogue*, the poet "establishes a mood of tension: What happens when Rome and the village come into conjunction?" Alpers, too, finds in these poems a dichotomous character, with tension between "public and private, high and low, epic and lyric."[9] One might add, too, that Virgil's allusions to Theocritus often combine elements from pairs of Theocritean poems (e.g., *Eclogue* 3 combines major themes of *Idylls* 1 and 5).

Such paradoxes infuse the entire book of *Eclogues*, apparent already in the poem's first lines:

> Tityrus, you, reclining beneath the covering of a spreading beech tree, contemplate the sylvan Muse with a thin reed; I am leaving the borders and sweet fields of my fatherland. I am fleeing my fatherland; you, Tityrus, lingering in the shade, teach the woods to resound with "Lovely Amaryllis." (1.1–5)

Meliboeus' words present a stark difference in fortunes: while he faces obligatory expulsion, Tityrus enjoys liberty to make music. Tityrus responds by explaining to Meliboeus how it happens that he can stay:

> Oh Meliboeus, a god has made this repose for me. For he will always be a god to me, often a tender lamb from my sheepfold will stain his altar. That one, as you see, has permitted my oxen to wander and me to play what I would like on my rustic reed. (6–10)

The young man, whom Tityrus regards as a "god," has restored not only property but also poetry, for repose (*otia*) does not connote merely rustic leisure, but to the reader familiar with its significance in Roman poetry it suggests time in the poetic workshop. Tityrus thus puts his political restitution on a par with his artistic expression, inspired and permitted by the divine properties of the young Octavian, whom the reader infers to be this unnamed god.

By contrast Meliboeus first focuses on his dispossession, only later querying the god's identity:

> Indeed I do not begrudge you; rather, I am amazed; to such an extent everywhere all round there is trouble in every field … I recall oaks, touched from heaven, predicting this misfortune for us if our mind had not been unlucky. But, still, tell me, Tityrus, who that god of yours is. (11–12, 16–18)

Though Meliboeus conceives of Tityrus' good fortune primarily in terms of property and cattle, Tityrus focuses on freedom, a concept linked to musical (and poetic) composition. Within a few lines we have gleaned an essential feature of Virgil's *Eclogues* and virtually all of his poetry. Virgil introduces the notion of dialogue between Tityrus and Meliboeus, offering two points of view, two experiences of life for two individuals, whose words encompass the dualistic notions of man and god, poetry and freedom, displacement and despair. Such dualism will emerge in a different form in the *Aeneid*, there called "two voices" by Adam Parry.

After Tityrus' description of his trip to the city, Meliboeus notes how fortunate his friend is: "Lucky old man, here among familiar rivers and sacred fountains you will seek out shade's cooling" (46). Implicit in these words is the fact that Meliboeus will not claim those fonts or shade, and he will state as much a few lines later:

> But some of us will go from here to thirsty Africa, part to Scythia, part of us to the Oaxes that takes up chalk as it goes and part of us will go deep among the Britons, who are divided from the rest of the world. Behold, will I be amazed to see, after a long time, the boundaries of my fatherland and, after so long, my impoverished hut's roof heaped up with turf – my realm – and my ears of grain? (64–9)

The balance of Meliboeus' imagined vision of exile from his beloved farm contrasts with Tityrus' vision of hope realized at the hands of the god/ man. These points of view represent two pathetically dissimilar experiences of life.

Eclogue 9 resumes this same theme. Lycidas, evicted from his property, engages in a dialogue with Moeris. Virgil chooses not to contrast how these characters differ with regard to their fates, but rather to show what effect the disruption both have suffered has on art in their lives, specifically how each is deprived of song. Each has lost memory, each craves the art he has lost. As Coleman puts it succinctly in his introduction to this poem, "music like farming has become one of the casualties of war."

As the poem begins, Lycidas inquires about Moeris' direction, "Are you going where the road leads to the city?" This question suggests a new direction in pastoral that engages urban themes. Moeris briefly describes the dire situation of property confiscations, to which Lycidas inappropriately retorts that he had heard that Menalcas' poetry had saved the local property holders' lands from such misfortune. Yet Lycidas' inept challenge to Moeris' initial description ("does such great evil fall on anyone?," 17) forces Moeris to rehash some of the details of his difficulty, to which he adds that his friend's songs had at least preserved his own life and that of Menalcas, whose presence is felt in the poem, even though he is not present.

Lycidas explains that earlier he had eavesdropped on Menalcas singing a song to Lycidas' love, Amaryllis. The song he quotes is by no means a love song to a woman but merely instructions for Tityrus about care of a flock. So inappropriate are the verses that Moeris feels compelled to correct Lycidas: "No," he says, "rather he [Menalcas] was singing verses for Varus, verses from a song that he has not yet finished" (26). Strikingly, however, the verses that Moeris cites are no more appropriate for a song to a young woman than the others were. Indeed, these words form part of a politically charged appeal to Varus to spare Mantua. Both Moeris and Lycidas allude to, but cannot quite recall, the work of Menalcas.

Lycidas' response is somewhat ill-timed, for in a self-effacing manner he invites Moeris to a singing contest. Having compared himself unfavorably to the urban neoteric singers Cinna and Varius (35–6), Moeris takes up Lycidas' indelicate attempt at genial banter:

In silence I reflect on it, in hopes that I can recall the song; nor is it an ignoble one. Come hither, Galatea; for what game is there amidst the waves? Here is glowing spring, here the Earth pours forth various flowers along the rivers, here the white poplar spreads over a cave and the pliant vines have covered the shady spots. Come hither; let raging waves crash against the shore. (9.38–43)

Although Moeris fancies himself a part of that "city group," paradoxically he cannot recall the words of the urban song. Their interchange points up the difficulty that these two characters have in adapting themselves and their poetic agenda to the poetry of the city, though such adaptation is ultimately possible, for Lycidas' words are those he should have cited for Amaryllis to hear when he mistakenly recalled Menalcas' song as being instructions for Tityrus about feeding sheep.

Virgil's use of the adjective *tacitus* (in silence) – a word he uses before the *Aeneid* only here and once in the *Georgics* (2.254) – helps to explain the situation of Moeris. The lines that Moeris was recalling "in silence" had, in Menalcas' original context, been part of an invitation to his lover to draw close ("come hither") and "let raging waves crash against the shore," which at the very least suggests the release of worry.[10] These are indeed the lines that Lycidas, "in silence," should have overheard Menalcas reciting to Amaryllis.

Though the poem ends with a somber reflection about the unreliability of memory, the conclusion also holds out hope for another song. That song belongs to Menalcas, the singer masked throughout this piece, who is the poet who remembers and whose verses about Galatea are memorable, for Moeris had recalled them. Such verses provide a basis for the poems that will triumph in transitioning pastoral from country to city:

> Here is the halfway point for us; for the tomb of Bianor is beginning to appear. Here, where farmers are clipping dense foliage, here, Moeris, let us sing; here bring your kids to rest; yet we shall come into the city. Or if we are afraid that the night should gather rain sooner, we may go singing the while, for the journey will grieve us the less for it. There, I'll relieve you of your bundle that we might wend our way singing. (59–65)

Though Lycidas' mentioning of Bianor's tomb evokes an image of death this is only the halfway point to the city and, whatever negative image a burial place might evoke, this one is in fact being passed by.

A more important reason for the reference to the "halfway point" and tomb, however, is Virgil's allusion to Theocritus' seventh *Idyll*, which featured a similar reference. Theocritus' character Simichidas speaks of Chalcon's lineage:

> [Chalcon] made the Spring Bourina with his foot, pressing his knee firmly on the rock; and next to it both poplars and elms, arched over and thick, weaved a covering with green leaves over a well-shaded grove. And we had not yet reached the halfway point in the road, nor did the tomb of Brasilas appear to us, when we came upon a certain goodly traveler, by the Muses' grace, Lycidas by name, a goatherd, nor did anyone who saw him not know that he was a goatherd, for he seemed exactly like one. (*Idyll* 7.6–14)

Even before Theocritus introduces Lycidas (also a character in *Eclogue* 9), Theocritus first explains that Chalcon had made a spring well up underfoot. With its lush vegetation and seclusion, this spring Bourina, which containing the Greek word for "ox" (*bous*) also evokes bucolic poetry, may have programmatic overtones, for springs are often seats of poetic inspiration. Theocritus' "ox" spring, Bourina, would seem here to rival the "horse" spring, Hippocrene, made famous by Hesiod; accordingly, Theocritus' poem transitions to a new poetic realm, Coan rather than (the more traditional) Boeotian. Bourina's nymphs equal Muses and the rustic figure Lycidas plays the role of poet. Thus, the seventh *Idyll* offers a transition to a new poetic vista suited to the new genre of bucolic.

Consideration of *Idyll 7* gives us insight for the contextualizing of the Theocritean material in Virgil's ninth *Eclogue*. Whereas Theocritus begins with the passing of the tomb and the halfway point in the road, Virgil closes with it. Theocritus' characters are leaving the city and going toward the countryside (e.g., the river Haleis, *Id.* 7.1–2), but Virgil's draw closer to the city (*Ecl.* 9.1 and 62). If Theocritus' tomb reference refers to the passing through of Hesiodic material and moving on to a new venue, then Virgil's imitation may betoken his own passing through (and even out of) the bucolic genre, as he moves toward "urban" poetry (or, better, "urbane," i.e., characterized by a refined style known as *urbanitas*). Accordingly, the content of *Eclogue* 10 resumes this theme, where Gallus embodies the urban poetry toward which Lycidas and Moeris journey.

In *Eclogue* 9, Lycidas quotes Menalcas, saying, "Daphnis, graft your pears; your grandchildren will pluck your fruits" (50). As a poetic descendent of Theocritus, Virgil honors his model by plucking the fruits of his poetic forebear and, in contrast to Lycidas and Moeris' failure to recall Menalcas, Virgil correctly recalls Theocritus' poetry, transforming it into a form acceptable in the city that stands ready to receive it. Virgil has grafted Theocritean pears through allusions to Theocritus' poetry, preparing the reader for the final poem in the collection, where Gallus, who represents urban poetry, is welcomed into the pastoral setting.

Eclogue 1 situates the bucolic genre in the Roman context: Virgil's *Eclogues* will be different from Theocritus' *Bukolika*, for they are not an escape from, but a dialogue between, the political realities of the *urbs* and the freedom of Arcadia. The complementary piece, *Eclogue* 9, redefines the genre in such a way as to look beyond itself, anticipating refined and urbane poetry that paradoxically will manifest itself in *Eclogue* 10's idealized rural poetic landscape and, beyond this collection, in the rural *urbanitas* of the *Georgics*. Thus, Virgil's movement from country to city

– or rather from *Eclogue* 1's self-proclaimed rustic Muse to *Eclogue* 9's anticipation of *urbanitas* – suggests an end to what Van Sickle has called the "Tityran mode." Lycidas, who had been in Theocritus unmistakably a goatherd, now advances toward Virgil's city, inviting Moeris to accompany him. This urban relocation is ostensibly caused by politics; it is, in reality, a poetic shift.

Eclogues 2 and 8

Eclogues 2 and 8, situated within the outer frame of *Eclogues* 1 and 9, form another pair and create a smaller frame that helps structure this poetry book. *Eclogue* 2 encompasses the story of the goatherd Corydon's homoerotic love lament for Alexis. As Coleman and other commentators have noted, *Eclogue* 2 is indebted to Theocritus' eleventh *Idyll*, whence Virgil drew not only the locale of Sicily for the setting but also details from Theocritus' self-absorbed Polyphemus for the portrait of Corydon. Corydon uses Polyphemus' words, while showing range also befitting other poetic figures.

One such figure is Orpheus, whose behavior Corydon imitates when he goes into the woods to lament. There Corydon "composes" a poem addressed to Alexis but actually heard only by the trees, like Orpheus' lament for Eurydice. Thus, Corydon neither awaits nor expects any response when he states that Alexis will eventually lament his pride: "white privets fall, black hyacinths are gathered" (18). In this verse there is more than a mere reference to the fashioning of garlands; the colors imply the roles that lovers play: white is the female color, while the dark refers to the male. Thus, to make Alexis jealous, Corydon suggests his willingness to don the female persona. All of this is, of course, mere conceit, as Alexis never hears Corydon's words.

Corydon soon decides to try another approach when he exaggerates his personal great wealth. Yet if he is a slave, as Coleman supposes, he could not have owned the "thousand lambs" that he boasts (21). His boasting and vain promises continue as he vaunts that he can offer gifts of roe fawns (40) and baskets of flowers brought by the nymphs. Corydon has entered into a fantasy landscape where he can transform Alexis into a superior musician (31) and himself into an Orpheus-figure.

Corydon is ready to take on any role, pursuer or pursued, to entice his Alexis, whose name fittingly enough means "he who wards off." When Corydon plays an aggressive role, his threat to Alexis, paradoxically, is that Corydon can himself play the passive role for Menalcas as easily as that of the aggressor in regard to Thestylis (43). Corydon also seeks to make Alexis jealous with his former girlfriend Amaryllis (14, 52). Beyond that, Corydon states that it would be better for Alexis to enter Corydon's fantasy landscape in the role of a singer, where the two of them can enjoy music and dialogue, not unlike Damon and Alphesiboeus in *Eclogue* 8.

In *Eclogue* 8, the narrator informs the reader that the two herdsmen mentioned above sing so well that they are capable of changing the course of rivers:

> We shall sing of the Muse of the herdsmen Damon and Alphesiboeus, at whom the heifer, forgetful of her grasses, marveled as they contended, at whose song lynxes were stupefied and rivers, changed, left behind their own courses; that muse of Damon and Alphesiboeus shall we sing. (8.1–5)

Alluding to river-changing poets such as Daphnis, Linus, and Orpheus, Virgil demonstrates Damon and Alphesiboeus' skill. In *Eclogue* 2, Corydon's quasi-elegiac lament to nature about his lack of success in enticing his lover had placed him in the tradition of Orpheus; nevertheless, Corydon's position had been on the "losing side" of that tradition, although his poem was excellent, for allusions to Theocritus' Polyphemus reveal that Corydon should be also regarded as a poet of Theocritus' caliber.

The poets of *Eclogue* 8, however, share a single Muse, as they sing an elegiac love song in pastoral mode. Damon seeks to entice a new lover, while Alphesiboeus wishes to bring one back. The latter uses one rendering of *carmina*, that of "spells," to achieve his goal of bringing back Daphnis, while Damon uses the other nuance of the same word, "songs," to evoke jealousy – like Corydon in *Eclogue* 2 – for his lost lover Nysa. Just as these two herdsmen use two aspects of *carmina*, they represent two aspects of Corydon's character from *Eclogue* 2.

Like Corydon, who in *Eclogue* 2 had lamented his plight to the woods, Damon begins with a similar complaint (19), hyperbolically adding the imminence of his "final hour" (20). His pipes are to play the verses of Mt Maenalus, the sylvan setting that hears the plight of lovers. Damon soon lays out the situation: Nysa, Damon's lover, has found a new beau, Mopsus, a turn of events that seems to Damon rather unnatural. In what Breed has posited as a parody of a wedding song, Damon taunts Mopsus, calling Nysa his "bride" (29). By echoing words from Theocritean *Idylls*

3 and 11, Damon evokes Corydon's comparison of himself with Theocritus' Polyphemus. These poems form a dialogue with each other through the shared Theocritean source. Dionysus, too, may be referenced behind the name of Damon's beloved Nysa, as her name was also that of the mountain where the infant Dionysus was reared by a nymph by the same name. Dionysus was himself famous for being a "new lover" of Ariadne when she had been abandoned by Theseus.

The poem now takes an introspective turn. Moving away from self-pity, Damon tenderly recalls first meeting Nysa as she was picking apples with her mother, when he was twelve years old (38–40). Although they were childhood sweethearts, now he knows how harsh Amor, the inhuman child of cruel Venus, can be (43–9). This leads to a third mother/child combination, namely that of Medea and her children, whom she kills (Nysa and her mother were the first such combination). Virgil has allowed for such a juxtaposition through an "apostrophe" (direct address) that provides an adequate transition between Venus and Medea:

> Savage love taught the mother [Medea] to stain her hands with the blood of her children. You, mother [Venus], are also cruel. Is the mother [Venus] more cruel, or that boy [Amor] more wicked? That boy is wicked; you too, mother, are cruel. (8.47–50)

The mothers mentioned are interrelated, for one is passion (Venus) and the other gives birth to the object of Damon's passion (Nysa), while the third (Medea) shows the lengths to which passion can drive a lover.

Damon now uses a series of impossible events (*adynata*), such as oaks bearing apples and the rivalry between types of songbirds, to describe the unnatural union of Nysa and Mopsus. The transition from songbirds to singing bards is easy enough, leading to a straightforward substitution of Orpheus for Tityrus: "let Tityrus be Orpheus," Damon sings, "let Orpheus be in the woods, let Arion be among the dolphins" (55–6). One recalls that Orpheus, like Dionysus invoked via Nysa's name, is the tamer of both the animal and botanic worlds. By placing Orpheus in the woods, where after Eurydice's death he performed his song that tamed nature, Damon again evokes Corydon's lament over Alexis' departure.

Damon's reference to Arion has a different kind of significance. While Orpheus died not for his song but for his homosexuality, Arion's swan song was anything but a finale, for, according to Herodotus (1.24.6), he was rescued by dolphins and transported back to Corinth. Accordingly, as Damon speaks of throwing himself into the sea, he introduces the theme of deliverance through the allusion to Orpheus, who nearly delivered Eurydice by song, and through reference to the story of Arion, the great singer who was miraculously rescued.

Though such allusive language offers hope for deliverance, Damon's words are less than hopeful:

> Let everything become the middle of the sea. Farewell, woods! Let me be cast headlong from the lookout point of a lofty mountain into the waters; you have this, the final gift of me, as I die. Cease, oh flute, now cease my Maenalian verses. (8.58–61)

One further bard alluded to here is Sappho, who out of her love for Phaon jumped from the Leucadian promontory. Fittingly, Alphesiboeus' song is presented from a woman's point of view for her lover Daphnis, the "divine" (45) and deified poet of *Eclogue* 5.

Following an invocation of the Muses, Alphesiboeus renders his song, or rather, his "spell" (the other meaning of *carmen*). Alphesiboeus has donned the female persona of Amaryllis, a witch-like character, to perform this magic ritual:

> Bring water and gird these altars with the soft woolen band and burn rich olive boughs and spiced, choice incense that I, by magic rights, may try to ward off the rational feelings of my spouse. There is nothing lacking except spells. Lead Daphnis home from the city, my spells, lead him home. Spells can even lead the moon down from the sky, Circe changed the comrades of Odysseus by spells, a cold snake is broken in the mead by enchanting. (8.64–71)

To make the connection with songs that betoken spells, Alphesiboeus specifically invokes Circe, whose magical powers transformed Odysseus' men in Homer. Amaryllis has thus become a Circe figure, appropriating the magical power that such a figure evokes.

The reason that Alphesiboeus' female persona wants to ward off her spouse is because a true lover cannot be rational; but, as Breed has noted, the fact that she is transgendered may also indicate that the relationship with Daphnis is meant to rival or supplant a "normal" spouse.[11] Daphnis is the legendary "classic" poet (*Eclogue* 5), on a par with Orpheus, poetically, and with Caesar, politically. As such, one can assume that only a unique power can draw him from the city.

To emphasize the magical aspects of his song, Alphesiboeus turns to a ritual involving threads and numbers: "I connect these three lines, distinct by their threefold colors, for the first time. ... A god rejoices in the uneven number ... Connect the three colors with three knots ... and say, 'I connect the bonds of Venus'" (73–5, 77–8). Such ritual language imitates closely Theocritus' second *Idyll*, in which Thestylis is instructed to strew the barley on the fire while dubbing it "the bones of Delphis" (2.21). But Alphesiboeus' "bonds of Venus" may also be designed to recall the mother-son relationship of Amor and Venus in Damon's song, just as the three threads may allude to the three mothers mentioned there.

In the next few lines, the ritual continues, with an interesting reference to burning the laurel tree as part of the ritual – interesting because the Greek word for laurel is *daphne*, a clever paronomasia upon the name of Daphnis. This tree, feminine in gender but sacrificed for a male namesake, complements the gender reversal of Alphesiboeus' persona:

> Such love had I for Daphnis as when a cow loves a bull and, weary from seeking him through the glades and the high groves, she lies down, lost, on the green swamp-grass next to the river of water, nor does it occur to her to give in to the late night; may such love hold him nor may there be a care for me to heal him. (8.85–9)

Whom does the cow represent? While the love at first seems to be that of Alphesiboeus' female persona, the precatory verbs in the last line of those cited above (89) suggest instead the emotional vantage point of Daphnis. The cow, therefore, befits either Daphnis or Alphesiboeus/Amaryllis, though by gender it should actually belong to neither.

After the next refrain of "Lead Daphnis home from the city, my songs, lead him home" (recurring nine times), Amaryllis casts Daphnis in the role of Theseus, whom Catullus had confirmed as the classic example of one who loves and leaves. The choice of words here certainly evokes that Catullan image (64.132f.), as Amaryllis states, "That faithless man once left these spoils for me, dear pledges of himself." Daphnis will himself become a prototype for Aeneas, who does this very thing in leaving Dido (*Aen.* 4.305), who will carry out similar magic rites using spoils left by Aeneas. Putnam once dubbed these spoils "pledges" of Daphnis' return.

For all her efforts, however, Amaryllis concedes that Daphnis cares not for spells. Even as she carries the ash, fire bursts out. Not sure how to interpret the omen, she prays that it betoken good:

> May it be a good thing! I certainly do not know what it is, and Hylax (the dog) barks on the threshold. Do we believe it? Or can it be that those who are in love themselves make up dreams for themselves? Cease now your songs, cease, as Daphnis comes from the city. (8.106–9)

The omen does indeed prove to be a good one, for Daphnis returns from the city. This ending should be contrasted with the final journey of the ninth poem, where Lycidas and Moeris make their way "to the city" (9.62).

The contrast with this poem and the second *Eclogue* is clear enough: both treat playfully a lover seeking a lost partner. The shared relationship of *Eclogues* 2 and 8 also sheds some light on the song of Alphesiboeus' transgendered persona. In *Eclogue* 2, Corydon's lament is homoerotic, whereas in *Eclogue* 8's first half, Damon's song is heteroerotic. Alphesiboeus' response, however, is neither and both. It caps the sequence of these songs by confusing the issue as a man playing a woman beckons home another man, Daphnis.

Let us consider a further level of narrative about *Eclogue* 8, beyond characterization. Near the poem's opening, the poetic persona addresses an unnamed person to whom this poem is dedicated:

> Whether you overcome now the rocks of great Timavus or you choose the shore of the Illyrian sea, will that day ever come when I may sing of your deeds? Will it ever be possible for me to carry through the entire world your songs alone worthy of the Sophoclean buskin? From you will be the beginning, for you will I cease. Receive these songs, undertaken at your bidding, and allow me to entwine around your temples this ivy amidst the laurels of victory that are already there. (8.6–13)

Coleman's view that the poem is "almost certainly addressed to Pollio" represents the opinion of most scholars. That Virgil may have had Octavian in mind, however, squares better with the geographical references, for Octavian was campaigning in Illyria in 35–33. The phrase, "your songs alone worthy of the Sophoclean buskin" would indicate that the dedicatee would have to be a playwright. Van Sickle and Clausen regard Octavian as the best candidate, since we know from the Suetonian life of Augustus (85.7) that Octavian composed at least one tragedy. The phrase "from you will be the beginning, for you will I cease" would therefore connote Octavian, who was bringing a new peace to Rome and was without doubt the young man and savior in *Eclogue* 1. Yet why is he unnamed? The reason may have to do with the nature of patronage. As we saw in the previous chapter, Virgil does not dedicate poetry to Rome's chief regent directly, but through another in his learned society of friends. That this is the case can be seen in the dedication of the *Georgics* to Maecenas.

Finally, let us consider Virgil's looking ahead in *Eclogue* 8. Virgil closes this poem with a call to a new style of poetry ("Let us rise up; the shade is accustomed to be heavy for singers"), an invocation that raises further questions. Do these words, as Van Sickle suggests, point toward a future work that will be the fulfillment of the quasi-*recusatio* of poem 8's dedication? Pastoral is moving toward the city, a direction in which at least temporarily it was already going in *Eclogue* 1, when Tityrus visited the young ruler-god. Without pressing generic associations too tightly, one can see that Virgil's poetry is in transition, as is also clear in *Eclogue* 9, in which the movement from the countryside to the city reflects a further step in this stylistic transition. The beckoning of Daphnis away from the city suggests bucolic's ironic "resistance" to that transition.

Eclogues 3 and 7

Arranged near the center of each of the *Eclogues'* two halves, poems 3 and 7 anchor the collection. The names of the characters derive from Theocritus and, as Theocritus does in *Idyll* 5, Virgil makes a singing contest the central feature of each poem. In Theocritus, a cup appears in *Idyll* 1, where the goatherd offers it as payment. That cup provides a model for two cups in this singing match, though in Virgil the cups become payment for a wager; as mentioned earlier in this chapter, the ecphrasis of these cups, too, is important for this poem.

Virgil begins *Eclogue* 3 with Meliboeus asking Damoetas about the flock before them, "Whose cattle is this? Can it be that of Meliboeus?" Damoetas responds that these cattle are Aegon's. Meliboeus then presents an anecdote about himself and Aegon as being rivals for Neaera. This exchange closely follows one in Theocritus' *Idyll* 4, thus situating it in a Theocritean context, as Virgil communicates to his reader immediately that this poem is a clear outgrowth of that tradition. Damoetas soon claims that Meliboeus desecrated a shrine by having intercourse there while the goats and nymphs looked on. After a bit of playful sparring also indebted to *Idyll* 4, Damoetas and Meliboeus agree on a prize of cups, a prize that is in fact never presented. Damoetas then invites Palaemon to adjudicate the dialogue that ensues:

D: Muses, begin from Jove, as everything is full of Jove; he cultivates
    the lands, for him are my songs a care.
M: And Phoebus loves me; for Phoebus, his own gifts are always with
    me, laurels and this lightly blushing hyacinth.

D: A playful girl, Galatea, seeks me with an apple, and she flees to
    the willows, desiring first to be seen.
M: But Amyntas, my flame, offers himself to me of his own accord
    so that now Delia is not better known to my dogs. (3.60–7)

The two songs are set in contrast from the very beginning, with different
genders of the desired lovers, along with different singers calling on different deities. Both lovers receive gifts (68–71), but the relationships
sour. Meliboeus indicates that all is not right with Amyntas when he
questions his lover's commitment as he is left "holding the nets" (75).

The shepherd-poets' attention now becomes deflected to another
interest, Phyllis, the lover of Iollas, who, as Coleman notes, is likely the
master of these two herdsmen. Damoetas wishes her to come for his
birthday, while Meliboeus speaks of her previous affection for him. Each
verse is point and counterpoint, forming playful banter that continues
until these singers revisit the topic of the lovers Amaryllis and Amyntas.
Soon, however, the conversation turns from rural Arcadia to the reality
of Rome:

D: Pollio loves my Muse although she is rustic; Muses feed a calf for
    your reader.
M: Even Pollio himself makes new songs; feed a bull, the kind that
    already lunges with his horn and sprinkles the sand with his hoof.
    (3.84–7)

Here the contrast between the rural setting and the urban reality is stated
explicitly, for Pollio is said to love the Muse in spite of her rusticity.
Menalcas counters Damoetas with reference to Pollio's poetic production, contrasting the bull – a weightier animal for a weightier genre, i.e.,
Pollio's writing of tragedy – with the "pastoral" calf mentioned by
Damoetas.[12] The subject of love returns through an association with a
bull that is gaunt as a lover: "Love is just as destructive a force for the
flock as it is for the flock's shepherd" (101).

The shepherds' banter comes to a close with twin riddles:

D: Tell me in what lands – and you will be a great Apollo for me –
    the space of heaven does not spread three elm trees more amply.
M: Tell me in what lands flowers are born inscribed with the names
    of kings, and you alone may have Phyllis. (3.104–7)

Though riddles had not been typical of the pastoral tradition, they are not infrequent in Roman comedy, as Fraenkel has shown in his classic study of Plautus. While scholars have spent a great deal of time trying to identify what the notion of "space of heaven" might indicate, few have looked to the question ("tell me in what lands") posed by these riddlers.[13] Menalcas' riddle clearly centers on the hyacinth flower; Damoetas' riddle is more perplexing. Clausen's note summarizes it nicely: both are ambiguous, but the first riddle would seem to call for an answer having to do with the concept of the sphere, such as that of Archimedes or Posidonius. The answer to the regional question, therefore, falls along east/west lines: in the west, Rome; in the east, Rhodes. Likewise, the second riddle's division between either Troy (according to one legend associated with Hyacinthus) or Sparta would follow a similar geographical separation. Such an east/west, Rome/Trojan distinction not only points up the poem's underlying dualism but also heightens the dichotomy between urban and rural, learned and rustic that characterizes these poems, as we saw in the case of the bull and the calf above.

In a final twist, which is perhaps a further riddle, Palaemon decides to award livestock instead of the cups. After stating that he is not one to judge so "great" a contest – though, generically speaking, it has been in fact a rather "delicate" contest – he pronounces that each of them is worthy of a calf, the smaller animal, indicative of "slight" poetry, which would be here the lighter genre of pastoral. At least for the moment, bucolic enjoys primacy of place among genres.

Eclogue 7, too, begins with small animals, whose size also befits the pastoral genre here. In that poem, Meliboeus tells the story of Thyrsis and Corydon:

> Corydon and Thyrsis had driven their flocks into one place, Thyrsis the sheep and Corydon the goats, whose udders were filled with milk. Both of these men were flowering in their age, both of them Arcadians, both equal in singing and both prepared to respond. (7.2–5)

The dialogue format offers a banter seen in Meliboeus' emphasis on the word "both" (*ambo*, line 4). Meliboeus repeats the word to describe the competitors in the contest: "both began to contend in alternating verses … Corydon bringing forth these, Thyrsis those" (18–20). The dialogic dualism inherent in the genre gives rise to the rhetorical give and take in which these two participate.

That these poets are Arcadians is distinctive of Virgil's adaptation of the genre. Though in Herodotus (1.66) Arcadians appear as primitives, some modern scholars have emphasized the "tender feeling" of Virgil's Arcadia.[14] Yet more than mere feeling led Virgil to adopt and transform that region: Virgil saw that Arethusa, a subterranean stream associated with poetic inspiration, could provide a symbol for the transference of Greek Arcadia westward. Specifically, Virgil imagines Arethusa to flow underground from Arcadia to Syracuse.[15] Linked, in part, by Arethusa, Virgil's Greek Arcadians, therefore, find themselves in a Sicilian landscape. When Meliboeus and Daphnis exchange glances, Daphnis even moves the landscape north: in setting up the parameters of the contest, he places the transferred Arcadia as far north as in Mantua, referring to the Mincius River as an aspect of this new vista.

Meliboeus reports their songs, as Van Sickle has shown, in an orderly manner, for both consist of forty-eight lines in neatly balanced quatrains, forming complementary pairs, a microcosm of this collection as a whole.[16] Corydon is said to have called on the Libethrides, nymphs of the Pierian region near the tomb of Orpheus; on Mt Helicon there is also a peak known as Libethrium, where the nymphs called Libethriae were worshiped. Corydon presents his proposed gifts of a boar's head, a bow, and stag horns to Artemis, one of whose sacred haunts was, in Callimachus, Arcadia (*Hymn to Artemis* 3.86–8). Thyrsis retorts by making vows to Priapus, the fecund god who comforted Daphnis upon his deathbed in Theocritus 18. Corydon describes the barrenness that occurs when a lover departs from the countryside, and Thyrsis matches this, noting that even the wine god can begrudge "the hills shade of his vine" (58).

The poem ends abruptly when Meliboeus declares his affection for and allegiance to the winner:

> I recall these things and that Thyrsis, conquered, strove in vain. From that time Corydon, Corydon is mine. (7.69–70)

Statements about recollection can suggest poetic indebtedness, and this one fittingly is attended by an allusion to *Idyll* 8.92, "from that time on Daphnis was first among shepherds." The repetition of Corydon's name harks back to Corydon's own words about himself in *Eclogue* 2, where Corydon had addressed himself about the madness of love. Through the repetition of that name, Meliboeus indicates both that the quality of *Eclogue* 2's lament is relevant to the current situation and that Corydon is a poet in the mold of the bucolic poet par excellence, Daphnis, who was the subject of Theocritus' address in *Idyll* 8.

The bucolic genre, of which these poems are especially typical, is therefore represented in a positive light by the association of one of its best flock-tending poets, Corydon, with Daphnis, the greatest bucolic poet in the genre's fantasy landscape. Now that the genre has been established, however, Virgil will take it in a new direction, one stylistically weightier and thematically more powerful.

Eclogues 4 and 5

Within the first few words of *Eclogue* 4, Virgil introduces this weightier theme, which anticipates his own future work, with a contrast between the low genre of pastoral and "greater things":

> Sicilian Muses, let us sing of things a little bit greater. The trees and humble tamarisks do not please everyone; if we sing of woods, let them be woods worthy of a consul. (1–4)

Although the poet opens with an invocation of the Muses of Sicily (i.e., of Theocritus) and elements appropriate to the bucolic vista, he soon invokes Rome's consul, the official head of state. Most commentators view this consul to be Pollio, the reference to whom in line 11 also suggests an approximate date of 41/40 BC for the poem.

"Worthy of cosmogony," however, would better describe the teleological return of ages that follows. With a probable reference to the famous comet seen after Caesar's death, known as the *sidus Iulium*, the sighting of which led to consultation of the Sibylline books, Virgil states that the final age of the Sibyl's song has arrived and a new order of ages is born:

> Now a new offspring is sent down from high heaven. You, chaste Lucina, cherish the new-born boy, because of whom the race of iron for the first time will cease and a golden race will arise in the entire world; now your Apollo reigns. (7–10)

Coleman notes that these lines recall an oracular pronouncement, from the Sibylline books (3.286), which prophesies that a king will be sent from heaven, an event to occur under Apollo's reign. This period is realized in Octavian's Rome, for as early as the 40s BC Octavian began to identify himself with this particular deity.

In *Eclogue* 4 the theme of the old becoming new ("there will be wars over again and great Achilles will be sent again to Troy," 34–5) is also important. Servius quotes the neo-Pythagorean philosopher Nigidius Figulus' discussion of separating out the gods and the ages. Such cosmogony dovetails with Virgil's apocalyptic vision, itself bolstered by the recent chatter in Rome about the significance of the *sidus Iulium*. Whatever the original source for such ideas may have been, the poem's subject matter is clearly focused on the person who will usher in a new age. In this regard, a connection of father and son is especially important:

> That one will receive the life of the gods and he will see heroes mixed with gods and he himself will be seen among them and he will rule the world made peaceful by the virtues of his father. But for you, lad, the earth without cultivation will pour forth little gifts first, with its fruit ivy wandering here and there and marsh lilies, mixed with smiling acanthus. (4.15–20)

The father's virtues will have brought about the peace that the son will now administer, as the earth yields its bounty through self-cultivating plants, with the ivy and acanthus among them. As Williams notes, such a notion of the land's fecundity being a gift to the child is not found before in Virgil.[17]

The familial reference with which Virgil continues his poem furthers the father/son association in connection with vegetation, by stating "as soon as you will be able to read the praises of heroes and the deeds of your father and to know what virtue is, the plain will become yellow, little by little, with soft ears of grain" (26–8). Such a description of cornucopian fecundity will later be translated into art, also seen in the acanthus and ivy that will later adorn the dado (lower frieze) of the Ara Pacis.

Yet the poem's power, as Norden noted nearly a century ago, lies not only in fecund images but also in its pervasive sense of destiny conveyed by the feeling of future challenges and the promise of prosperity. Virgil continues with further prophecy:

> The snake, too, will perish, as will the herb, deceptive with its poison. Assyrian spice will spring up everywhere. But as soon as you will be able to read the praises of heroes and the deeds of your father and to know what virtue is, the plain will slowly turn yellow with soft ears of grain and the reddening grape will dangle on uncultivated bushes, while harsh oaks sweat dewy honey. Nevertheless, a few traces of our ancient deception will obtain. (4.24–31)

It is no surprise that some in the early church interpreted this child as the Christ, for his coming transforms nature and kills the "snake," an important symbol of the evil over which the Messiah triumphs in Christian theology. The degree of acceptance was debated among various church fathers. Eusebius tells us in his biography of Constantine, Rome's first Christian regent (4.32), that that emperor once presented at an ecclesiastical council meeting a Greek translation of this poem, with the notion that it should be seen as heralding Christ's birth. Yet even before Christendom, the poem's power could be seen in its strong sense of hope pinned upon the presence of a single individual.

In that positive sense the poem looks back to the verses of *Eclogue* 1, in which Tityrus described his encounter with the young man whom he had already proclaimed to be divine (*Ecl.* 1.6–7). We saw there a twofold vision of Octavian, who was both a political figure and, to Tityrus, a god. In *Eclogue* 4, however, for all its hope, its description of the golden age is qualified: "the optimism generated by the *sidus Iulium* had been disappointed by subsequent events. A further period of discord and war must first be endured" (Coleman, ad 4.36). Coleman seems to regard Virgil's words as predictive of the tension that will ensue in the 30s between Octavian and Antony, culminating at Actium. From such conflict, *Eclogue* 4 suggests, peace will come.

One result of the imagined peace is the self-dyeing wool of lambs ("nor will the wool learn how to deceive various colors, but the ram himself in the meadows will change his fleece with sweet red dye and now with the saffron yellow; of its own accord scarlet will clothe the grazing lambs," 4.42–4). Even if wool-dyeing can be viewed as betokening decline, as some scholars have suggested, Virgil's tone is clearly more affirming. In the midst of this high-flung prophecy, multicolored sheep offer a light moment.

After this almost humorous vignette of self-coloring flocks, the poem closes with a powerful image, as the poet calls upon the boy himself:

> Begin, lad, recognize your mother with a smile; ten months have brought to your mother long weariness. Begin, lad: him at whom his parents have not smiled neither a god will deem worthy of his table nor a goddess of her bed. (4.60–3)

This fated child, whom the narrator has urged to come quickly (48–52), is told to smile upon his mother to be worthy of divine association. The adjective "worthy" thus frames the poem. This poem would be worthy not only of Pollio but also of the young man, Octavian, who had been suffect consul in 43 and who enjoyed the status of "son of a god" (*filius diui*). He thus could himself be deemed worthy of the table of a god and bed of a goddess, provided that he know and emulate the deeds of his father (27) and receive now his charge (60). In any case, the notion of worthiness of consul and child frames the optimism and power of this poem of a future hope.[18]

If *Eclogue* 4 embodies hope, its complement, *Eclogue* 5, commemorates death, specifically that of Julius Caesar, suggested by the lament for the figure of Daphnis, as Hubbard, Alpers, and others have noted. Most scholars since antiquity have accepted the identification, made as early as Servius, of Daphnis with Caesar. Leach states the case very clearly:

> Allusions to the death of Julius Caesar … are quite explicit. The mourning of Daphnis' mother is that of Caesar's divine mother, Venus. The groaning of the Carthaginian lions recalls Caesar's special patronage of that city, which he had restored and recolonized under her ancient name. The agricultural images might suggest Caesar's relationship to Italy, which supported him in the face of senatorial Rome. Daphnis' *tumulus* in the forest suggests Caesar's monument in the Forum, erected by his supporters shortly after his death. (*Vergil's* Eclogues 188)

If we accept Leach's analysis, a further question arises as to why *Eclogue* 5 follows the prophetic fourth *Eclogue*, inasmuch as Caesar's death must happen before Octavian can begin to reign. Yet one must keep in mind that *Eclogue* 4 is a future prophecy and as such can defy temporal boundaries.

Furthermore, the fourth poem is in the prime position as far as an ordering system even mildly indebted to Pythagorean principles goes, as the number four represents the fulfillment of the *tetraktys*, the sum of which is the powerful number ten. Its first ten lines, which culminate with a proclamation of an Apolline age, could even represent a miniature *tetraktys* within it.[19]

The content of *Eclogue* 5, too, supports a connection with *Eclogue* 4. In *Eclogue* 5, Menalcas and Mopsus agree to sit down to exchange songs in an informal singing match. Mopsus responds to Menalcas' urging by stating that he will recount the contents of a song that he had inscribed on a tree (13). The lines that he recalls catalogue the benefits Daphnis had brought to his environment (20–32), followed by the fact that Daphnis has died:

After the fates took you, Pales herself quit her fields, and so did Apollo himself. From the furrows, to which we entrusted a huge barley crop, often arise the unhappy tares and the sterile wild oats. (5.34–7)

Clausen notes that the repetition of the intensive pronouns "himself" and "herself" puts the minor Roman deity on par with a god from the Greek pantheon. As Leach suggests, a reference to Daphnis' tomb and epitaph furthers an association of Daphnis and Caesar. Although we do not know the words of Caesar's epitaph, Mopsus renders Daphnis' epitaph when he calls for a tomb for Daphnis:

I, Daphnis, lie here in the woods, known from here even unto the stars; I myself was the guard of a most comely flock, and I myself was comelier still. (43–4)

After responding that Mopsus' poem is a welcome solace, Menalcas, too, takes up the Daphnis theme, describing the dead master as now deified (56–7) and hailing the dawn of a new golden age that has come as a result of his deification (60–4).

Coleman has stated that "it is incredible that anyone in the late 40s could have read a pastoral poem on this theme without thinking of Caesar." He might have added, "and Octavian," for the reference to a boy being "a second one from that man" (49) and worthy to be celebrated in song has overtones of succession (54). Now, in a parallel relationship with Pales (34), Daphnis himself is put on par with Apollo, for each will have two dedicated altars (65–6) and established rites, much like those dedicated to the deities representing the sustenance of life, Ceres (bread) and Bacchus (wine). The poem closes with mutual praise, an exchange of gifts and Menalcas' reference to "his other poems" (*Eclogues* 2 and 3). Menalcas offers Mopsus a "fragile reed" symbolic of poetic composition, as Mopsus does the same by giving Menalcas a shepherd's crook.

In sum, *Eclogue* 5's death of Daphnis, symbolic of Caesar's death, has an interesting structural and thematic association with *Eclogue* 4. Combined, *Eclogues* 4 and 5 embody a dualistic relationship between life and death. In *Eclogue* 4, this new life and hope rests upon the child who, if not Octavian himself – so tight an association would be, admittedly, a minority view – is at least representative of the optimism associated with Octavian's nascent reign.

Eclogues 6 and 10

The opening of *Eclogue* 6 consists of the best example in Virgil of a *recusatio* (refusal to write epic):

> When I was singing of kings and battles, Cynthius (Apollo) plucked my
> ear and admonished me: Tityrus, it is right that the shepherd feed fat sheep,
> that he sing a fine-spun song. (3–5)

These lines are concerned with generic associations, as a fine-spun song
betokens the delicacy of Alexandrian composition, whereas kings and
battles reflect more traditional martial epic. Virgil is thus called back from
a future project to the current one, the composition of *Eclogues* in the
Alexandrian fashion.

Virgil follows this amusing picture of his call to keep to his poetic
agenda with a more sober address of the person who was likely responsible for the confiscations of the property used to pay off Octavian's
troops. That person was Alfenus Varus, a Roman jurist who served as
consul suffectus (consular replacement) in 39 BC. From the Greek idyllic
world comes poetic banter, with Apollo teasing his bard about genre
amidst the harsh politics of the Italian landscape.

Not long after the *recusatio* directed to Varus (3–12), Virgil uses the
verb "to see" (*uidere*) for the fourth time in thirteen lines in an apostrophe. In this context he creates an inviting mythical landscape:

> You would see fauns and beasts sporting in meter,
> And next rigid oaks shaking their treetops;
> neither does the crag of Parnassus rejoice so much in Phoebus,
> nor Rhodope and Ismaros so much in Orpheus. (27–30)

Sporting fauns, the familiar territory of Parnassus and Rhodope and a
drunken satyr are all aspects of the bucolic landscape of *Eclogue* 6, in the
midst of which Silenus has been bound with garlands (19) and is required
to sing ("Let me go, lads; 'tis enough to have seemed to be able; listen
to the songs you desire," 24f.). Under mild compulsion and smeared
ritually with black mulberries like a fertility god, Silenus renders a song,
in a familiar style:

> For [Papa Silenus] was singing how seeds of earth, winds, and sea had
> been brought together through the great void, and seeds of smooth fire,
> too; how in these first things all first beginnings came together and how

the soft sphere of the earth itself congealed; then, how land solidified, how it shut Nereus in the sea and little by little took up the forms of things; and now the lands would be amazed to see new sunshine higher above and how rains would fall when the clouds come together, when the woods began first to arise and now and then animals wandered through hitherto unknown mountains. (31–40)

This is not merely a "good yarn" of the sylvan setting but a cosmological poem in the long tradition of Greek poetry on nature (*peri physeos*). The most recent installment in this tradition, some fifteen years before the *Eclogues*, is Lucretius' epic-length poem *De Rerum Natura*, a cosmological and philosophical treatise presented in the sweet, "honey-lipped cup" of poetry (1.936–42).

Though Silenus' poem first (32–40) purports to be of this same ilk, it turns out rather to look more like that of some of Lucretius' neoteric contemporaries, Calvus or Cinna. Their work went well beyond cosmogony to incorporate the world of old mythological stories. Ovid's *Metamorphoses* (published AD 8) offers perhaps the best example, while before Virgil, there was Catullus 64 (ca. 54 BC) on the marriage of Peleus and Thetis. Virgil would also have known Cinna's *Zmyrna*, of which only a few fragments survive. There were other poems of this type in circulation, as well.

Such poems were highly urbane, and it is just such a poem that Silenus composes:

He tells of the tossed stones of Pyrrha, the Saturnian realms, the birds of the Caucasus, and the theft of Prometheus. He adds to these at what spring the sailors had cried out for the abandoned Hylas, how the whole shore was exclaiming, "Hylas, Hylas"; and he consoles Pasiphae for the love of the white bullock – she would have been fortunate if herds had never existed. Ah, unlucky maiden, what madness took hold of you! (41–7)

Silenus' stories have transitioned from cosmological didactic epic to the urbane level of the neoterics, with tales of Pyrrha, Prometheus, and Hylas. His song thus moves from the world of pastoral to that of the city's latest trend in poetry. Thus it is less than surprising that Silenus brings one of those very neoteric poets into the traditional poetic landscape:

Then he sings of Gallus wandering by the streams of the Permessus and how one of the sisters guided him into the Aonian mountains; and how the entire chorus of Phoebus rose up for the man; then, how, with his divine song, the shepherd Linus, bedecked in his hair with flowers and with bitter parsley, spoke to that man: "The Muses give you these reeds – come, take them – which they once gave to the old Ascraean, whereby he was accustomed, with song, to lead the rigid ash trees down from the mountains." (64–71)

Gallus represents the best of Rome's neoteric tradition, here receiving the fruit of Greece's didactic tradition, represented by the Hesiodic reeds in a setting reminiscent of Hesiod's encounter with the Muses in the *Theogony*. These reeds, and with them this tradition, have grown out of the inspiration of the Grynian grove, originating with Phoebus himself. Linus has received them through the hands of Hesiod, the old Ascraean, who hailed from Ascra near Mt Helicon. Through Theocritus they are transmitted to Virgil's verse and, now, on to Gallus, who in the context of this poem is treated as a new Orpheus, a neoteric who is welcomed as part of the pastoral tradition.[20]

But Gallus is not a part of the bucolic tradition. Virgil's inclusion of Gallus is an aspect of a strategy of reversal (*oppositio in imitando*), an assertion of Virgil's allegiance to neoteric principles, as Gordon Williams has shown, not an appeal to Gallus to become a bucolic poet. Virgil is, therefore, not so much declaring Gallus a part of the pastoral world as Virgil is carving out his own place as a neoteric poet within the pastoral tradition. Gallus' role here is similar, then, to his role in the tenth *Eclogue*, where Coleman aptly notes that Virgil's invitation to Gallus to write pastoral need not be taken at face value.

When the words of Papa Silenus in *Eclogue* 6 come to a close, the urbane neoteric Gallus is welcomed into a rural setting of no small significance, namely the seat of all poetic inspiration. Not surprisingly, therefore, as the narrative persona shifts to indirect citation of the rest of Papa Silenus' song, the themes reflect the very kind of poetry that Gallus represents:

> Why shall I speak of Scylla, Nisus's daughter, whom the story attended that she, girt as to her white loins with barking monsters, harassed the Dulichian ships and in the deep whirlpool, ah, she ripped to shreds the timid sailors with her sea hounds? ... All those things that once, when Phoebus was practicing them in song, that blessed man heard and bade the laurels of Eurotas to learn, he now sings, and the valleys, struck, bear them to the stars, until he ordered them to lead the sheep back to the stables and to count up their number, and evening came, though Heaven did not want it to. (74–7, 82–6)

Only here at the poem's conclusion do we return to the rural setting in which Papa Silenus is the singer. The poem within the poem is the story of a poet within another poet's song, just as the internal landscape of Permessus and Helicon finds its counterpart in the valley and the laurels of the Eurotas. While Papa Silenus is the rural poet in the rural setting, his song reveals a heavy debt to the neoterics of Gallus' day, very possibly to Gallus himself.

Eclogue 10 is the natural complement to this poem, not only because together they frame the second half of the collection but also because both concern Gallus and both deal with the question of poetic allegiance and generic shifts. We saw above, in *Eclogue* 6's pastoral context, Virgil weaves into Papa Silenus' song didactic and neoteric elements, with Gallus inducted into the poetic hall of fame.

In *Eclogue* 10, Gallus has a different role; having wandered into the bucolic genre, he finds himself hemmed in by sheep (16). While snub-nosed goats continue to graze (7), Virgil describes Gallus' lost loves, mourned even by the laurels and tamarisks (13). Gallus is greeted by many mythological figures associated with that genre (Menalcas, Apollo, Silvanus, Pan). With an epigrammatic pronouncement, Gallus asks the Arcadians to sing of his loves and claims that he could have wished to have participated in their genre in which he would have found different loves (38–41).

Instead, he merely wastes his love on war. His loss parallels the situation of his lover, Lycoris, who has also gone far from Rome, following a soldier entirely different from Gallus (46–9). Therefore, Gallus says, he will sing pastoral, pining in the woods and inscribing his amorous adventures upon trees where his love will, quite literally, grow. Inasmuch as Gallus' body of poetry was entitled *Amores*, the reference would seem to suggest, as Conte has noted, that Virgil's Gallus has inscribed his own work upon the pastoral genre.

After this brief reference, however, Gallus bids farewell to the woods, noting that no matter how far he might push the genre, love must prevail:

> Now again neither the wood nymphs nor their very songs please me; oh you very woods, give way. My labors cannot change her; not even if I should drink in the middle of the cold the Hebrus and undergo the Scythian snows of the wet winter or, when the bark, dying, should dry in a high elm tree, would I guide the sheep of the Ethiopians under the constellation of the Crab. Love overcomes all things: let us, too, all yield to Love. (62–9)

Virgil's paronomasia of the *moriens liber* ("dying tree bark" or "a dying book," 67) offers a poignant metaphor for the end of the bucolic genre, at least as far as Virgil's participation goes. Furthermore, the reference to shepherding in archetypally distant Ethiopia (68) suggests that pastoral poetry has been pushed to the furthest limits of the genre. Entering the bucolic landscape and dabbling with pastoral themes does not provide a shelter from ubiquitous love (69), to which Gallus' ultimate loyalty belongs, for he is an amatory neoteric in the tradition of Catullus, Propertius, and Tibullus.

That we have come to the end of the genre is made even clearer by the lines that immediately follow, as the focus moves from Gallus within the genre to Virgil, whose poetic persona – in a manner recalling the characters from Theocritus' *Idyll* 1, such as the keeper of the vineyard who decorates a cup, or the old fisherman who mends his nets – suggestively weaves a basket:

> This will be enough, divine Muses, for your poet to have sung, while he sits and has woven a basket from the slender hibiscus. You will make these things the greatest Gallus, for Gallus, whose love for me grows as much every hour as in the new spring the green alder shoots up. Let us rise up; the shade is accustomed to be heavy for singers, the shade of the juniper is heavy; shade harms the fruits, too. Come home sated, ye goats, come; evening approaches. (70–7)

By beginning this final section with the phrase, "this will be enough," Virgil would seem to suggest that both the genre and the collection have come to an end. Furthermore, the lines that follow intimate Virgil's own impending generic shift, as Virgil calls upon his poetic persona to "rise up" (*surgamus*). Stephen Hinds has elsewhere demonstrated that this verb can be a generic code word, as it is in Ovid's *Metamorphoses*, where it suggests epic.[21] "Shade" (*umbra*) is a polyvalent term, ranging from the darkness of the Underworld to poetic production. Here the latter seems to be emphasized, while in the *Aeneid*'s last line the former significance is prominent; Virgil closes the *Georgics*, too, with a reference to shade. Prevenient of the word's import in his subsequent work, Virgil emphasizes the word by repeating it here three times. That it may point toward epic is also suggested by its close association with *grauis* (heavy), used twice here, an adjective that, in a context such as this where a self-consciously poetic discussion is being undertaken, suggests epic narrative.

In short, Virgil's injunction of himself to "rise up" because shade is accustomed to be heavy for singers and harmful to fruit, suggests that, just as Gallus cannot leave amatory poetry for the pastoral world, Virgil cannot ignore the epic impulses that he feels calling upon him. These epic impulses are heavy and shadowy, and they will lead ultimately to the death of an epic warrior. Yet, for the present, goats are sated and evening approaches. It is time for Virgil and his goats to go home, his goats to their pens, and him to his next poetic project, didactic epic.

Notes

1 Cf. Kathryn Gutzwiller, "The Evidence for the Theocritaean Poetry Books," in M. A. Harder, R. F. Regtuit, and G. C. Wakker (eds.), *Theocritus* (Gröningen, 1996), 119–48.

2 Charles Martindale, "Green Politics: The *Eclogues*," in *The Cambridge Companion to Virgil*, ed. Charles Martindale (Cambridge, 1997), 120.

3 Brian W. Breed, *Pastoral Inscriptions: Reading and Writing Virgil's* Eclogues (London, 2006), 156. See also C. Gallazzi, "P. Narm. inv. 66,362: Vergilius, Eclogae VIII 53–62," *ZPE* 48 (1982), 75. M. Geymonat, "Ancora sul titolo delle Bucoliche," *BICS* 29 (1982), 19, highlights papyrological evidence that the individual *Eclogues* had names independent of their ordering; James E. G. Zetzel, "Servius and Triumphal History in the *Eclogues*," *CP* 79 (1984), 141; Joseph Farrell, "Asinius Pollio in Vergil *Eclogue* 8," *CPh* 86 (1991), 204–11.

4 John Van Sickle's thorough study, *The Design of Virgil's* Bucolics (London, 2nd edn., 2004), 209–13 *et passim*.

5 Several references to Orpheus, the legendary poet who descended to Hades to rescue from death his beloved Eurydice, may advance an Orphic–Pythagorean connection whereby Virgil secures his place in the poetic descent through Pythagorean ideas from Orpheus. The opening line of the collection may offer a hint: the combination of the first two words of the collection, *Tityre, tu* … may softly echo the word *tetraktys*.

6 Mario Geymonat, *Il Grande Archimede* (Bologna, 2008), 24, 105f.

7 Jeffrey Wills, *Repetition in Latin Poetry* (Oxford, 1996), 461–72; cf. Van Sickle (2004), 222f.

8 Wendy Steiner, *The Colors of Rhetoric* (Chicago, 1982), 42. See also W. T. J. Mitchell, *Iconology: Image, Text, Ideology* (Chicago, 1986), 99.

9 Michael C. J. Putnam, *Virgil's Pastoral Art: Studies in the* Eclogues (Princeton, 1970), 35; Paul Alpers, *The Singer of the* Eclogues: *A Study of Virgilian Pastoral. With a New Translation of the* Eclogues (Berkeley, CA, 1979), 114.

10 So Solodow (1977): "the waves beating the shore represent the opposite of pastoral, the incessant turmoil of political life" (764); the verb *sine* (let) would thus suggest the discarding of that concern. The image of waves crashing on a shore could possibly also have erotic connotations.

11 Breed (2006), 47–8; cf. Coleman, ad 66–7.

12 Eleanor Winsor Leach, *Vergil's* Eclogues: *Landscapes of Experience* (Ithaca, NY, 1974), 178, regards the animals as symbolic of the poets. For the association of animal size with genre, see Holzberg (2006), 113. See also Clausen, ad loc.

13 E.g., Michael C. J. Putnam, "The Riddle of Damoetas (Virgil *Ecl.* 3.104–105)," *Mnemosyne* 18 (1964), 150–4; D. E. W. Wormell, "The Riddles in Virgil's Third *Eclogue*," *CQ* 54 (1960), 29–31.

14 Bruno Snell, *The Discovery of the Mind: The Greek Origins of European Thought*, tr. T. G. Rosenmeyer (Cambridge, MA, 1953), 283. Cf. Glbert Highet, *Poets in a Landscape* (New York, 1967), 50–1.

15 Cf. S. J. Harrison, *Generic Enrichment in Vergil and Horace* (Oxford, 2007), 60–5.

16 Van Sickle (2004), 70.

17 Gordon Williams, *Tradition and Originality in Roman Poetry* (Oxford and New York, 1968), 277.

18 Gerhard Binder, "Lied der Parzen zur Geburt Octavians: Vergils vierte Ekloge," *Gymnasium* 90 (1983), 119; cf. also Holzberg (2006), 48. Caesar had published commentaries on his military achievements; if the son were to be Octavian, the statement that the son would be able to read the exploits of his father (26–7) would also befit this association.

19 Van Sickle (2004), 62–5, offers a careful analysis of the structure of these first ten lines.

20 Cf. Harrison (2007), 62–4, who views Gallus as an elegiac lover here introduced into the pastoral world.

21 On *surgo* in Ovid's *Metamorphoses*, see Stephen Hinds, *The Metamorphosis of Persephone: Ovid and the Self-conscious Muse* (Cambridge, 1987), 21–4.

4

The *Georgics*: A Repast of Wisdom

The poem privileges mystery, not solution; complexity … not certainty.
Christine Perkell (The Poet's Truth, 191)

The georgic narrator's very act of teaching signals the necessity to reconceptualize a supposedly traditional knowledge and disseminate it through markedly different channels of communication.
(Alessandro Schiesaro, The Roman Cultural Revolution, 89)

Virgil's *Georgics*, composed between approximately 36 and 29 BC, consists of four books on farming that not only offer didactic instruction but also include pithy dictums, observations, and lessons pertaining to both agriculture and life. Ostensibly treating farming, these poems reveal how the farmer's struggle with nature can instruct the reader about the human experience. This collection is arranged symphonically, with an ebb and flow characteristic of Virgil's entire corpus. The quotations cited above hint at the *Georgics'* style and substance. Each book touches on political realities, encompasses themes of death and life, and transitions between moments of gloom and optimism. Rich in precepts, this collection places before the reader a repast of wisdom.

As he begins the first of his four movements toward such wisdom, Virgil poses a series of indirect questions. The addressee is Maecenas, Virgil's patron and friend:

> What makes the crops happy, under what star, Maecenas, it is best to plow the earth, and to join vines to elms, what is the care of oxen, what tending is needed for keeping a flock, how much skill for keeping thrifty bees – I shall now begin to sing. (1.1–5)

The book's first line ends with the word "earth" (*terram*), a word that befits the earthy question that Virgil asks. In this poem, which Perkell suggests "privileges mystery," Virgil will posit indirect questions and present indirect answers. Each book in this collection treats life born of the earth and offers the reader wisdom, if often stated circuitously, about life in the natural world and often in the company of other human beings.

The *Georgics* is a deliberately structured work: the first book treats crops and weather signs; the second, vines and trees; the third, oxen and flocks; the fourth, bees and a song. We saw in the last chapter how the final *Eclogue* divulges song's ability to produce Gallus' right of entrance into Helicon; the final *Georgic* goes further, culminating in song's capacity to overcome death by imparting wisdom. This last element, the transmission of wisdom through song, permeates all four *Georgics*. Though Virgil begins with a brief reference to song (1.5), he greatly amplifies this theme at the close of book 4.

Agricultural poetry was not a new idea. Hesiod's eighth-century didactic poem *Works and Days* (the abbreviated Greek title of which is *Erga*) treats agricultural themes. Hesiod was, even for Virgil, the archetypal farmer – poet; Nicander, who wrote a poem whose importance for Virgil is revealed by its title *Georgika*, also provided inspiration for Virgil. Virgil's poetic agenda, however, is different from Hesiod's, whose *Erga* emphasizes hard work and moral choices; it is likely to have been very different from Nicander's lost poem, as well.

To impart wisdom, the *Georgics* moves back and forth between positive and negative imagery. Even if instruction in wisdom acquired by working the soil is the primary focus of the *Georgics*, dualism, too, remains important, manifest in the shift between the *Georgics'* disheartening and affirming moments.

Georgic 1: Bread and Circuses

After presenting his poetic agenda for the work, Virgil invokes several deities, including Ceres and Liber, representing bread and wine and metonymically associated with *Georgics* 1 and 2, respectively. Virgil then turns to the principal focus of the poem's opening:

> And even you, Caesar – one of the councils of the gods will soon certainly receive you – whether you should wish to attend to the city and countryside, and the greatest sphere of the earth, girding your temples with your mother's myrtle, should accept you as the author of fruits and the potentate of storms, or you should come as a god of the vast sea, and sailors worship

your spirit exclusively: ... give easy passage and assent to my bold beginnings and, having pitied rustics like me who are ignorant of the way, go and now get used to being called upon in prayer. (24–30, 40–2)

Octavian (Caesar) garners as much adulation as all the other deities combined. Lucretius had opened his *DRN* with a similar invocation, there directed to Venus, who symbolizes life's generative force. Now the focus is on that goddess' ultimate heir through the Julian family line (*gens Iulia*), which in political terms is the family that sustains Rome. Octavian has greater sway than Liber (i.e., Bacchus), and by the late 30s, offers the political stability necessary to secure Rome's supply of grain (Ceres).

On the heels of this lofty invocation, Virgil embarks upon a sensual description of farming: earth crumbles as mountains pour forth cold streams and "the plow glistens when rubbed in the furrow" (46). Grain and vines grow abundantly, an image that provides a thematic reference to Ceres and Bacchus. The earth, rich in clods (64f.), is ready for human cultivation.

Over four hundred years before Virgil, Pindar had used the clod as a symbol of fecundity.[1] Virgil's clod symbolizes the earth's bounty, even if the yield is not always plentiful. Virgil expands this image to comprise cultivation of fields, including crop rotation and stubble burning. He then returns to the clod itself:

> He aids the fields much who with his rakes breaks sluggish clods and drags over them wicker harrows; nor does golden Ceres look upon him from high Olympus in vain; and he, too, aids his fields who, with his plow turned back, again crosswise cleaves the ridges that he causes to rise once the plain has been furrowed; he continuously masters the land and commands the fields. (94–9)

Virgil places himself outside of the narrative with an impartial, military tone, affecting detachment by referring to the farmer in the third person while at the same time deftly including material from two of his poetic forebears in Alexandrian style. He includes material drawn from Hesiod, who had once urged his reader to "perform the work that pleases Demeter" (*Erga* 299–301). Virgil also alludes to Callimachus, who in his *Hecale* had referenced Hesiod,[2] reseeding his text with traditional material that gives a religious aura to the new context, an aura backed by traditional language. Virgil thus contextualizes his adaptation in a line of descent from his poetic forebears.

Irrigation, too, is an aspect of Virgil's allusively rich account, to describe which he presents a simile that in Homer had represented Achilles' rage against the Scamander, "as a man who conducts water from a dark spring, guiding its flood to his plants and groves" (*Il.* 21.257–8). Virgil restores this simile to its agricultural context, as the battle of the Homeric warrior begins to be transformed into the battle of the farmer. In contrast to Homer's bloody scene in the Scamander, *Georgic* 1's beautiful waters cascade in a waterfall in a tiny grotto:

> As it falls, that water rouses an echoing roar through smooth stones, and with its bubbling streams regulates thirsty fields. (109–10)

Here we find a vignette presented from ground level, drawing the reader's attention downwards: the furrows, which are in part the result of the farmer's battle against nature become, in this microcosm, rivers that transport life-giving liquid to the fields.[3] This less-than-perfect world demands the farmer's ingenuity and relies on hard labor that begins with Jove, who first caused the fields to be cultivated (121). Such a tonal shift reflects the flux between positive and negative that characterizes the *Georgics.*

Virgil emphasizes nature's bounty: honey once flowed from trees, while rivers teemed with wine (136–46) in a passage that harks back to Hesiod's Golden Age. Yet, as humanity progresses, a balance between natural resources and human resourcefulness emerges, as humans ultimately become less humane, ever adapting to hard work until "iniquitous labor has dominated everything" (*labor omnia uicit / improbus* 145–6). This is a far cry from a positive view of the dignity of a hard day's work and, not surprisingly, the tone of this passage becomes increasingly gloomy.

En route to that sense of foreboding, the reader learns that Ceres (grain), too, must be cultivated through toil. Here there is no tribute to Ceres in the manner of Hesiod, who had instructed his reader to pray to the goddess "to make Demeter's ripe and holy grain heavy" (*Erga*, 466). Virgil, by contrast, has his text take on a more negative quality that recalls similar shifts in tone in the *Eclogues.* The negative trend continues with Virgil's presentation of the rustics' agricultural "weapons"; thus, the notion of labor being on a par with war obtains. Although the farmer can prevail through labor, it is the iniquitous type (*improbus*) to which Virgil attributed such potency. The emphasis on sheer effort advances the increasingly ponderous tone: "all things have hastened by fate to a worse estate" (199–200).

The reader's attention is, however, diverted to astronomical signs by which to sow, in the vein of the agricultural treatises of Cato and Varro. Virgil describes the earth's zones from its poles to the equator (233–9). If this sweeping geographical assessment of the world, indebted to works such as Eratosthenes' *Hermes*, is technically extraneous to the theme of plowing, it is nevertheless vital: the wise man must not merely know how to farm but understand the laws of nature that frame farming.

With an elevated shift in tone, Virgil describes the household of the farmer in winter season:

> Meanwhile, the farmer's wife, consoling her long work with a song, sends the tuneful comb over the threads or cooks down the sweet juice's liquid with Vulcan's fire … Winter is a lazy time for the farmer. In frosty weather farmers mostly enjoy their produce and arrange parties to share joyously their bounty with one another. Festive winter issues the invitation and loosens cares, just as when ships, heavy laden, come into port and joyous sailors place garlands on the sterns. (293–5, 299–304)

In the first chapter of this book we considered the description of the old Corycian gardener from *Georgic* 4, a scene similar in terms of domestic simplicity. This passage portrays a satisfied life, foreshadowing the portrait of the farmer at rest, with which the second book closes. The farmer and his wife find contentment in their daily tasks: she sings as she weaves and cooks, while he organizes a party. Though there is always work to be done, this domestic tranquility gives the farmer's life a rhythm that perhaps counterbalances *labor improbus*.

Like a composer whose symphony might have sudden shifts in mood and tempo, Virgil abruptly moves to a chilling description of a raging storm and seasonal change (311–27) that lead to the uncomplicated worship of Ceres. After the storm, birds chirping signal the image of a new day. Yet the tone of the first book shifts negatively yet again, as Virgil describes solar warnings based on Aratus. The narrator urges the farmer/reader to remember: "it will profit you *to remember* this [the sun's signaling atmospheric change] the more, when he [the sun] now goes down from vast Olympus" (450f.). This verb of recollection (*meminisse*) is as important for the the reader as for the farmer, as inclement weather is associated with political unrest:

> The sun will give you signals. Who would dare to say the sun is false? Often he also warns us that dark upheavals impend and deception and hidden wars are brewing. When Caesar was killed, the Sun even pitied Rome when

he covered his shining face with black darkness and an impious generation feared night eternal. Although at that time Earth, too, and the sea's expanses were giving signs, as were loathsome dogs and ominous birds. (1.463–71)

The notion of remembering is extended when the farmer's recollection parallels that of the Roman citizen as avian and solar signals mark Julius Caesar's murder. Various numinous portents, from sweating statues to speaking cattle to wells that serve up blood, confirm the loss (477–85). On the political side, Germany, Rome's violent adversary, has taken note of Rome's weakened condition (474, 499). Through the veiling of his face, the Sun confirms the unnaturalness of Caesar's death.

The hope for the future rests upon Caesar's successor, whom the poet refers to as "the youth" (line 500), as he had in *Eclogue* 1. Yet in closing *Georgic* 1, Virgil will go further, addressing Octavian as Caesar and thus as Rome's potentate:

Now for a long time has the palace of heaven begrudged you to us, Caesar, complaining that you care about men's triumphs. Wherefore, here right and wrong have changed places: there are so many wars in this world, so many appearances of evil, nor is there any fitting honor for the plow. With farmers removed, fields are overgrown, and curved sickles are forged into a strong sword. Here does the Euphrates, there does Germany, incite war; neighboring cities, with laws between them broken, take up arms; impious Mars rages throughout the entire world. (1.503–11)

Emphasizing Rome's plight, Virgil moves from issuing the farmer warnings to admonishing the citizen. With the powerful phrase "the many appearances of evil," Virgil notes how morality has been perverted. Rome's circumstances reflect those of the farmer, "removed" from his field for military service, with his pruning hooks transformed into weaponry. Mars' raging crowns this gloomy picture, anticipating also the image of circus chariots that "have poured forth from the starting gates and give space; holding onto the reins to no avail, the charioteer is carried along by the horses, and the chariot fails to obey the reins" (512–14). The first book's tone has shifted from order to disorder: from grain (as bread), which offers sustenance, we have come to the unruly circus, where the competitors have lost control.

Virgil marks this pessimistic picture with an Alexandrian touch, for, as discussed above in the first chapter, Virgil closes this book with a reference to the Euphrates River. This is, at one level, a nod toward Ventidius' campaign against the Parthians in 39 BC. At another, however, as Scodel and Thomas once noted (discussed in Chapter 1), Virgil's placement of the river's name is here strategic, clearly evoking Callimachus (*Hymn* 2.108).[4] As such, the Euphrates reference serves as a subtle assertion of Virgil's adherence to Alexandrian principles, perhaps even a *recusatio* of the epic genre. Even when Virgil eventually does fully engage the epic genre in the *Aeneid*, he will do so with Alexandrian dexterity.

Georgic 2: In uino, ciuitas

The second *Georgic* begins with an invocation of the wine god with whose properties this book is concerned. The deity is addressed both as Bacchus (2) and father Lenaeus (4), the aspect of the godhead associated with winemaking, affirmed by an association with Dionysius, through the features associated with tragedy: "Come here, O father Lenaeus, and with me dip your naked legs, with buskins removed, into the new wine-must" (7–8). This invitation for the god to move from tragedy, symbolized by actor's boots (buskins), to winemaking reflects Virgil's poetic program: the god of the stage is appropriated to an epic subgenre (so Thomas, ad 7–8). As Mynors notes (ad loc.), the phrase "with me" and the invocation of the god of the winepress offer a personal touch and fondly suggest the vintage season anticipating the book's sanguine, if not quite satisfying, ending that contrasts with the unruly conclusion of *Georgic* 1.

The poet begins with a brief catalogue of uncultivated trees, soon showing the farmer's intervention through grafting. After addressing Maecenas (40f.), Virgil expands the image: "fruitful slips are inserted; in a short time a huge tree surges to the sky with happy boughs, and it is amazed at its new leaves and fruit not its own" (79–82). Although this is technically impossible, and thus done for effect without pretense of credible instruction, grafting may suggest a metaphorical illustration of Alexandrian poetic composition borne out in the lines that follow. After naming trees that produce their own fruit, Virgil touches on vines that generate various different types of grapes:

> But innumerable are both the species and their names, and indeed it does not make any difference to reckon them by number. He who would wish to know this would similarly wish to tell how many grains of sand of the Libyan shore are stirred by the Zephyr or, when the East wind falls rather violently upon the ships, would wish to know how many Ionian waves wash upon the shore. (2.103–8)

Commentators have noted that Virgil here grafts into his text a sprig of Catullus c. 7, where Catullus answers his lover's question about the optimal number of kisses by stating, with Archimedean precision, that the number would have to be like "the number of Libyan sands of Cyrene" (7.3–4). In Virgil's hands, the number of wines have replaced kisses, and in place of Catullus' reference to "thirsty Jove," Virgil describes Ionian shores pounded by gale-driven waves.

The variety of wines gives way in subsequent lines to exotic places and their produce, with peoples mentioned coming from as far as Scythia (sc. Gelonus) or Ethiopia, evoking the lands' remoteness as had Meliboeus in *Eclogue* 1. While the prose author Theophrastus would have offered Virgil an important model for unusual lands,[5] a further poetic allusion to Catullus may be operative here, for his eleventh poem describes distant places. The traveling exploits of Catullus' poetic persona stand in sharp contrast to the amatory exploits of his mistress, who has no feelings for her various partners. Catullus' physical foreignness is met by her spiritual distance with a destructive result:

> Nor let her look back upon my love, as before, a love that by her own fault has fallen, just as a flower on the edge of the meadow, after it has been touched by the passing plow. (ca. 11.21–4)

Virgil's use of this passage as a model for his own enumeration of the variety of wines goes beyond a simple connection between love and wine, as we see in the previous allusion. Rather, he fashions a list in the manner of Catullus, evoking indirectly Catullus' final agricultural image. Virgil closes his catalogue of locations with a description of a flower:

> The tree itself is huge and much like a laurel in appearance – if it were not tossing about another scent, it would be a laurel: by no means do its leaves fall in any wind, and its flower clings particularly fast; with it Medes treat their breath and malodorous mouths and offer aid to the elderly when they have difficulty breathing. (2.131–5)

In contrast to Catullus' mowed flower, Virgil's bloom holds fast and the laurel-like tree produces a healing medication – fittingly so, as the laurel was the plant of Apollo, who was also the god of healing, poetry, and music. The melancholy recollection of Catullus' feigned travels, his toppled flower, and Lesbia's exotic lovers are replaced with exotic places, a tenacious bloom, and medicinal healing. Though more positive, Virgil's passage is also less passionate, even quasi-prosaic. Such a tone may be engendered by the fact that Virgil also imitates Theophrastus, whose text preserved a corrupt reading revealed by Virgil's adaptation of it.[6]

Virgil's paronomasia of "Medes who medicate" (2.121f.) allows him to compare such exotic lands with Italy in the so-called *laudes Italiae* (praises of Italy). For Roman triumphal processions, animals are either well disciplined (e.g., the war horse, 145) or sacrificed (e.g., the bull, 146–7). In Italy, "spring is eternal and summer occurs in months not her own; the cattle breed twice, the tree is twice productive in fruit. But there are no fierce tigers here" (149–51).

Though other Roman agricultural writers, such as Cato and Varro, had included similar praises of Italy,[7] Virgil defines Italy not on her own terms but with regard to how she is different: Italy is not Bactra or India or Lydia. This "not *x* but *y*" pattern is an aspect of Virgil's dualistic style, with Italy's self-definition in part emerging in terms of what she is not. Such approbation however, that expresses value in terms of comparison, leaves the reader with the feeling that Italy's worthiness is less than self-contained, in spite of the peninsula's bounteous aquatic resources, ample shoreline, mineral wealth and, finally, famous families.

Among those families, the names of Decius, Marius, Camillus, and Scipio would have had a ring as familiar to a Roman as Churchill to an Englishman or Kennedy to an American. Virgil's list closes with a direct address to Octavian himself:

> You, too, greatest Caesar, a victor already on Asia's farthest shores, now repel the weak peoples of the East from Rome's citadels. Hail great mother of fruits, Saturnian land, great mother of men! Having dared to open sacred springs, for you I embark on the themes of ancient praise and art, singing the Ascrean's song through Roman towns. (2.170–6)

Octavian's greatness manifests itself in his capacity to subjugate far-off places and repel foreigners. By contrast Virgil will daringly employ a foreign song in the vein of the Ascrean Hesiod. Virgil's song will look to the remote, Saturnian past.

Could Virgil's praise of the most ancient realm that had no need of labor be subversive to the *Georgics'* general tone, which makes work a central, though not unequivocally good, aspect of the post-Saturnian human condition? Though, we shall see at the end of book 2, men can live in a quasi-Saturnian state that holds the seeds of Rome's destiny, in the *Georgics* there is no perfect Garden of Eden. Rather, one finds, here and there, an uneven progress. The connection of Saturn with agriculture through derivation of his name from the Latin word for "sown" seed (*satus*) might suggestively connect the god of cornucopian prehistory with the labor of sowing seed, but such sowing, the reader now knows, will involve iniquitous labor.

From the lofty *laudes Italiae*, Virgil returns to reality, considering various soils. Cattle, too, need land, and Virgil cites examples ranging from Tarentum in the south to the "lost" plain of Mantua in the north (198–99). Mention of Virgil's hometown presents a poignant reminder of the confiscations of the early 30s, a prominent theme of the *Eclogues*. Having introduced this painful subject openly, Virgil now considers it against his discussion of the dark earth:

> Black earth, rich beneath the crushing plowshare, and characterized by crumbly soil – a feature that we replicate by plowing – is usually best for grain. Not from any plain will you see more wagons drawn by slow oxen coming home, nor land whence the angry plowman has hauled off wood and overturned groves idle for many years. He has utterly uprooted the ancient homes of birds; their nests abandoned, they head for the sky, but the rough plain glistens beneath the plow driven into it. (2.203–11)

The displaced birds not only metaphorically capture book 2's tension between progress and nature but, coming within ten lines of the pathetic reflection on Mantua, they also offer a poignant parallel to the Mantuans' displacement. The land is subject to an angry plowman and is symbolically violated by the driven plow (211). Thomas notes that violent tones qualify even the *Georgics'* gentle moments.

Virgil closes out this section by noting how the volcanic flow of Vesuvius has enriched the local earth. In accordance with Varro's advice in the *De re rustica* (1.9), various soils are divided up according to their suitability for growing either grain or vines, while the farmer is to remember how to lay out the vineyard:

> Give space to the rows; nor less readily, when the trees have been positioned, let every row square to the nail's width once the line has been cut. As often in a mighty battle when a lengthy legion has unfolded its ranks and its column has taken its stand in the open plain, and the battlelines have been separated and all the land pulsates far and wide with the gleaming bronze, nor yet do they engage the horrible battles, but Mars wanders uncertain amidst the two armies. (2.277–83)

Here Virgil delicately echoes Lucretius' description of an army on a hill-side as beheld from a great distance (*DRN* 2.323–32). Lucretius' army, representing atomic motion, gleams on the plain as its sound wafts toward the distant viewer. Virgil, by contrast, describes a stationary and orderly army that has not yet commenced fighting but is on the brink of doing so. While Virgil's uncertain and wandering Mars possibly acknowledges the underlying disorder of Lucretius' atoms, Virgil's tidy rows offer a different image: what had been in Lucretius the disorder of natural process, now, under human supervision and care, is a strategy for harnessing nature.

Virgil considers some particulars by feigning conversation with the reader: "You would ask, perhaps, what the depths are for the trenches; or whether I would dare to entrust the vine to a shallow furrow" (*G.* 2.288–9). Here Virgil adapts a simile from *Iliad* 12 in which Homer describes two warriors as oaks whose roots could hold up to the elements (132–34). Virgil restores to earth what had been a simile derived from agriculture. This illustration of the placing of a plant in its proper spot offers a playful reseeding of the Homeric original.

After various admonitions, Virgil introduces a line that speaks about a "rival":

And let not any other author – however wise he might seem to you – persuade you to turn the stiff earth when the North wind blows. Then winter hems in the fields with frost and, when the seed is cast, it does not suffer the frozen root to plant itself in the soil. The best planting time for vines is when, in warming spring, the white bird has come, hateful to long snakes, or in the first chill of autumn, when the swift-moving sun does not yet touch winter with his horses, and summer is now passing. Spring is even useful to the groves' leaves, spring is useful to the woods; in spring the lands swell and demand procreative seeds. (2.315–24)

Who is "any other author" mentioned in line 315? Varro would be a possibility for Virgil has already in this book alluded to Varro's advice on soils. A writer of prose, Varro speaks of the planting of vines, urging the farmer to consider each plant's nature and to choose the most suitable time and the place in the field "as to what part of the sky each area looks up, so as to suit the season in which each thing most easily grows" (*R.R.* 39.1–3). Though Virgil playfully feigns to correct his contemporary, he actually adapts Varro's prose.

This didactic tone gives way to Virgil's lush description of spring, which involves intercourse between Heaven and Earth:

> Then the all-powerful Father Heaven descends unto the lap of his joyous spouse with fecund rain and, mixed with her great body, the Great One nourishes all their offspring. (2.325–7)

Such a description of sexual potency is not exclusively Virgilian, as this very presentation stems from a Lucretian passage on the regenerative power of the springtime (*DRN* 1.250–56). Though the details show a debt to Theophrastus (*De causis plantarum* 3.4–6), Virgil's didactic tone here is indebted to the *De Rerum Natura*, as his use of the common Lucretian phrase *quod superest* ("as for what remains," 2.346) also attests. The technical world of farming is always close at hand, as Virgil touches upon the practicalities of proper fertilization and drainage (346–53).

In the section that follows, Virgil extends the association of the planting of the vine. Now the development of vine dressing suggests a connection with the rise of civilization. Virgil makes this connection by shifting his focus to the origins of Greek drama, with an excursus on Bacchus (388–96). He then enlarges on primitive Rome's adaptation of the dramatic arts:

> Even Ausonian farmers, a race sent from Troy, play in disordered verses and, with uninhibited laughter, they put on shaggy faces from hollowed out tree bark and call upon you, Bacchus, with their happy songs; for you they hang soft little masks from tall pines. Hence does every vineyard come of age with abundant fruit. (385–90)

The name Ausonian, here referring to Trojans, suggests Rome's ultimate origins and thus anticipates the end of *Georgic* 2, where a prototype of Rome will emerge. More importantly, Bacchus is connected with the rise of this civilization: where Bacchus goes, the arts and fecund abundance go also. But civilization has its problems, and Virgil is here describing a civilized but far from perfect world. Bacchus, we shall see shortly, can bring trouble, too.

A reminder that this world is less than a utopia lies in the vinedresser's hard work (*G.* 2.397–400; 418). The Latin word *labor* occurs here thrice in a span of fifteen lines (397, 401, 412) with advice appropriate to the hard worker: "be the first to dig the land, the first to burn the cast off twigs, and first to bring the poles under cover" (408f.). Virgil follows these instructions with marked repetition (known as anaphora): "now vines are bound, now the vineyard returns the pruning-knives and now the last vine dresser sings of rows completed" (416f.). In the midst of this frame, which begins with the word "first" and ends with the job completed, one finds a piece of practical wisdom: "Praise a big farm, cultivate a small one" (412–13).

Virgil soon commences a discussion of the usefulness of various trees for making houses, ships, and spears, all objects of military or civilized life. Milling serves as a symbol for the rise of civilization:

> Nor does the light alder, sent down the Po, not swim into the raging wave; nor do the bees not also establish their swarms in the hollow bark and belly of a rotten oak. What equally memorable thing have the gifts of Bacchus brought? Bacchus has even given reasons for fault; he overtook with death the raging Centaurs, Rhoetus and Pholus and Hylaeus, who threatened the Lapiths with a huge wine bowl. (2.451–7)

From trees carrying a community of bees and the perhaps uncertain prospect of milled lumber for civilized life, Virgil transitions to an even more ambiguous aspect of civilized society: wine and its intoxicating power. In this passage, famously dubbed by Servius *uituperatio uitium* (*uini*), "scolding of vines (wine)," wine is rebuked because it produced such scurrilous behavior in the Centaurs that the Lapiths retaliate. Passages with such outrageous and ultimately negative incidents, as this one has, mitigate the more harmonious moments in the *Georgics*. No passage in the *Georgics* paints an unblemished picture of life: here we see that even the gift of wine can have negative consequences.

The focus now comes back to farmers, who are "too fortunate, if they should know their own blessings" (458), for the earth yields them its produce unbidden. Yet the reader knows better, for the earth requires work, as is evidenced in the farmer's unrelenting effort. This farmer lives simply, not in a lofty mansion (461–5) and, though he may from time to time enjoy quasi-Lucretian quietude (467), he does so because he reveres his forefathers and has kept the rites of gods (473).

A setback in the movement toward civilization comes when the reader learns that Justice has quit the earth (474), a theme associated with transgression found also in Catullus (64.398) and going back to Hesiod's *Erga* (200–2), which included material on which Virgil drew for his invocation of the Saturnian age – preparation, Thomas notes, for the muted crescendo with which the book culminates. Before that finale, Virgil invokes the Muses (475–82) and dons the persona of a wise teacher, offering a portrait of rustic philosophical contentment: "Happy is he who knows the causes of things and has placed all fears and inexorable fate under his feet, along with the cry of greedy Acheron" (490–2). While the phrase "causes of things" evokes the title of Lucretius' *De Rerum Natura*, the line that follows is even more evocative of that poet, for, as Mynors shows, Lucretius purports to subjugate fear and fate (*DRN* 1.78). Yet for Virgil in this passage philosophical contentment alone is not enough: one must go beyond Lucretius; one also needs a mystical proto-Saturnian aura.

Lucretian authority allows Virgil to establish such an aura, the setting for which is characterized by rural values that run contrary to the insufferable hustle and bustle of the forum. Virgil pulls the reader back toward the prototypical Saturnian realm. The farmer does not enter the halls of kings (504) or drink from a jeweled cup or sleep on fancy bedspreads; rather, he is content with his friends and family:

> His sweet children hang upon his kisses, his chaste home keeps its purity, his cows distend lactating udders, and on the happy field his plump goats butt one another with opposing horns. He himself keeps festival days and, when the fire is in their midst and his comrades crown the mixing bowl, they spread out on the grass. He calls upon you, Lenaeus, and he pours a libation, affixing to an elm the shepherds' contests of the swift lance. Next they strip their hardened bodies for the rustic wrestling. This is the life the ancient Sabines once cultivated. This is the life of Remus and his brother; thus Etruria waxed strong, no doubt, and Rome became the fairest of things. (2.523–34)

The image of this happy farmer stands in stark contrast to Lucretius' maudlin portrait of the man who dreads death because he might lose the joy of family:

> Now no happy home will welcome you, neither will your very lovely wife or sweet children rush to snatch kisses from you nor will they touch your chest in quiet sweetness. (*DRN* 3.894–6)

In contrast to the notion that sentimentality is no reason to fear death, Virgil points up the importance of family and communal life. The community of Virgil's farmer presents a prototype of *ciuitas* that develops over a wine bowl shared among friends. The building blocks of Roman civilization are here in the beauty of the rustic life uncomplicated by the societal demands of Virgil's own day. One such building block is the games that will ultimately become the central feature of Rome's circuses. This image of competition itself competes with the image of the out-of-control charioteer that closed *Georgic* 1. Such a portrayal of life looks back to that of "old Sabines," who had lived years before Virgil's time (532), just as it looks ahead to Augustan Rome.

Characteristically, Virgil introduces tension amidst an apparent respite from woe. Rome's founders are ominously termed "Remus and his brother" (533), phrasing that cannot be dismissed as mere periphrasis. Were this passage an unqualified march toward Rome's greatness, one might have found in it Romulus, not Remus (Romulus' brother whom he murdered for leaping Rome's wall in violation of his statutes [Livy 1.3.10f.]) as the character mentioned. Accordingly, when Virgil states that from these origins "Rome became the fairest of things, and surrounded her seven citadels with a single wall" (534–5), the informed reader thinks quite pointedly of the death of Remus at Romulus' hands – a variation characteristic of the ebb and flow that is the rhythm of Virgil's wisdom – a reminder that the cost of progress is dear.

Virgil has transitioned this book from the toil of planting vines to the joy of drinking its vintage. With that shift the farmer has moved to a quasi-Saturnian, proto-Roman moment of joy qualified by the difficulty associated with the broader implications of civilized life (*ciuitas*). Such joy is neither borne out of the ideal of the Epicurean school of philosophy that advanced the notion of undisturbed freedom from worry (*securitas*), nor is it a response to worrisome insecurity, engendered by Rome's pervasive political dominance. Instead, Virgil offers a moment in which the farmer and the reader can find a moment of rest. The festive scene that closes *Georgic* 2 offers just such a moment, a glimpse of *ciuitas* that societal life affords, as family and friends gather around a wine bowl, suggestive of prosperity and harmony, though these ideas are themselves qualified by the strife of Rome's founding brothers and farmers' toil.

Georgic 3: Civic Promise and Rural Catastrophe

The third book's invocation focuses on two figures, both seemingly rural but with urban connections:

> You, too, great Pales, and you, shepherd of Amphrysus, worthy to be remembered, we will sing, and you, woods and streams of Mt. Lycaeus. The rest, which would have captivated idle minds with song, are themes now all too common. (3.1–4)

✱ rural yet urban connections ✱

Though woods and brooks suggest rusticity, the reader knows that Pales is not only rural but also, through association with Rome's rustic foundation (21 April), paradoxically suggestive of the *urbs*. Likewise, the reference to Apollo as the shepherd of Amphrysus (i.e. "Apollo the of flocks") is, on the surface, rustic; yet Apollo was, at the time of the *Georgics'* composition, also the patron deity of Octavian. Thus, in Pales and Apollo, urban and rural themes come together, as do also the apparent opposites of grand epic and Alexandrian delicacy, for Virgil claims to sing rural themes. An allusion to the Italian epic poet Ennius, however, shows that this is not to be a book simply about rural themes. Virgil allusively adapts Ennius' famous epitaph that decries lamentation because the poet flits "alive on the lips of men":[8]

> The path must be tried, whereby I, too, can lift myself from the ground and fly, a victor on the lips of men. Provided only there be life remaining for me, I will be the first to bring down the Muses to our fatherland from the Aonian peak; I will be the first to bring back to you, Mantua, Idumaean palms, and on the verdant field I will put a marble temple next to the water, where the vast Mincius wanders with its sluggish river bends and its banks fringed with tender reeds. Caesar will be in the middle for me and he will possess the temple. For him, I, a champion clothed in Tyrian purple, will drive a hundred four-horse chariots along the stream. For me all Greece, leaving the river Alpheus and the groves of Molorchus, shall compete in races and with raw-hide gloves; I myself, head adorned with the leaves of a cropped olive, will bring gifts. (3.8–22)

The third book's introductory verses here continue, Thomas points out, with a "non-refusal" (anti-*recusatio*) to embrace epic themes; indeed, Virgil even may obliquely anticipate his later epic production, as he claims to draw Greece for a fresh game in Italy. Thus, he moves allusively from Ennius to Hesiod, who hailed from Boeotia (viz. the Aonian peak), whence Virgil claims to transport the Muses from Greece to Italy, as once Naevius had claimed (cf. Gellius 17.21.44).

Virgil's procedure, however, is highly self-referential: *he* is the victor, *he* will be the first to bring the Muses from the Aonian (Hesiodic) summit to Mantua, and *he* will be the first to "bring down" (*deducam*) the palms of Idumea (i.e., Israel). The Latin verb is *deducere*, a coded word that suggests "producing in Alexandrian fashion." This Alexandrian brushstroke is apt, as Thomas has shown, for the reference to Idumea seems to come from a lost line of Callimachus. The reference to Molorchus, too, is drawn from Callimachus, specifically his celebration of his patron,

deducere

Queen Berenice (*Aetia* 3); by this allusion Virgil delicately claims that he, too, has a powerful patron in Caesar (i.e., Octavian).

Accordingly, as Virgil begins the second half of the *Georgics*, he vaunts a connection to the master teacher, Hesiod, to the master stylist, Callimachus, and to the master Roman epicist, Ennius. Yet such an opening points beyond mere style to political reality, as well, for Caesar is "in the middle" (16) both figuratively and, for the *Georgics* as a collection, literally. Having allusively brought Greece to Italy, Virgil now shifts the focus to Caesar (Octavian). Though Virgil is the victor in Tyrian purple driving a chariot, which now he, as charioteer, controls – one might recall the helpless charioteer at the end of *Georgic* 1 – the person at the center of things is Caesar, just as he had been at the center of *Eclogue* 1.

Virgil's persona offers gifts in Caesar's honor, even sacrificing to him as to a god, which befits the young monarch, for he will have a temple, an image that harks back to Pindar's description in his first *Olympian*. The doors of *Georgic* 3's temple bear images suggesting the breadth of Octavian's sway (31–32) and the poet-craftsman even fashions "statues that breathe" (34), in the tradition of the famous Greek artist Phidias. Yet Virgil's temple surpasses its Pindaric predecessor, for it parallels the grand building program of Octavian himself and may even anticipate the grandeur of Virgil's future poetic production:

> Soon I will gird myself to sing of the burning battles of Caesar and to make his name famous through as many years as Caesar is removed from the Tithonus' origin. (3.46–48)

Such a work will ultimately be realized with the composition of the *Aeneid*. Earlier, Virgil had referred to the reward of victors at the Olympic games; the breeder who would win that prize must be especially selective as to the mare's form. The discussion of horse-breeding resonates with Virgil's own driving of the chariot with which the third book opens. It also anticipates the book's poignant conclusion describing equine and bovine death (*G.* 3.498–514).

Just after this prologue's allusive presentation of a future poetic project and quasi-religious picture of Octavian, Virgil engages universal issues with a gnomic statement:

> Each best day of life flees wretched mortals first. Diseases come, as do sad old age and labor, and harsh death's cruelty snatches them away. (3.66–8)

notice how animals : humans are converged

I would say he is creating sympathy

Virgil thus begins his book also with an awareness of the fleeting quality of life. As the book progresses, we shall see that there will be little distinction between the plight of human beings and other animals. Just as Lucretius' exposition of philosophical tenets may prepare the reader to face the reality of death in the *De Rerum Natura*'s finale, so Virgil's blending of human and animal in book 3 prepares the reader to extend the metaphor of destruction in book 3 into the human sphere. This metaphor will contrast with the close of book 4, in which bees are also put on a parallel with human existence.

Accordingly, Virgil's treatment of horses includes aphorisms equally suited to humans: the farmer is not to indulge ignoble old age (96); there is no rest for horses, as their love of victory is strong (110). Virgil's description of bulls' passion and rivalry also suggests a convergence of man and animal: "every single race on earth of men and beasts ... rushes headlong to madness and passion: love is the same for all" (242–4). Such passion is evident in the equine condition of *hippomanes* (mare madness), engendered by the desire for sex that Venus gives to each species (268). This craving manifests itself as the dripping from the mare's groin, sought by scheming mothers-in-law as an ingredient for potions.

To indicate a shift in subject matter to smaller animals, Virgil opens the book's second half with a second proem:

> But meanwhile time flies, it flies irrevocably, while we, captivated by love, carry on with details. This is enough on herds; the other part of my task remains, to drive on woolly flocks and shaggy goats. Here is my labor; hence, brave farmers, have a hope for praise. Nor am I doubtful about how great a thing it is to master these matters with words and to add this honor to "slender" things. But sweet love draws me on, over the deserted slope of the Parnassus; I delight to roam over this land, where no circuit of those before me turns, with a "gentle" slope, toward Castalia. (3.284–93)

The "slender" things and Mt Parnassus' "gentle slope" (*molli ... cliuo*) reveal Virgil's Alexandrian allegiance – these adjectives are Alexandrian code words – as had the verb *deducere* at the opening of *Georgic* 3. Virgil uses the leitmotif of a race to explain how his poetic persona strives in a competitive poetic world and he employs the expression "drive on" (*agitare*) to connote the driving on of the flock. Mynors notes (ad 386) that this verb, which can also be used for chariot driving, is "a very forcible word for the shepherd's activity." Such competition may reflect the Alexandrian practice of *aemulatio* or playful rivalry. Virgil states clearly the importance of victory in words; his competitors in this race are his forebears, those who are "before him" (*priores*).

Having established himself in the poetic landscape, Virgil again invokes Pales (294), turning his discussion to husbandry:

> As I begin, I declare that sheep feed on grass in gentle pens, until in due course leafy summer returns, and that you strew the hard land below with much straw and handfuls of ferns, lest the frozen ice harm the gentle flock bringing scabies and unsightly foot-rot. (3.295–9)

Holzberg has argued persuasively that smaller animals connote a generic shift from the feel of grand epic that opened the book, where "grander" animals such as horses and oxen were prominent. The second half of the book, however, treats smaller creatures and therefore betokens indebtedness to the slighter style of Callimachus. Thus, Virgil twice uses the same coded adjective, "gentle" (*mollis*, 295, 299), that he had used only moments before in reference to Mt Parnassus.[9]

The care of sheep and goats begins with a description known as a *locus amoenus* (pleasant locale) in which the flocks find rest, water, and shade.[10] Virgil juxtaposes such an inviting place with regions of climatic variance: Libya is blistering (339), while Scythia is frigid (449). In the final analysis, Scythians at least have in common with Romans the celebration of life in their homes, enjoying wine and sharing happiness in a manner not unlike those of Virgil's compatriots (376–80). Such a description emphasizes the universality of the human experience.

After presenting an account of genetic dominance, Virgil focuses on two small animals. Dogs offer protection from potential brigands (406–8) and assist in the hunt (409–13). The snake, however, is dangerous, sometimes requiring fumigation (414–15). Snake venom provides Virgil with an easy transition to the disaster associated with plague. The poem now shifts to its most negative moment. Having reasserted his role as teacher, Virgil explains in the authorial first person how disease makes its way into animals' marrow. As Lucretius does with great irony ("death fills all the holy shrines of the gods," *DRN* 6.1272), Virgil notes the ineffectiveness of prayer:

> Still, there is no fortune for these labors handier than if someone could cut open with a blade the head of the boil; its harmfulness is nourished and lives by hiding within, so long as the shepherd refuses to put his healing hands to the wound and just sits there, demanding of the gods better omens. But, too, when the discomfort, having slipped into the deep marrow of the bleating lambs, rages, and dry, parching fever feeds on their limbs, it is best to ward off the fiery heat. (3.452–9)

In a book that opened with the image of Apollo as "shepherd" (*pastor*), this reference to the shepherd's weakness is a matter of dualistic disparity, in part because Apollo is also a healing deity. A starker contrast, however, lies in the fact that the shepherd had, just a few lines before, been portrayed as highly capable; here he has no success and must resort to prayer.

The plague takes the animals so rapidly that they cannot be sacrificed (486–93). This irony is extended to the futility of medicine. Wine, "the solitary hope of healing for the dying" (510), poured into the ill animals' mouths also fails, leading only to grotesque self-mangling (514). Thus, good things such as wine prove to be useless, and Virgil wants his reader to realize that there is no easy way out or hope of salvation in such dire straits. Now the plowman, elsewhere "angry" (2.207) or "harsh" (4.512), is described as "sad" (3.517). Virgil's narrative voice shows dismay, questioning the benefit of labor. The poet's wisdom is palpable as he does not back away from life's hard questions; these pertain to despair and suffering, both animal and human.

The conflation of man and animal is advanced as the poet explains that men must take over the animals' work:[11]

> Therefore men wretchedly scratch the land with rakes and bury the seed with their very nails, and through the high hills they drag the creaking wagons with their straining necks. (3.534–6)

The plague that wreaked havoc among human beings in Lucretius and Thucydides here destroys animals. Men are transformed into brutes as they don hide coverings and take up the beasts' labor. Even physicians such as the centaur Chiron (550) cannot help the dying. Half-human and half-animal, Chiron metaphorically bridges the gap between man and beast. Ironically, this connection is heightened as men unwisely don the pelts of the diseased animals, a harmful act in the vein of the story of Deinira's venomous gift to Hercules. Hercules' bride gave him a coat, tainted with the blood of the centaur Nessus, that caused his demise. Now humans suffer, like Hercules, from contact with tainted pelts.

Georgic 3 closes with a crescendo of pathos and despair. Though men have not become animals in a bestial sense, their toils are now those of animals. All creatures can be victims of disease and religious excess. Animals fall to disease at the altar; men, too, die without hope, having lost their sense of purpose. Were the *Georgics* to end here, Virgil might have surpassed even Lucretius for the ending with the most pessimistic *tour de force* in ancient literature.

Georgic 4: The (Parallel) World of Bees

In book 4, Virgil treats apiculture, using bees as an analogy for human society. Virgil opens this final book with an economical proem:

> Forthwith I will follow up with the heavenly gifts of honey from the skies; of this part, too, Maecenas, take note. The spectacles of tiny things are fit to be marveled at by you; great-hearted leaders, the character of an entire nation and its pursuits, clans and battles – in due order these will I sing. The work here is on the slight side; but the glory is not slight, if inauspicious godheads permit and Apollo, when called upon, hears me. (4.1–7)

This invocation forms a ring composition by citation of Maecenas' name, for he is addressed in the second line of both the first and fourth books, while in the second and third books Maecenas is mentioned in precisely the forty-first line. As Thomas notes, the invocation of Maecenas allows the content of these books to be emphasized in different ways. *Georgic* 1 sets forth the agenda for the entire poem; there, Maecenas is addressed at the inception. The fourth *Georgic*'s content will be the culmination of the poem as a whole, and Maecenas again is acknowledged straightaway. The proems of *Georgics* 2 and 3, however, are different: *Georgic* 2 focuses on wine's civilizing influence, with an address to Dionysus, Bacchus, and Lenaeus. That book treats trees and the vine, and Maecenas is named only after those themes are established. In the opening of *Georgic* 3, the focus is on Roman civilization, defined afresh by the one who is "in the middle" of the work, Caesar himself, who has a temple and is celebrated by a chariot-driving Virgil. In the two central books, the address to Maecenas is delayed, as his role is secondary to the central focus of each prologue.

For book 4 the focus will be on bees and their civilization with its own national character. In the midst of his discussion of this civilization, Virgil includes a miniature epic (sometimes called an "epyllion") that will emphasize the theme of renewal. The adjective "slight" (*tenuis*), like his use of the adjective *mollis* (gentle) in *Georgic* 3 and his allusion to Aratus' use of *lepte* (slender) in his acrostic in *Georgic* 1 (discussed in Chapter 1), makes clear that Virgil, in Alexandrian style, will tell the story of bees, used by Callimachus as a metaphor for the poet (*Hymn* 2.110–12).[12]

The bees' home is sheltered from wind and sportive goats. Led out by their "kings" in the springtime, the bees remain near the hive, where abundant shade and water form a *locus amoenus* of lush surroundings

(8–32). The hive itself is a practical structure, which the farmer need only ensure be sealed (33–50). A brief account of the two "kings" and their warring factions follows:

> The kings themselves, in the midst of the battle lines, with marked wings, carry great courage in their tiny hearts, ever so determined not to give ground until the ponderous victor has compelled one side or the other to retreat in flight. (4.82–5)

Virgil goes beyond Varro's description of swarming (*R.R.* 3.16.29–31) to include a small story about the quashing of apian strife (86–7). When bees clash to choose a leader, the flinging of sand settles the battle. Though such dust tossing might seem "half humorous," Mynors notes, it turns out to be a serious motif in this section (96–7), as a wayfarer, who is compared to the inferior class of bees, emerges spitting dirt from his mouth:

> For other ugly ones have an unsightly appearance, just as when a wayfarer comes, parched, out of the deep dust and from his dry mouth spits dirt. Others, shimmering with gold, shine with its glitter on their bodies, covered evenly with golden droplets. This is the more capable breed; from these at a fixed season you will draw sweet honey – it is not so sweet as it is smooth and ready to overcome the harsh taste of Bacchus. (4.96–102)

The dust that settled the bees' skirmish now takes on a more serious tone, evoking the way that the earth can harm. The parched (98) wayfarer is nearly subdued by his need for a drink; conversely, the honey that will come from the "better" bees will subdue drink (102), of which this parched wayfarer would savor but a sip. Instead, covered with dust, he represents the inferior bee whose king is not fit to govern.

From this description of the bees' struggle to choose the superior king, it is not difficult to imagine a parallel with the struggle between Octavian and Marc Antony that characterized the period during which most of the *Georgics* was being written. Nevertheless, the political metaphor of battling bee-kings should not be over extended, for the king bee's wings are clipped to keep the swarm from migrating (106).[13] This advice, not found in the earlier discussions of Varro or Aristotle, allows Virgil to move his text away from a bald association with Octavian and Antony to the superb excursus about the Corycian gardener, discussed in the first chapter. The transition to that passage breaks up the details of beekeeping as the image of dueling kings passes away; the Corycian gardener emerges as a sage figure, who embodies uncomplicated wisdom and the value of hard work.

Virgil has not, however, finished with bees, whose society seems to be based on a blend of Plato's *Laws* and *Republic*, sharing children in common while conducting life subject to written laws. Yet Virgil broadens the scope: Plato's ideal state, with its written code, is outstripped by Roman culture, which prided itself on adherence to law and hard work.[14] In describing their industry, Virgil introduces his comparison of the tiny bees to the Cyclopes in their forges with the phrase, "if one may compare small things to great" (176); in the first *Eclogue* (1.23) Rome had been similarly compared to smaller cities. Furthermore, apian society encompasses Rome's finer attributes: cooperation (184), respect for ancestors (209), and loyalty to the ruler (210–18). Finally, the narrator even refers to the bees as *Quirites*, "Roman citizens" (201).

Following speculation about the bees' divine nature, Virgil describes how even bees can be afflicted, explaining how death comes to the hive. Having described the illness and ways to cure it (251–80), Virgil then couches the eventuality of the bees' death in a conditional clause: "if suddenly the entire race shall have failed [for the keeper] and he will not have the means to call back the stock of a new line" (281–2). Unlike book 3's close, this text does not dwell on death but focuses on the bees' regeneration, recounted in the subsequent section.

Known as the Aristaeus epyllion, this tale encompasses the story of Proteus, the sage consulted in *Odyssey* 4 by Menelaus. Virgil's rendition of the Proteus tale is characteristically Alexandrian, consisting of a tale within a tale. The story begins with Aristaeus complaining to his mother, Cyrene, about the loss of his hive (321–32). His soliloquy, modeled on that of Achilles to Thetis in the *Iliad* (1.348–56), closes with a somber request:

> Come on then and, with your very hand, uproot my happy woods, bring destructive flame to my stables, kill my crops, burn my plantings and wield a strong axe against my vines, if such disgust with my honor has taken hold of you. (4.329–32)

Aristaeus' invitation for his mother essentially to undo the content of the *Georgics* is hyperbolic in the Homeric manner. Further epic qualities can be seen in the catalogues of nymphs and rivers that follow, and a Homeric connection is emphasized when Virgil describes Cyrene's welcoming of

Aristaeus to a banquet (4.276–81), an event comparable to Telemachus' being entertained in *Odyssey* 4 (55–8).

In this epic context, Cyrene offers explicit instructions, which fittingly echo those given by the nymph Eidothea to Menelaus in *Odyssey* 4. Aristaeus is to go to Proteus, who speaks only under duress. Twice described as a *uates*, meaning both poet and seer, Proteus tells Aristaeus the story of the greatest poet, Orpheus, whose tale may allude to Gallus since, Servius says, all references to Gallus were removed from *Georgic* 4 at Augustus' command. Horsfall has shown how unlikely a literal reading of the Servian proposal is, and others have seen Servius as muddling *Eclogue* 10 with *Georgic* 4. In any case, Orpheus could, qua poet par excellence, symbolize all great poets, among whom Gallus would be a recent exemplar; as such, Virgil may implicitly acknowledge his friend in the *Georgics*.[15]

A shape-shifting wisdom figure, Proteus explains the connection of Aristaeus with Orpheus: Aristaeus pursued Eurydice on her wedding day, causing her to be bitten by a snake. Explaining how Orpheus' song of lament opened a way to the Underworld, Proteus describes Orpheus' descent with a miniature ecphrasis that anticipates Virgil's much larger description of the Underworld in *Aeneid* 6. This passage includes an account of the shades that flock like birds, followed by the bleak picture of unwed children laid to rest before the faces of their parents.

After a portrayal of the Underworld in a manner commensurate with Homer's account in *Odyssey* 11, Proteus pithily recounts Eurydice's return to Orpheus, followed by the lovers' ascent and farewell:

> What great madness has ruined us, Orpheus, both you and wretched me?
> Behold, a second time the cruel Fates call me back, and drowsiness
> encompasses my swimming eyes. And now, farewell! I am carried away,
> hemmed in by vast night and, as I stretch out my weak hands to you, alas,
> I am no longer yours. (4.494–8)

Ironically, Eurydice calls attention to her own eyes, the organ by which Orpheus has caused her second death; conversely, Orpheus, whose voice gained access to the Underworld, does not respond. Though in Proteus' elliptical treatment we have not actually heard the voice of Orpheus himself, we now learn that he wishes to say more (501–2) as he grasps after Eurydice's flitting shade.

Orpheus' lament that follows shortly is modeled on Penelope's (*Odyssey* 19.512–15). Virgil's Orpheus is presented as a nightingale mourning her lost chicks dragged harshly from the nest by a farmer's plow (511–13). With Alexandrian erudition, Virgil reminds us in his account of the nightingale's song that we are still reading the *Georgics*, for we recall this plowman from the second book (210f.), where his plowshare had displaced birds from their nests. Now Orpheus' birdlike song cannot save him, though after his death his decapitated head's warbling tongue will continue to hymn his lost lover (4.526).

With the close of his account, Proteus rapidly plunges into the sea, leaving Cyrene to interpret his tale for Aristaeus: the nymphs, who were angry over Eurydice's death, are to be appeased. The instructions are explicit: four altars, four sacrifices over a period of ten days, and the offended nymphs will relent in their anger. This epyllion, a poem within the larger poem of the fourth *Georgic*, thus ends with corrective instruction given by the *uates* Proteus, as song brings about restoration of order.

Conclusion: Recapitulation, Regeneration and Repast

In his description of the bees' regeneration, Virgil cleverly recapitulates the major themes of each *Georgic*, themes that, taken together, point toward a repast of wisdom for the reader. This description begins when Aristaeus returns to the grove, where he finds a portent:

> He comes to the shrine and he raises the altars in the manner that had been explained, leading four outstanding bulls with excellent form and as many heifers with necks untouched by the yoke. Afterward, when Aurora had brought on her ninth rising, he renders Orpheus funeral offerings and returns to the grove. But here they see a portent, sudden, and amazing in the telling: through the rotting internal organs of the cows, bees buzz within the whole belly and teem out from the broken ribs. They are drawn together in immense clouds and from the tree top they now commingle, hanging from pliant boughs as a cluster of grapes. (4.549–58)

This "portent" accords with result of the *bougonia*, the regeneration of the hive which would have been a procedure known by Virgil's readers. This regenerative phenomenon was as ancient as the story of Samson's riddle in the Old Testament book of Judges. Virgil's words are as riddling in their own right: he presents four lines of instruction (296–97), where four windows are to face the four winds, a description that, Thomas suggests, may hark back to the pre-Socratic atomistic philosopher Democritus. Further, these windows permit a view back from the four books of the

Georgics to Virgil's immediate didactic predecessor, Lucretius, whose poem had ended with death; through Virgil's "window" reference, he continues the didactic legacy, enhancing it by having the final book end with not death but regeneration.

The *bougonia*'s theme of regeneration offers a partial and still indirect answer to the indirect questions of the first *Georgic*'s prologue: for the immortal race of bees, life must necessarily return. To lead up to such regeneration, Virgil has used four books, paralleled by the four sacrifices or the four windows of the structure for the *bougonia* that introduced the story of Aristaeus. Out of the toxic rotting flesh of book 3 comes a reinstatement of the life of bees, whose civilization resonates at least in some ways with that of Rome. Yet any optimistic reading of this regeneration, such as that advanced by Bovie many years ago, is qualified by the poem's darker moments, and a tight comparison of the bee community with Rome must not be pressed too hard.[16]

Virgil's structural nexus, if complicated, does much more than merely give the work coherency. The first half of the *Georgics* had been about plants, the second half about animals. The first half had celebrated bread and wine, the second half meat and honey. Taken together, these are the components of a Roman meal. Yet the food that Virgil wants to put before his reader is not merely a dinner such as the old Corycian's simple fare, the bounteous winter festivities of the farmer and his wife (1.293–304), or the farmer's party at the end of the second book (2.505–40). Such quasi-festive vignettes are qualified by negative moments that occur even at the most optimistic occasions, such as the disturbing tone of the phrase "Remus and his brother" (2.533) found in the midst of the farmer's celebration at the end of book 2. If, in light of their varied mood, the four *Georgics* are not such a festive meal per se, they nevertheless present the components of such a meal – bread, wine, meat, and sweet honey – offering at least the potential for a feast. Yet that feast does not consist merely of harvested items to eat; it is a repast of wisdom.

In the *sphragis* that follows this recapitulation, Virgil reflects on Octavian's political power vis-à-vis the poet's literary agenda. In contrast to Octavian's military exploits, Virgil has been singing:

> I kept singing about the cultivation of fields and of cattle and about trees, while great Caesar thunders in war along the deep Euphrates and as victor gives laws throughout the willing nations and builds a road to Olympus. At that time sweet Parthenope was nursing me, Virgil, when I was

flourishing in the pursuits of inglorious leisure – when I played with the songs of shepherds and, in the boldness of my youth, sang of you, Tityrus, beneath the covering of a spreading beech tree. (4.559–66)

Fields, cattle and trees correspond to the weather signs, grapes, and cattle's flesh mentioned just above in lines 555–8, again delicately alluding to the *Georgics* as a whole.

Virgil has imbued these four books with the poetic code of Alexandrian *epos*. When he mentions the Euphrates six lines from the end of the book, as we saw in Chapter 1, Virgil is abjuring epic, whereas Caesar has been engaged in "epic" activities. Meanwhile, Virgil, in a rare autobiographical moment, is flourishing in leisure's pursuit of poetry (463f.). "Is poetry less glorious than imperialism?" Griffin once asked. "In the sphragis ... Virgil has found a way of agreeing that it is, which at the same time ... implies that it is not."[17] Thus, in the *Georgics*, all things are qualified: empire comes with a cost, life cannot come without death, and Virgil's poetry does not embrace imperial glory without qualification. Though sometimes understated, the wisdom that these books encompass is expansive in nature and is promulgated amidst the characteristic oscillation between recklessness and control, toil and moments of joy, as well as death and regeneration. After the *Georgics*, when Virgil resumes his work as a poet, his mission will be to craft what is for him an entirely new sort of *epos*, alluded to at the opening of *Georgic* 3, when he described the temple that he will place by the Mincius' banks. "It is tempting," Thomas writes (ad 3.1), "to see the reference to a future epic" capturing, "as no other passage of Virgil does, the moment at which the inevitability of the *Aeneid* must have come to him." Having laid a foundation of wisdom, Virgil turns to just such a poetic mission.

Notes

1   Pindar, *Pythian* 4.34–41. Cf. Richard Thomas, "Virgil's Pindar?" in Peter E. Knox and Clive Foss (eds.), *Style and Tradition: Studies in Honor of Wendell Clausen* (Stuttgart, 1998), 99–120.

2   Noted by Thomas (1988), ad 95–6, but not by Mynors (1990), ad 96; cf. Don Folwer, "Subject Reviews: Latin Literature," *G&R* 38 (1991), 240.

3   So Thomas notes (ad 104), "the Virgilian battle is to be fought against nature."

4   Ruth S. Scodel and Richard F. Thomas, "Virgil and the Euphrates," *AJPh*
    105 (1984), 339; cf. ch. 1; J. Bayet, "Les Premières Géorgiques de Virgile
    (39–37 av. J.C.)," *RPhil* 4 (1930), 139f.; Mynors (1990), ad 1.509.

5   *Historia plantarum* 4.2–11. On Theophrastus, cf. Richard Thomas, "Prose
    into Poetry: Tradition and Meaning in Virgil's *Georgics*," *HSCP* 91 (1987),
    229–60.

6   Thomas (1987), 230.

7   Cato, as cited in C. Julius Solinus, *Collecteana Rerum Mirablilium*, 2.2;
    Varro, *R.R.* 1.2.3–6; Sophocles, *Oedipus at Colonus*, 668–719; see Richard
    Thomas, *Virgil:* Georgics, 2 vols. (Cambridge, 1988), 230.

8   E. H. Warmington, *Remains of Old Latin*, vol. 1 (Cambridge, MA, 1935),
    402, Epigram 10, *Nemo me lacrimis decoret nec funera fletu/faxit. Cur?
    uolito uiuos per ora uirum*; cf. G. Williams (1968), 451.

9   Niklas Holzberg, *Virgil: Der Dichter und Sein Werk* (Munich, 2006), 113f.;
    on *mollis*, cf. Hinds (1987), 21–3, 127, 141 n. 58.

10 *G.* 3.322–38. See Gerhard Schönbeck, *Der locus amoenus von Homer bis
    Horaz* (Heidelberg, 1962); further, Ernst Robert Curtius, *European
    Literature and the Latin Middle Ages*, tr. W. R. Trask (New York, 1953),
    195–200.

11 Cf. Servius, ad *G.* 4.219.13–16 and Varro, *R.R.* 3.16.5. Cf. Jasper Griffin,
    "The Fourth 'Georgic,' Virgil, and Rome," *G&R* 26 (1979), 61–80; and
    Monica Gale, "Man and Beast in Lucretius and the *Georgics*," *CQ* (1991),
    415 *et passim*. Cf. Thomas (1988), ad 3.215–16.

12 Richard Hunter, "Winged Callimachus," *ZPE* 76 (1989), 1. On Virgil's
    Alexandrianism, see M. M. Crump, *The Epyllion from Theocritus to Ovid*
    (Oxford, 1931), 195–242; David O. Ross Jr, *Backgrounds to Augustan
    Poetry: Gallus, Elegy and Rome* (Cambridge, 1975), 26f., 76.

13 Eva Crane, *World History of Beekeeping and Honey Hunting* (London,
    1999), 278.

14 The Twelve Tables were the most important ancient Roman legal code. Cf.
    Nevio Zorzelli, "Poetry and the City: The Case of Rome," *CJ* 86 (1991),
    313, 323. Cf. also A. H. F. Lefroy, "Rome and Law," *Harvard Law Review*
    20 (1907), 606–19; Thomas Habinek, "Sacrifice, Society, and Vergil's Ox-
    Borne Bees," in *Cabinet of the Muses: Essays on Classical and Comparative
    Literature in Honor of Thomas G. Rosenmeyer*, ed. Mark Griffith and Donald
    J. Mastronarde (Atlanta, GA, 1991), 209–23.

15 Horsfall (2000), 86–9; cf. W. B. Anderson, "Gallus and the Fourth *Georgic*,"
    CQ 27 (1933), 36–45. Cf. Putnam *Virgil's Poem of the Earth: Studies in the*
    Georgics (Princeton, 1979), xi; Thomas (1988), 1: 15–16; Farrell (1991)
    253–6; David O. Ross Jr, *Virgil's Elements: Physics and Poetry in the* Georgics
    (Princeton, NJ, 1987), 229.

16 Smith Palmer Bovie, "The Imagery of Ascent–Descent in Virgil's *Georgics*,"
    AJP 77 (1956), 337–58. Cf. Julia T. Dyson, "*Caesi Iuuenci* and *Pietas*

Impia in Virgil," *CJ* 91 (1996), 277–86. Dyson thoughtfully qualifies this vignette of regeneration: "slaughtered bullocks ... like Dido in the Underworld, say much by their silence. It is characteristic of Virgil's art that the same phrase should convey both harmony and discord, triumph and murder" (285).

17 Jasper Griffin, "The Fourth *Georgic*, Virgil and Rome," *G&R* 26 (1979), 72. Cf. also R. G. Austin, "*Ille ego qui quondam* ...," *CQ* 18 (1968), 107–15.

5

The *Aeneid*: Mission and *Telos*

Virgil has the capacity to sing … of the strong ships of Caesar,
who now stirs to action the weapons of Trojan Aeneas and the walls
that were put in place on the Lavinian shores. Yield, Roman writers,
give way, Greeks! Something greater than the *Iliad* is being born.

Propertius (*Elegies*, 2.34.61, 3–67)

And, by Hercules, though we shall yield to Homer's heavenly and
immortal nature, so even there was greater care and diligence on
Virgil's part, because he had to labor the more and, insofar as we
Romans are outstripped by Homer's outstanding passages, perhaps
we measure up in terms of Virgil's stylistic evenness. All other poets
will trail behind these at a great distance.

Quintilian (*Inst. Or.*, 10.86.4–7)

More than half a century after Propertius, Quintilian speaks of a conversation in which Domitius Afer compares the *Aeneid* to the *Iliad*, touting Virgil's stylistic evenness but ultimately favoring Homer. Nevertheless, Afer finds merit in Virgil's care, diligence, and labor. Quintilian may simply be referencing Alexandrian erudition, one of the principal differences between Virgil and Homer. Yet before we consider Virgil's application of Alexandrian standards to the *Aeneid*, let us examine the fundamental difference between his literary epic and Homer's orally transmitted poems.

Virgil manipulates the Homeric tradition, steering his epic toward a particular goal or *telos*, one attuned to contemporary historical consciousness in a more complex way (or at least a more deliberate way) than Homer. Whereas Homer presents his Trojan war as a major historical event, his depiction does not culminate in a *telos*, a goal with significance beyond the narrative, such as if the war were a fated plan for either the

Greeks or the Trojans or pointed toward some sort of cultural renewal. Accordingly, Odysseus' journey home (*nostos*) in the *Odyssey* is not teleological to the same degree that Aeneas' voyages are in the *Aeneid*.[1] Odysseus embarks upon a journey that entails personal adventures.

The *Aeneid*'s *telos* is vastly different, looking beyond Aeneas to Troy's rebirth, which lies outside of the epic's narrative but is made clear in the opening verses:

> I sing of arms and a man, who first, exiled by fate, came from the shores of Troy to Italy and to the Lavinian coast; much was he tossed, both on lands and the deep by the power of the gods, all because of the mindful wrath of savage Juno; and much did suffer, too, in war, until he would found a city and bring his gods to Latium, whence the Latin race, Alban fathers, and walls of high Rome. Muse, make me remember the reasons – in what aspect of her wounded godhead, or aggrieved at what thing – that the queen of the gods impelled a man, so distinguished for his devotion, to wend his way through so many disasters and to undergo so many labors. Does such great anger belong to divine spirits? (1–11)

In this outline of his poetic program, Virgil establishes Aeneas' mission. He also reveals a debt to his predecessors and situates his work within the Roman context. The first three words (*arma uirumque cano*) contain concise classical allusions to both Homeric epics, "the man" (*uirum*) to the *Odyssey* and "arms" (*arma*) to the *Iliad*. The poem's two halves appear to imitate each of these epics, beginning with Aeneas' journey westward, which parallels Odysseus *nostos* in the *Odyssey* and culminates in the war in Italy, which recapitulates the *Iliad*.

Alexandrian erudition is also at play in the poem's opening words, the first three letters of which present an acronym of the title of Livy's *A.U.C.*, or *Ab Urbe Condita*, the first pentad of which was published near the time Virgil began work on the *Aeneid* (29 BC).[2] Such an acronym is apt, for while Aeneas does not found Rome proper, his transference of Troy to Italy lays the foundation on which the city must be built. When Virgil writes the *Aeneid* he is not striving merely to demonstrate how sophisticated his poem is in comparison with all those that came before. Rather, as scholars such as Conte and Barchiesi have variously demonstrated, Virgil's learnedness is an aspect of his development and expansion of the epic code. Thus, the *Aeneid* is both classical, harking back to Homer, and informed by Alexandrian erudition, as is evident from the many learned allusions that enrich this poem. Such dualism is characteristic of this poem, with its juxtaposition of Greek and Roman

Figure 5.1. The Pantheon in Rome (ca. AD 126). Drawing by Mary Claire Russell.

material, its blending of myth and history, and its ktistic (foundational) emphasis, as Rome's future grows out of the remnants of Trojan society.

About a century and a half after the *Aeneid*, the Emperor Hadrian accomplished a similar feat of dualism when he rebuilt the Pantheon (Figure 5.1), a major structure of the Campus Martius on the site of Agrippa's temple of the same name. The inscription on the architrave ("Marcus Agrippa made this") and the Hadrianic façade's likely similarity to the Augustan original encourages the reader of the inscription to think that this building was a part of the Augustan milieu, as either the original edifice or a renovation of it.[3] Though the veneer of Hadrian's temple largely replicated Agrippa's, the design that lies beyond the façade was different. Whereas Agrippa's temple likely had a rectangular interior room (*cella*) with a statue group representing the twelve major Roman deities placed at its far wall, the Hadrianic building was thoroughly different: its vast rotunda, which still stands as one of Rome's finest monuments, featured individual niches for each deity. The overall effect would have been one of both familiarity and innovation.

The *Aeneid* is similarly innovative and imitative. The prologue's opening theme of national origin is to be understood in terms of the epic code derived from Homer. When, in the prologue, Virgil recounts briefly Aeneas' departure from Trojan shores, he reflects his own indebtedness to and departure from his Homeric source. If the first page announces the poem to be a Homeric imitation, the reader will soon realize that it is not simply a repetition of the two Homeric epics, as Virgil's use of the first person "I sing" instead of an invocation of the omniscient Homeric muse ("Sing, O Muse") also suggests.

The directional words "to Italy and to the Lavinian coast," as Klingner noted many years ago, reveal the epic's teleological nature. The reader immediately learns where Aeneas is going, what challenges he will have to endure and even why he must endure them. With the phrase "the mindful wrath of savage Juno," Virgil shows that he is not afraid to engage the matter of human suffering. Virgil will broach this issue as the epic unfolds around the main character, Aeneas, who undergoes much suffering, informing the reader and Aeneas himself about the pathos of the human experience.

The suffering that Aeneas undergoes results from divine anger. The word that Virgil uses for "anger" in his prologue is *ira*, which, along with *furor*, serves as one of the key terms for wrath in the poem. Apart from the problem of divine anger, Aeneas' struggle in part involves his own *furor* and *ira*, which he seeks to harness for the preservation of those loyal to him in the fulfillment of his mission, a desire that stems from his deep-seated devotion (*pietas*). Anger stays with the hero throughout the epic, emerging in full force in the poem's final scene, where it serves as a vehicle of either just reprisal or personal vengeance, depending upon how one interprets the poem.

Aeneas' suffering is also at times a product of his humanity. In grappling with this complex issue, Aeneas appears to be a slow learner or reluctant leader: he tarries in Carthage and too heavily relies on his father at times, for Anchises' interpretation of oracles does not always prove reliable. Yet these human traits also make a credible "modern" hero, for he accepts his destiny only insofar as it is thrust upon him; as he will later confess to Dido's shade (6.460), Aeneas often obeys the gods unwillingly. His quest is not for the old Homeric glory (*kleos*) but for a higher cause; still, in his quest for that cause, Aeneas shows human fallibility.

Also prominent in the prologue are some of the qualities that will characterize Aeneas throughout the poem: a capacity for endurance and deep devotion. The word *pietas*, usually best rendered "devotion," connotes Aeneas' quality of unswerving loyalty, a kind of endurance within the realm of social obligation. To secure a place for his devoted hero in the epic tradition, Virgil endowed the *Aeneid* with the traits of the other learned works of its day. Like Apollonius' Jason, Virgil's hero is on a quest, yet Aeneas' quest is far grander than the search for the golden fleece. The *telos* of Aeneas' mission is the reestablishment of a nation, which itself undergoes redefinition of its identity in the course the journey with Aeneas. Along the way, Aeneas must have numerous experiences and even suffer so as to learn to be not merely heroic but humane.

Book 1: Mission and Safe Haven

Immediately after his prologue, Virgil lays out the most basic theological presupposition of the poem: the goddess Juno, angered by the unfaithfulness of Jupiter, who had brought an object of his affection, the Trojan boy Ganymede, to Olympus, and by the fact that Aphrodite had been judged more beautiful than herself by the Trojan prince, Paris, seeks revenge upon the Trojans for her slight. To achieve this, Juno, the goddess of marriage, employs Aeolus, the king of the winds, with the promise of an attractive nymph to marry (71–5).

Aeolus' winds create a squall. Virgil's storm description, a *topos* (typical narrative feature) often found in epic, is arranged so as to suggest confusion. In the midst of the storm's chaos, Aeneas raises his hands and cries out:

> O three and four times blessed, you whose lot it was to perish before your fathers' eyes beneath Troy's high walls! O son of Tydeus, bravest of the Greek race, could I not have fallen and have poured forth my life by your right hand on the plains of Troy where savage Hector now lies, under the spear of the son of Aeacus, where huge Sarpedon lies, where the Simois rolls so many shields and helmets and strong bodies of heroes, snatched beneath the waves (94–101)

Aeneas' first words are not only memorable but filled with memories, specifically epic memories. In this passage Aeneas is the poet's spokesman, recalling Homeric precedents; he goes beyond this, even wishing to have perished at Troy, i.e., in the *Iliad*. As he is delivered from the storm, so he is delivered from the constraints of old epic tradition and made free to set out on a new epic adventure that will lead him to a defined epic goal.

That new adventure begins when Aeneas, having survived the storm and procured provisions for the survivors, encourages his disheartened men:

> My friends (for we are not ignorant of evils hitherto), you who have suffered more serious things, god will grant an end even to these. You have approached the Scylla's raging and deeply resounding crags and have experienced the rocks of the Cyclopes, as well. Now buck up your courage, put away grievous fear. Perhaps it will be sweet to recall even these events one day. Through various disasters and trials we make our way toward Latium, where the fates show us a peaceful abode. It is right that the realm of Troy rise again there. Endure, and keep yourselves safe for favorable developments. (198–207)

In contrast to Aeneas' first words during the sea storm, these more optimistic comments feature the (ultimately Aristotelian) notion that there is value in the memory of past trials.[4] Virgil's epic advances beyond the Homeric points of reference to the teleological notion of Rome's founding. Thus Aeneas' sufferings are not merely subject to chance but form a critical aspect of the story, connecting the mythical past with Roman history. One must continually bear this connection in mind as Aeneas' adventures unfold.

The description of Latium as a "peaceful abode" echoes the Epicurean poet Lucretius' description of the abode of the gods (*DRN* 3.18). Aeneas does not consider such a "heavenly" place out of reach; nevertheless, the narrator does qualify Aeneas' hopeful reference: "so with his mouth does he speak and, though ill with great cares, on his face he feigns hope, forcing his grief down deep in his heart" (208–9). These lines reveal Aeneas' inner struggle, showing that he is not beyond suffering.

Virgil's gods do not enjoy Epicurean security: as he lays out Rome's future in his response to Venus' query about Trojan destiny, Jupiter shows his concern for Aeneas' future (234–6). Aeneas will reign three years, his son, Ascanius (or Iulus), will reign thirty, and his successors three hundred in Alba Longa before Romulus will establish Rome and "give the Romans their name from his own" (277). Their unlimited dominion (*imperium sine fine*, 279) anticipates religious and political developments under Augustus, such as the closing of the gates of war, a sign of peace throughout Roman territory (292–4).

The interspersing of scenes from Olympus with mortal affairs is sustained, as Virgil shifts the focus to Aeneas' exploration of the African land, in the course of which he encounters Venus, his mother, disguised as a huntress. Their interchange is coy, with a belated recognition scene (anagnorisis); Aeneas' failure to recognize the goddess perhaps even conveys a hint of comedy. Still, her words include information critical for understanding how the first four books will unfold. Venus explains that Dido rules in Carthage, offering details about the death of the queen's husband, Sychaeus, at the hands of Pygmalion, Dido's brother. These details predispose Aeneas to be sympathetic to the queen. Virgil connects the present narrative with narrative of the epic past through an ecphrasis of a frieze on the temple of Juno, which Aeneas and Achates observe as they enter Carthage. The frieze reveals the battles around Troy:

> He sees the battles of Ilium in order and the wars known now by their reputation through the whole world, the sons of Atreus and Priam, and Achilles, savage to them both. There he stood and in tears spoke: "Achates, what place now, what region on earth is not filled with our labor? Look, there is Priam. Here, too, praise has its own rewards. There are tears of things, and mortal things touch the mind. Put away your fears; this fame will bring you some sort of safety. (456–63)

Aeneas' interpretation might seem surprising, given the fact that the artwork depicts the fall of his city. From it, Aeneas counterintuitively infers a positive reputation for the Trojans, while, in his exegesis, he reveals the depth of his pathos. Dido, too, knows pain, explaining as much when she meets those of Aeneas' men who have washed ashore separate from him and present themselves at Carthage: "Not ignorant of evil, I am learning how to help the wretched" (630). One recalls that Aeneas had reminded his men that they, too, were not ignorant of evils (4.198); both of the chief protagonists of books 1 and 4 share in the knowledge of suffering.

The reader spends a sizable portion of the first book seeing through Aeneas' eyes. Hidden in a cloud, he beholds Dido's hospitable reception of his men. He soon emerges from the cloud, becoming the object of everyone's gaze and, in particular, captivating Dido as Apollonius' Jason had Medea (*Arg.* 3.253) or Odysseus had Nausicaa in *Odyssey* 6. As Odysseus had recounted his wanderings in the Phaeacian court, Aeneas does so at a feast in Dido's palace, to which Ascanius brings gifts that ironically foreshadow Dido's doom. One is a dress of Helen, whose illicit affair with Paris parallels Dido's with Aeneas. Another, a necklace, has a haunting quality, as it had belonged to Priam's daughter Ilione, who sought to preserve Troy's royal line by offering her son, Deiphilus, in place of her younger brother, Polydorus, who would have been the rightful heir to the throne. An exchange of a brother and nephew will be an aspect of Aeneas' encounter with Dido, for his half-brother, Cupid, replaces Ascanius upon his return. As Putnam has shown, these gifts are therefore apt, vis-à-vis beauty, love, and deception.

Book 1 ends as Dido plays with Ascanius (i.e., Cupid) in her lap (718), whereby Love's poison infuses her and she forgets Sychaeus, her former husband (720). This book has set the stage not only for the encounter of Aeneas and Dido but for the epic as a whole by emphasizing themes of dualism (king/queen, Troy/Carthage, storm/safe haven, Juno's wrath/Jupiter's plan) and mission (e.g., through Jupiter's encouragement of Venus). If that purpose sometimes becomes muddled, it nevertheless remains vital, even when Carthage begins to become a comfortable haven confused with the "peaceful abode" (206) where Aeneas belongs. First, however, Aeneas, must recount Troy's fall.

Book 2: Memories of the Fall, Visions of the Mission

Aeneas is the narrator of the material of the second and third books. He opens his lengthy exposition in book 2 with the emotional expressions "lamentable," "wretched," "tears," and "grief," all within the first twelve lines. In such terms does Aeneas describe the fall of the city, while also emphasizing the mission beyond the city's demise. Having mentioned the Greeks' feigned departure (2.27–8), Aeneas tells of the Trojan horse and Laocoon, the priest of Neptune, who warns against the gift presented by the stray Greek, Sinon.

To introduce the horse to the city, Sinon falsely claims that the Greeks left him behind as a sacrifice required by the seer Calchas. Though Quintus Smyrnaeus and Tryphiodorus, both of whom write later than Virgil, feature the character and thus possibly recall a model predating the *Aeneid*, Virgil's casting of Sinon in this prominent role may well have been innovative. Virgil may have chosen the character for the suggestive possibilities associated with his name. The seventeenth-century commentator de la Cerda puts forth the notion of paronomasia upon the Greek verb *sinomai*, meaning "harm" – though the vowel "-i-" is long in the Greek word and short in the character's name – while Bernard Knox connects it with a sinuous serpent.[5] Ironically, the components of Sinon's name (*si* and *non*) are the Latin words for "if" and "not," words that occur in this passage, as Aeneas tells Dido with regret about the Trojans' tragic refusal not to follow Laocoon's advice:

> And, if the fates of the gods, if their intention had not been against us, he would have prevailed upon us to raid the Greeks lair with the sword, and Troy would now be standing, and you, high citadel of Priam, would abide still. (54–6)

Such irony obtains, for Laocoon, who has told the truth, is killed on the very altar where he was to sacrifice, while Sinon, who lies about being released from sacrifice, is welcomed as an honorary Trojan (1.148f.). Laocoon's death is also ironic in that, despite his position as a Priest of Neptune, he and his sons die as they are eaten by snakes sent from the sea.[6] Laocoon's death is rendered in numerous artistic depictions, among which a statue from the Vatican Museum, dating to about the same time as the *Aeneid*, stands out. His death leads to Troy's destruction, in the midst of which a vision of Hector clarifies Aeneas' mission:

> Alas, goddess born, flee … Troy entrusts to you her sacred rites and household gods; take them as comrades of your fate, seek for them great walls which you will establish when at last you have wandered the sea completely. (289, 293–5)

Hector's references to flight, traversing the sea, the transfer of gods, and the foundation of new walls resonate with book 1's prologue. The future is indebted to the past, as the hero's present action toward the fulfillment of his destiny is informed by his memory.

This fulfillment of destiny begins with Aeneas' rush to arms. Aeneas confesses to his imprudence: "mindlessly I take up arms, nor is there sufficient rationale for arms" (314), to which he adds, "madness and wrath cast my thought headlong, and the notion that death in arms is a beautiful thing gives me strength" (316–17). Such confessions show an aspect of Aeneas' character that makes him an all-too-human hero, suggesting both his often irrational anger and fear at Troy being under siege (363).

Such irrationality is emphasized as Achilles' son Pyrrhus' breaches Priam's home (484). This character's destructive nature is emphasized both through nominal paronomasia (i.e., a play on the Greek word *pyr* "fire") and the simile that likens him to a puffing snake, ready to strike. Aeneas then describes the horrific scene of Priam's demise, emphasizing his final vision:

> By lot this death bore him away as he watched Troy burn and Pergamum fall, once proud ruler over so many peoples and lands of Asia. Now he lies there, a huge trunk on the shore, a head plucked from shoulders and a body without a name. (554–8)

This vision of Priam like a hacked trunk evokes the execution of Pompey, who was mangled after his loss at Pharsalus (Servius, ad 557). Less brutal visions follow: first, Aeneas' of Helen, which produces in him a desire for retribution. A vision of his mother Venus, however, checks Aeneas' hand, for she permits him yet another vantage point: he now sees Neptune, Juno, and Pallas at war (608–23).

From these fantastic visions, Aeneas' focus shifts to that of his family. After Aeneas' plea to Anchises to accompany him, a tongue of fire licks the hair and temples of young Iulus (684–86); then a shooting star appears (695–8). This last event is interpreted positively by Anchises, whose initial refusal gives way to renewed faith.

Aeneas' escape with Ascanius, visible on Greek vases as early as the fifth century BC, becomes an even more widely circulated motif in Roman art after Virgil, as a coin of 47 BC reveals (Figure 5.2).[7] Virgil reinterprets this legendary event's significance in terms of the preservation of history, religious values, and a better future. As the poem unfolds, Aeneas' act of preservation points toward the future in Latium. Furthermore, in the sixth book, Anchises, who symbolizes the past, will explain the future.

At his behest (711), Aeneas' wife Creusa follows, as Aeneas leads his retinue from the city. By the time they reach the specified grove, however, Creusa is lost. Frenzied, Aeneas searches for her, only to encounter another powerful vision: Creusa's shade now speaks prophetic words – happy circumstances, a kingdom, and a future wife (783) – that offer consolation but little comfort. Finally, Aeneas returns to his men at Creusa's behest.

Figure 5.2. Silver denarius of Caius Julius Caesar, reverse (UMKf04277). Copyright ©
Museum of Cultural History, University of Oslo, Norway. Photographer P. G. Maurtvedt.
Used by permission.

Book 3: Fiction and Reality

Throughout book 3 Aeneas recounts his adventures on his journey from
Troy to Italy and his actions separating the allurements of the past
from the reality of the destiny that lies ahead. By the opening of book
4, Dido will have fallen in love with the hero who, to her misfortune,
has become intent upon his destiny.

Aeneas' adventures do not begin auspiciously. When he tries to found
a city, called Aeneadae, in Thrace, he encounters a bad omen: a myrtle,
dripping blood because Aeneas thrice plucked at it, is inhabited by the
spirit of Ilione's slain brother Polydorus, who warns Aeneas not to settle
there. A consultation of Apollo on the island of Delos provides direction,
though Anchises misunderstands the god's oracular response, believing
Crete to be the Trojans' place of origin referred to in the oracle. When
the Trojans settle there, as Horsfall notes (ad 137), Aeneas plays the role
of lawgiver and colony founder (oecist) apportioning houses to his
people. But a plague shows this, too, to be the wrong choice. The Penates
(gods rescued from Troy) appear to Aeneas to clarify the situation: the
land is to be Hesperia, specifically Italy, Dardanus' birthplace (167).
Thus, the notion of the poem's *telos* obtains and is refreshed from time
to time. For example, when Aeneas comes to the Strophades, the Harpies'

home, the Harpy Celaeno speaks ominously to Aeneas, prophesying that no walled city will be granted to Aeneas before the Trojans eat their own tables (257), a prediction fulfilled in book 7.

The climax of Aeneas' journey in book 3 is Buthrotum, a place of paradox, not a new Troy, but a "toy Troy."[8] Buthrotum is nearly in Greece, but not quite; seems like Troy, but is only a replica; and its king, Helenus, sounds Greek, but is not. Ironically, Helenus, a seer taken captive after the fall of Troy, only became the leader of this settlement because of the death of his Greek captor, Pyrrhus. Hector's wife, Andromache, Pyrrhus' war prize, is now Helenus' wife.

Approaching the city, Aeneas beholds Andromache, who, deeply moved to see him, asks whether he is real or a phantom; her ambivalence reflects the uncertain reality of this city. She first treats Aeneas as a shade, asking if he has seen Hector (312). Convinced that he is not a shade, she tells him how she was given to Helenus by Pyrrhus. Andromache and Helenus have a chance artificially to recreate the past, fashioning themselves as a new Hecuba and Priam.

Helenus, though trapped in the past, in his traditional role as seer (*uates*) affirms Aeneas' destiny. The tension between future and past in this passage is also emphasized by the parting gifts that Andromache offers Ascanius:

> Receive these things, too, boy, that they may be for you mementos made by my own hands and may call to witness the abiding love of Andromache, Hector's wife. Take the final gifts of your own people, you who are the lone surviving image for me of my own Astyanax. He had eyes like these, hands, features. And now he would have been about the same age as you, a young man. (486–91)

Andromache, literally and figuratively, cannot let go of the past. Describing herself as "Hector's wife," she sees in Ascanius her own son, and offers him reminders of her earlier existence. Aeneas' response (493–505) is inadequate because he cannot fully indulge Andromache in her fictional world. He tries to comfort her by emphasizing the immediate satisfaction that her new Troy brings: though his own vision ever recedes, she has hers now (497).

After Aeneas' departure from Buthrotum, the vision of Italy becomes reality (522f.). The place name "Italy" is repeated thrice as the Italian peninsula comes into view (524f.). Castrum Minervae, a settlement in Calabria known to the geographer Strabo (6.281), is the first settlement that Aeneas says the Trojans see:

Here I saw the first omen, four horses with a white sheen in a grassland grazing on the broad plain. And Anchises, my father, cries, "O foreign land, you are bringing war: it's war for which the horses are armed, war does this herd threaten. But, still, those same four-footed beasts were once accustomed to come under the chariot and to bear bridles that are in harmony with the yoke; there's hope for peace, too. (537–43)

Though Anchises jumps to the conclusion that the horses betoken war, he must soon think again, reflecting on the fact that horses can also bear the yoke; thus strangely he adds, "there's hope for peace, too." Anchises, it seems, is an imprecise interpreter, which in part accounts for the length of time that Aeneas spends trying to find the land of his destiny.

As they sail through the gulf of Tarentum, Aeneas and his men pass the Homeric Scylla and Charybdis. Their arrival at Etna even introduces a character allegedly from Homer's *Odyssey*, Achaemenides. Aeneas mercifully accepts this Odyssean "survivor" and now, like Odysseus, Aeneas' retinue flees the giant Polyphemus (660f.), as Achaemenides elucidates these Homeric realms.

The book ends with the death of Anchises. The instruction that Aeneas desires from his father, at least temporarily, comes to an end, though Anchises will return in a powerful scene in book 6. No longer an apprentice, Aeneas seems now to have learned from his father what he has needs to don the mantle of the Trojans' sole leader.[9]

Book 4: Love and Destiny

The phrase "but the queen" starkly and powerfully opens the fourth book. Although here he begins with an adversative conjunction, Virgil more typically uses a temporal subordinator, such as "when," or "meanwhile" for this purpose. The Latin adversative *at* (but), used only here in a book's initial position, is followed in each case by the word *regina* ("the queen," Dido), dividing the book into three dramatic "acts" (or perhaps three plays in a dramatic trilogy). Such divisions suggest the disjunctive nature of the amatory relationship of Aeneas and Dido that further develops in this book.

The flames that burned Troy in book 2 now figuratively burn Dido herself, offering an appropriate symbol of the depth of her passion for Aeneas (4.2). Anxiety destroys Dido's rest and she lacks inner peace (*securitas*). The passionate and anxious Dido is not capable of serenity, which in book 4 is sometimes described in terms of unattainable Epicurean tranquility.[10] Thus, themes of adversity, anxiety, and passion characterize this book, as demonstrated by Dido's initial conversation with Anna, her sister, who fans the flames of passion by encouraging Dido to forget her dead husband, Sychaeus (34). As Apollonius' Medea had at the bidding of her sister Chalciope, Dido banishes shame at Anna's urging.

To heighten the sense of futility, Virgil's narrative voice breaks into an apostrophe to the reader about the ignorance of seers, an expression that harks back to a similar one in Lucretius. As one might expect, given the Lucretian tone, Dido visits the altars of the gods to no avail and vainly offers prayers (65–6). Like a wounded doe, Dido wanders about neglectful of her duty, as Carthage's urban progress is halted.

As so often happens in the *Aeneid*, human events are explained in terms of divine actions behind the scenes. Juno approaches Venus to work out a plan to be hatched during a rainy hunting expedition aimed at driving the couple into a cave:

> Dido and the Trojan leader come into the same cave. Earth first and Juno, the marriage goddess, give the signal. The fires flashed and the air acted as a witness to the wedding, as the nymphs ululated on the highest peak. That day was the first of death and the first of evils, the very source of them. Dido is not moved by appearance or reputation, nor any longer does she regard her love as secret. She calls it "marriage"; with this term she has concealed her fault. (165–72)

As Feeney has shown, the question of matrimony is a matter of each character's perception.[11] Dido considers herself Aeneas' wife, a view not untenable given the fact that nature in this scene reflects aspects of a typical Roman marriage. Her misunderstanding, which marks the first day of her demise, leads her to be open about their relationship, which gives rise to rumor, described in an ecphrasis.

Virgil portrays Rumor (Fama) as having a multiplicity of feathers, eyes and mouths in the vein of Homer's Strife or Hesiod's Typhoeus. Gossip about Dido and Aeneas spreads even to the Gaetulian king Iarbas, one of Dido's rejected suitors. Iarbas prays to Jupiter, which prompts Jupiter to dispatch Mercury to call Aeneas back to his mission (236). Mercury demands that Aeneas have regard for Ascanius to whom "Italy and the Roman land is owed" (275). The vision of the future that Mercury puts forth must supplant Aeneas' temporary enjoyment.

The middle third of this book encompasses a splendid psychological drama, introduced with the repetition of the phrase, "but the queen" (296). Dido soon claims to have discerned Aeneas' intention:

Did you hope to be able to hide such malice, faithless, and in your silence
to slip away from my land? Does neither our love nor the right hands that
we exchanged, nor Dido, about to die a cruel death, restrain you? ... Are
you fleeing from me? ... by our wedding, by our fresh wedding vows, if
have I well deserved anything from you, or if anything of mine was sweet
to you, pity this falling house and reject that plan of yours, I beg, if there
is still any place for prayers. (305–8, 314, 316–19)

Dido invokes her "wedding ceremony" performed in the cave, revealing
through her language that she sees her separation from Aeneas as parallel
with that of Theseus and Ariadne, described in Catullus' sixty-fourth
poem. Dido spells out the dire consequences: Iarbas will now close in
on her, as will her estranged brother Pygmalion (325f.). Dido wishes that
she might only have carried a child by Aeneas; if so, she would at least
have "tiny Aeneas" to commemorate their love.

Aeneas' response is his longest speech in the poem. He begins with
the juxtaposition of the Latin pronouns "I" and "you," stating that he
shall never forget her, but flatly disavowing marriage. Given a choice,
he says a bit callously, he would never have left Troy, the unstated impli-
cation of which is that he would still be with Creusa. He adds a further
stinging revelation: his true love is Italy, and he even accuses Dido of
"jealousy" (*inuidia*, 350). With one of the poem's most cited half-lines,
Aeneas concludes his speech by avowing his obedience to divine
command: "I am seeking Italy not of my own accord" (361).

In comparison with Aeneas' detachment, Dido shows great emotion,
deploring his faithlessness and vowing to haunt him like a fury. "Shaken
by love" (395), he returns to his men, who work feverishly to complete
preparations for departure. Dido, nevertheless, asks Anna again to inter-
vene: "Go as a suppliant, sister, to address the haughty enemy" (424).
The oak-like (441–6) strength of Aeneas' resolve contrasts sharply with
Dido's stirring request for "empty time" (437). Snubbed again, Dido
rages like a character on stage, specifically Orestes as he is hounded by
furies, seeing visions (471). Though Dido instructs Anna to prepare a
pyre to burn the reminders of Aeneas, she intends otherwise.

In the final section, again beginning "but the queen" (504), Dido
places an effigy of Aeneas on the pyre. Attended by an Ethiopian priestess, she makes sacrifices with one shoe off and dress untied, gestures of
ritual observance. She then presents the first of two emotional soliloquies:
reviewing her poor choices and Trojan treachery, she considers her
options before confessing that her "pledge, promised to Sychaeus' ashes,
was not kept" (552).

Aeneas is portrayed as certain about his departure as Dido is about death (554, 564); nevertheless, Mercury again warns him, this time in a dream. Inspired, even afraid, Aeneas rouses his men to departure, and then, in a line symbolic of the end of the physical relationship, "draws his thunderous sword from the sheath and cuts the mooring cables" (579–80). One need not press too hard the archetypal association of swords and sheaths. Aeneas is moving on, soon to "celebrate" with his men (*ouantes*, 577), just as Dido had predicted he would (543).

In her second soliloquy, twice as long as the first, Dido asks herself, "Do only now your impious deeds touch you, unhappy Dido? ... Could I not have pulled apart his seized body and scattered it on the waves? ... or served up Ascanius as a dinner for his father's table?" (596, 600–2). These "ghastly acts of vengeance" allude to well-known myths, identifying Dido with mythological characters such as Procne, who served up to her husband their son as dinner.[12] Dido ultimately concedes her fate was impossible to avoid, as her use of the phrase "deeply clinging boundary stone" in reference to the intractable nature of her situation suggests (614) – a phrase Lucretius had used to express natural law (*DRN* 1.77, 1.596, 5.90, 6.66). Nevertheless, Dido pronounces a curse on Aeneas, presaging the long-standing antagonism between Rome and Carthage, which would produce three Punic wars.

At the height of this passionate scene, Dido speaks from atop the pyre:

> I shall die unavenged, but let me die. In this way, it is pleasing for me to go to the shades below. Let the cruel Trojan drink the flame in with his eyes from the deep, and let him bear the omens of my death with him. (659–62)

Using Aeneas' sword, she takes her life; the fact that the sword is foaming adds an erotic twist to this final act of passion (665). Juno then sends Iris to cut Dido's lock, an act meant to grant her soul passage to Hades.

If Aeneas utterly fails at any point in the poem, it is chiefly in his relationship with Dido. Nowhere else is the pathos greater or the decisions harder, as Dido and Aeneas' story enjoys characteristics of high drama. Dido is a tragic heroine in the mold of Euripides' Medea and Phaedra; her final soliloquies and scenes of lament contribute to the book's dramatic quality. As Conte puts it, these two Euripidean characters and their language "have entered into the [Virgilian] text and contaminated it with different registers; ... Virgil, the epic poet of pathos, learned from [dramatic poets] how to grant space to those individual voices, making himself their witness and their champion."[13] No literary vignette, save the passion of Christ, has had wider influence on text, art, or musical composition. The humanity of book 4's characters represents the best of Virgil's literary creation.

Book 5: Names and Games of Identity

In book 3, Anchises had incorrectly identified Crete as the place for Trojan walls to rise, while Buthrotum later also exemplified what the new Troy should not be; even Aeneas' dalliance at Carthage presented a possible erroneous alternative for the mission's *telos*. In book 5, Virgil brings the issue of cultural and national identity to center stage through the themes of competition, the desire for stable existence, and various nominal associations.

This book's quest for Roman identity begins when Aeneas' helmsman Palinurus, strategically placed at the beginning and end of this book, urges a return to Sicily, the not-quite-Italian island that symbolizes Aeneas' westward migration toward a new identity. In Sicily Aeneas is greeted by a character whose ethnic identity is also ambiguous. Half-Trojan, half-Sicilian, Acestes has become fully Sicilian. After greeting him, Aeneas addresses his assembled men in terms of their identity: "sons of Troy (*Dardanidae*)" (45). Yet these Trojans are, like Acestes, now in Sicily, where the transformation of their identity to Roman is advanced by the games that celebrate Anchises' shade. Based on the athletic competition in Patroclus' honor in *Iliad* 23, the games for Anchises close a chapter in Aeneas' Trojan past while also bringing Trojan and Roman closer together by explaining etiologically the Roman festival of Parentalia, celebrated each February by Augustus in memory of his adoptive parent, Julius Caesar.

Most competitors in the naval games, which open this event, have an etiological connection with Roman families:

> Driving the swift Pristis with eager oars, Mnestheus comes, soon to be the Italian Mnestheus, from which name comes the family line of Memmius, and Gyas drove the Chimaera, with its huge mass, practically a city, which the Dardan youths, in triple rows, push on, oars surging together in three rows; and Sergestus, from whom the house of Sergius holds its name, is carried by the huge ship Centaur, and in the sea-colored Scylla comes Cloanthus, whence is your family, Roman Cluentius. (116–23)

As the race unfolds, Cloanthus prevails because he observes the gods. Second place goes to Menestheus, while Sergestus, who is wrecked on the rocks in the race, finds compensation with a consolation prize. These names broadly evoke aspects of Roman character. Mnestheus, the progenitor of the Memmii, avoids disgrace, which is appropriate as his honorable clan would encompass many Roman leaders including Gaius Memmius, the anti-aristocratic tribune of 111. Lucretius' *DRN* was dedicated to another of his descendants. Sergestus, the forefather of the gens Sergia, barely extricates his ship from the rocks and limps into port. In light of the ruinous behavior exhibited by Lucius Sergius Catilina (Catiline) that occurred during Virgil's childhood, such extrication is precisely what that family had to do. The Arch of the Sergii, located in Croatia not far from the Italian border, was erected after the battle of Actium, in which conflict the bravery of another descendent restored the family name.[14]

Gyas, not identified by Virgil with any *gens*, behaves ignobly, throwing his helmsman overboard (174). As a competitor in the ship race, Gyas desires victory too strongly; he fails to merit a future Roman name and recedes into the background.[15] Those from whom Rome will descend show that they are worthy to be forebears through their character exhibited in the contest.

Further competitions advance and enhance this quest for identity:

> From all quarters come Trojans and Sicanians mixed, first Nisus and Euryalus … next followed regal Diores, born of the amazing line of Priam; following this man came Salius and, at the same time, Patron, of which two men one was an Acarnian, the other from Arcadian bloodline, of the Tegean clan: then came two youths, natives of Sicily, Helymus and Panopes, accustomed to the woods; they were comrades of aged Acestes. (293–4, 296–301)

The wide range of backgrounds here indicates Sicily's unique suitability to the blending of nationalities. Trojans are mixed in with people different from themselves in a cultural amalgamation. The prizes that Aeneas offers reflect such diversity: Cretan weapons (*Aen.* 5.306), an Amazonian quiver with Thracian arrows (311–12) and an Argolic helmet (314). Such regional variety enriches the Trojan redefinition, a redefinition that must take place as Virgil directs this book toward the poem's goal of Troy's rebirth as Rome.

The next event, a boxing match, modeled on a similar type found in Homer and Apollonius, features the young and vociferous Trojan Dares and the Sicilian pugilist, Entellus, who wears the gauntlets of his teacher, Aeneas' half-brother Eryx. Aeneas' blood ties with this region – noted by Palinurus (24), Dares (412), and Iris (630) – both connect and distinguish Trojans and Sicilians. Entellus' ultimate victory enhances such a dualistic tension, for it is a victory of the skill of the old Entellus over the prowess of the Trojan upstart, Dares.

Dares' claim to fame springs from his having encountered both the Trojan Paris and the immense boxer Butes, a descendant of the famous fighter Amyclus. Though commentators tell us Butes is found only here, that same name is used to describe a lover of Aphrodite by whom she conceived Aeneas' half-brother, Eryx (Diodorus, 4.23, 83). Thus, Virgil has connected both these fighters and their cultures: Dares' victory over Butes associates him nominally with Eryx and thus with Entellus, who himself is a true Sicilian.

Such a connection also produces tension. Having twice tauntingly called Dares "Trojan" (417, 420), Entellus now can right the record of the defeat of his mentor's father, Butes. Through the reference to Butes, Virgil brings the boxers' stories together to such an extent that, when Entellus falls, both Trojan and Trinacrian youths cry out (450). After Aeneas' judgment, Entellus offers Eryx the prize bull to sacrifice, a fitting gesture as this could be viewed as a kind of grudge match for the late Butes, Eryx' father and Dares' victim. Entellus makes Eryx a "better sacrifice," which closes this episode.

The final set of competitions in Anchises' honor culminates with games in which no competitor is described in terms of national origin. Eurytion and Hippocoon, contestants in archery, are not familiar names. Though one can infer from Eurytion's background that his brother Pandarus is a Trojan and Hippocoon's patronymic Hyrtacides may suggest that he is the brother of the Trojan Nisus, no clear distinction between Trojan and Sicilian is made.

When Acestes' arrow breaks into flames and Aeneas gives him the first prize in the archery contest, Aeneas' decision is disputed. Eurytion, the challenger, ultimately defers to Acestes' status as the elder statesman of what now seems a unified group. The prize offered by Aeneas to Acestes, a mixing bowl, which had been given to Anchises by a Thracian king as "a reminder and pledge of affection" (538), is apt, for its function as a mixing bowl suggests blending and evokes also the wine of hospitality that Acestes had once offered Aeneas (1.195).

The parade of Trojan boys that follows anticipates the future pageantry of the Roman *lusus Troiae*. Well disciplined, these youths conduct a lavish display that demonstrates proto-Roman battle efficiency (5.587). Though this parade caps the funeral celebration, its very artificiality is exploited as a second theme of the book emerges, namely the quest for true identity. That quest is not meant to end in Sicily.

Juno, however, wants to end it there, dispatching Iris, who, appearing as the Trojan woman Beroe, is another example of identity "reversal" in this book. As Beroe, Iris rouses the Trojan women to desire a new home immediately. Their propensity to embrace this immediate vision and to yield to despair emulates the spirit of the chorus of Euripides' *Troades*, which admonishes Hecuba to give up and board ships. Virgil's Trojan women, however, give up by attempting to burn the ships to achieve the building of "walls," a foundational symbol. The fallen Troy, lamented with resignation in the *Troades*, is to be reestablished *now* in Sicily by reversing the action of the conclusion of Euripides' play.

Virgil's Trojan women behave collectively in the manner of a single forsaken woman ("all with one voice," 616). The fevered pitch of fury comes upon these women even after a new character, Pyrgo, is introduced to expose Iris' ruse (645). Pyrgo's name continues the verbal game that Virgil had begun in the races. "Pyrgo" represents a quasi-homonym with part of the name of Pergamum, and is similar to the Greek word for a city's tower (*pyrgos*). Accordingly, inasmuch as her name recalls the tower of Troy, Pyrgo is the right woman to unmask the identity of Iris, who advances the notion of building walls (631). In addition, Pyrgo, whose name also contains the Greek word for fire (*pyr*), is uniquely equipped to counter Iris's fire and to call attention to Beroe's fiery eyes, which reveal godhead within (648).

Ascanius' arrival, however, brings the women back to their senses (670–3). Addressing them, he summons up the women's former confidence about their mission, and when he tosses his mock-battle helmet, he discards a "false" emblem: the child-like image of a false-replacement Troy should be similarly discarded. In any case, his casting off the helmet parallels the end of the women's false vision. The women now can shake Juno from their hearts.

One of the Trojans, old Nautes, urges Aeneas to accept Acestes as a counselor, noting Acestes' "Trojan" origin; further, Nautes suggests that Aeneas allow those whose ships were destroyed – advice that befits the giver since *nautes* means "sailor" in Greek – "to have their walls" (717) under Acestes' leadership in a new city, Acesta. Encouraged by his father's spirit (722–40) to accept Nautes' counsel, Aeneas founds a temple to Idalian Venus (i.e., Venus of Mt Idalia on Cyprus) on Mt Eryx, a geographical incongruity that caps the blending of incongruous elements in book 5.[16]

The book now comes full circle, with Palinurus on the deck of Aeneas' ship engaged in conversation. Palinurus, whose name (Greek *palin* "back" and *ouros* "fair wind") is consistent with the pattern of names appropriate to characters that we have seen, dies as a result of mistaken identity, for Somnus comes to him under the false identity of Phorbas and induces him to fall asleep. Hurled into the sea, he swims to the Italian shore and is killed, "one for many" (815), a sacrifice agreed upon by Neptune and Venus in the lines that introduce this final episode. Thus, Palinurus' death opens the way for Aeneas' passage to Italy; it also imbues the mission with pathos, symbolizing the cost, in terms of human loss, of the rebirth of the nation of Troy.[17]

Sicily is the penultimate stop in Aeneas' wanderings toward the Italian peninsula. It is not a peninsula, but an *insula*, the proximate island and an approximate goal. Sicily is the place where various identities come together, where Trojans practice to become Italians. It is a training ground for Roman identity, not a region of mere nostalgia, like Buthrotum. Yet this Roman testing ground also provides a consolation prize for the weary, who have striven but have left their ultimate quest unfinished.

Book 6: Past Presenting Future

Book 6 begins with the Trojans' arrival in Italy at Cumae, where, in the precinct of Apollo, Aeneas admires the temple doors made by Daedalus. The master craftsman would have portrayed his son Icarus, Virgil writes, but grief prevented him. This book is framed by the death of young men: Icarus' here, and that of the young Marcellus near the book's end, where he appears in the parade of future heroes known as a *Heldenschau*, presented to Aeneas in the Underworld by his father Anchises.

To begin the journey to visit his father, Aeneas enters the Sibyl's cave, where he offers a prayer that resumes book 5's central theme of struggle for identity:

> Now, finally, we take hold of the receding shores of Italy; may Trojan fortune have followed just this far. You, too, gods and goddess all, against whom Ilium and the vast glory of Troy once stood, now should spare the

Trojan race. And you, o most holy priestess, knowing of the future – I am not asking for realms that the fates do not owe me – grant the Trojans to settle in Latium, along with Troy's wandering gods and disturbed divinities. (61–8)

While clearly Trojan fortune has been unfavorable so far, that may be in part because fortune has been "Trojan" up to this moment; Aeneas' prayer thus might suggest a further step in the transformation of Trojan into Italian, a change this book richly unfolds.

The Sibyl's Apollo-inspired prophecy explains the cost of such change: "I see wars, chilling wars, and the Tiber foaming with much blood" (86f.); another Achilles awaits in Latium (89). This statement, which lays the groundwork for the "Iliadic" half of the *Aeneid*, has an ominous tone but also offers hope, for the Sibyl states that help will come from an unexpected quarter, a Greek city (97).

Aeneas' one request to visit his father will afford an opportunity for a dialogue between past and future. Bringing about that visit, the Sibyl tells him, is to be a thoroughgoing challenge, for though the descent to Hades is easy, the return is not (126–7). Even before he begins this quest, Aeneas must first bury Misenus, a fallen comrade.

Guided by Venus' doves to a requisite golden bough, Aeneas sets out on his descent into the Underworld. Initially, the bough "hesitates" as Aeneas plucks it from the tree (211); one may infer that Aeneas is here, as elsewhere, a surprisingly human hero, one barely suited to the enormity of the tasks that he faces.

For Aeneas' descent, Virgil offers a catalogue worthy of Hesiod (*Theogony* 211–15) consisting of distressing characters crouching at Death's entranceway, each of whom brings trouble to mortals, among whom are Centaurs, Harpies, and the three-headed dog Cerberus. The striking description of the blazing eyes of the ferryman Charon, contrasts vividly with the gloomy vision of children's pyres that their parents behold (6.308). Aeneas then encounters his former helmsman Palinurus. When Aeneas inquires about Apollo's apparently unfulfilled promise of safe passage to Italy, Palinurus explains that the divine promise had been kept: washed ashore alive, he met his death at the hands of hostile natives.

The Sibyl's disclosure of the bough convinces Charon to give Aeneas safe passage. Soon they come to the *Lugentes Campi* ("Mourning Fields") where suicides reside (442). From among those who have so died, Dido emerges, following the gender-changing Caeneus, who had originally been a woman but in life was changed to a man. It is curious that Virgil places this figure, who did not take her own life, among the suicides. The reason might be that, in Alexandrian fashion, the poet simply uses Caeneus to highlight Dido's ability to transition between gender roles; one recalls that Virgil had labeled the queen a "woman leader" (*dux facti erat femina*, *Aen.* 1 364). Caenis, who as a result of male aggression had been transformed into a man (Caeneus), has in death become a woman again. This offers a reversal of the fate of Dido, whose affair with Aeneas in a sense restored her status as a "woman," and as a scorned woman thus was compelled to commit suicide. Now, reunited with her husband, Sychaeus, Dido completes her regression to her former identity as the wife of Sychaeus:

> Among these women Phoenician Dido was wandering in a large forest, fresh from her wounds. When the Trojan hero first stood near her, and recognized her, dim in the shadows, he was like a person who, at a new moon, sees or thinks he has seen the moon rise through the clouds. He poured out tears and spoke to her with sweet love: "Unhappy Dido, was the report true, then, that came to me that you had died by the sword? Alas, was I the cause of your death? I swear by the stars, by the gods and if there is any faith beneath the earth, unwillingly, o queen, did I depart from your shore. (450–60)

Caenis is not the only interesting association in this passage. Whereas, in book 4, Dido had cast Aeneas in the role of the Catullan Theseus by calling him faithless and likening him to someone raised by tigresses, Virgil brings his allusion to Catullus full circle with the words "unwillingly, o queen, did I depart from your shore." Speaking thus, Aeneas incongruously compares his departure from Dido to that of a famous lock of hair that had belonged to Berenice of Alexandria, another African queen. That shorn lock achieved fame by being miraculously placed among the stars, a story that was the centerpiece of Catullus 66 (and a lost poem of Callimachus, which was Catullus' model). The comparison is odd, and suggests at the very least Aeneas' uncomfortable position; on another level, that of Alexandrian allusion, it may even be a humorous reference.

Aeneas' incredulity fails to satisfy Dido, whose unresponsiveness highlights his failure in the relationship. Aeneas' trailing Dido contrasts with her bestriding her responsive husband Sychaeus. The notion of Aeneas' following at a distance also ironically parallels Creusa's lagging behind Aeneas upon his departure from Troy (2.725). Now he is unable to keep in step with his former love, and she slips away from him as he had once outpaced Creusa.

The Underworld discloses additional figures from Aeneas' past. While Greeks shudder, Trojans greet Aeneas before he passes Tartarus, where the greatest sinners reside. Aeneas soon plants the golden bough to gain access to the Fields of the Blessed, where pious men and poets sing songs worthy of Apollo. Aeneas and the Sibyl approach Anchises, whose greeting recapitulates Aeneas' reliance on duty and devotion. Aeneas vainly grasps at his father's shade, as he had that of Creusa in book 2.

Anchises first explains the concept of metempsychosis (transmigration of souls), a Pythagorean notion that Socrates advances, for example, in Plato's *Phaedrus* and *Phaedo*; the notion of a preexistent fully formed identity perhaps even goes further back than Plato. Anchises tells his son how the River Lethe induces forgetfulness of previous existence (6.714–15). Having explained his eclectic philosophical system, Anchises expands upon an array of figures, beginning with Aeneas' successors. Throughout this *Heldenschau*, the juxtaposition of the adjectives "Dardanian" and "Italian" (756–7) evidences the transformation of Trojan to Roman (761–3) that began in book 5. Anchises notes the first foundation of the Trojans in Italy is to be Alba Longa, well known to Virgil's audience as Rome's birthplace. Cairns has argued that the list of Alba Longa's first rulers establishes a monarchical precedent for Roman imperial governance, with myth blending into history as the narrative comes closer to Roman historical and geographical reality. Place names, such as Nomentum and Fidena, offer historical authority. Finally, "famous Rome" (781) is named, characterized by her walls and hills.

Ascanius' alternate name, Iulus, affords an obvious enough connection with Julius Caesar and thus, Augustus. Not even Hercules or Bacchus will have greater sway than Augustus, who will usher in another Golden Age (792–3) and whose authority harks back to the old kings of Rome. Anchises summarizes the accomplishments of the kings until the regal period comes to a close, with the introduction of the consulship by Lucius Brutus (817–18), who is paradoxically described as "haughty" (*superbus*). To the reading Roman the transfer of this adjective to Brutus must have sounded revisionist, for it is normally attributed to the Tarquinian king whom he expelled.

From the rivalry of Brutus and Tarquinius, Anchises transitions swiftly to that of Caesar and Pompey. Other late republican figures are also named, from the Gracchi to the Scipios to Fabius Maximus. Anchises culminates this list with an admonition to Aeneas:

You, Roman, remember to rule the peoples with your power (for these
will be your arts), to impose custom upon peace, to spare those humbled,
and to vanquish the proud. (851–3)

This is an important moment of transformation from Trojan to Roman.
Aeneas is pronounced "Roman" by Anchises, with a gnomic admonition
about how to do what Romans do best: rule. At the poem's close, both
aspects of his instruction are still in the reader's mind, if not in Aeneas,'
as well.

This exhortation, rich in wisdom, might well have completed this
catalogue. Yet Anchises adds some additional information. Aeneas' father
specifically focuses on the young Marcellus, who, though slated to be
Augustus' successor, died too soon (23 BC). The melancholy of Virgil's
poetic voice in this section is pronounced, revealing a sense of pathos
that would have undoubtedly been in harmony with the reading Roman's
sorrow over Marcellus' death.

This *Heldenschau* is sometimes compared to the statues that would
later adorn the Forum Augustum, construction on which began during
the *Aeneid*'s composition. Inscriptions (*tituli* and *elogia*), approximating
Anchises' descriptions of each figure to Aeneas, adorned the Forum's
numerous statue bases. The Forum Augustum, like the *Heldenschau* of
Aeneid 6, affirmed Roman identity, the very thing Aeneas grapples with
here, situated in the context of the ebb and flow of life and death, father
and son, future and past, Trojan and Roman. In such a dualistic context,
Anchises' words of wisdom, on which Aeneas must draw to fulfill his
destiny in the poem's second half, prepare Aeneas for his subsequent
mission.

To embark on that mission, Aeneas departs from the nether realms,
passing through the ivory gate of false dreams. The other gate mentioned
is fashioned out of horn and is, we learn in this context, reserved for true
shades. The most obvious explanation for his choice of gate is that Aeneas
is not a true shade and therefore could not exit through the gate of horn.
Yet by closing the epic's first half with only these two choices for Aeneas'
departure, Virgil introduces a troubling question that will remain in the
reader's mind well after Aeneas returns to the living, in Anderson's words,
"more Roman than Trojan."

Book 7: Home and Hostility

Virgil moves from the tender account of the young Marcellus that closes
the sixth book to a brief but touching description of the death of Caieta,

Aeneas' childhood nurse. Through an apostrophe to Caieta, Virgil tells how her name has come to signify a portion of the Hesperian coastline. As Horsfall notes in his learned *Aeneid* 7 commentary, her passing is a symbol of a further break with Troy.

Although book 7 introduces the Iliadic half of the *Aeneid*, Aeneas never fully loses his association with the homeward-bound Odysseus. Aeneas' ships thus skirt Circe's island from which come eerie sounds that recall Homer's account of the goddess' abode. A fresh prologue sets the stage for much of the second half's action:

> Come now, Erato, and tell who the kings were and of the times, what state of affairs existed in ancient Latium, when the foreign army first struck upon Ausonian shores. I will unfold and I shall recall the beginnings of the first battle. You, goddess, advise your poet. I shall tell of terrible wars, battle lines and kings driven to funerals by pride, the Tyrrenean band and all Hesperia driven to weapons. A greater order of things springs to life for me, I move a greater work. (37–44)

Virgil's choice of Erato to inspire his work stems in part from the precedent of Apollonius' *Argonautica*, the second half of which begins identically ("Come now, Erato"). Though her name connotes love, Erato befits books 7–12's "terrible wars" (40), for the ensuing rivalry centering on Lavinia – betrothed to Turnus but destined to be Aeneas' wife – parallels Odysseus' with the suitors. Commentators have noted that Lavinia stands as a Penelope figure, although unlike Penelope, her personality is only brushstroked. As in the *Odyssey*, a rival suitor will emerge.

Setting the stage, Virgil explains that the region's king, Latinus, lacks a living male heir. His daughter, Lavinia, is betrothed to the Rutulian prince Turnus, but portents point toward wrongful betrothal: a swarm of bees over a sacred laurel presages foreign domination, while Lavinia's hair catching fire is interpreted as an omen of war (7.79–80). An oracle, too, suggests that Lavinia is not to wed Turnus (96–101). Meanwhile, Aeneas receives verification that this is the land promised to him: his men hungrily devour crusts of bread that Ascanius jokingly refers to as platters or tables (116), fulfilling Caeleno's prediction from *Aeneid* 3.

Aeneas' first diplomatic action is to send a sizeable embassy to king Latinus, the description of whose "august" palace (170) reflects the house of Augustus on the Palatine, which was similarly a repository of antiquities. Receiving the embassy, Latinus recounts that Dardanus, the Trojan forebear, hailed from Italy before coming to Troy via Samothrace

(205–11). This detail confirms Aeneas' journey as an Odyssean *nostos* (homecoming), but with a ktistic (foundational) twist: this Odysseus-figure returns "home" to reestablish his lost home upon the land of his ultimate origin. Revoking Lavinia's betrothal (253), Latinus invites Aeneas to wed her, believing him to fulfill a prophecy of his forebear, Picus.

Turning his attention to the divine workings, Virgil recounts Juno's deployment of the fury Allecto, whose provenance consists of strife, to break the peace between the Trojans and Latins. Allecto transforms one of her serpent locks into a necklace that inspires Bacchic frenzy in Amata, Latinus' queen, who thus declares Aeneas to be another Paris. Calling attention to Turnus' Greek genealogy, Amata interprets Turnus to be the "foreigner" of Faunus' prediction; his Greek origins allow for a new Trojan war between "Trojan" Aeneas and "Greek" Turnus.

In the guise of Calybe, Juno's aged priestess, Allecto comes to Turnus, her next victim, at his Ardean home. Similar to the way that Callimachus' autophagous Erysichthon had treated Demeter when she appeared as the priestess Nicippa (*Hymn to Demeter*, 42), Turnus rudely dismisses Calybe. In so doing, he reveals his own style of self-destructive appetite, if less obvious than that of Erysichthon. He speaks in Homeric platitudes, stating, "wars must be waged by men" (7.444), a dictum that recalls a similar sentiment of Hector (*Il.* 6.492). Yet in this context the aphorism becomes an affront that provokes a furious response. Allecto sends two snakes that overcome him; when he awakens from his trance, he has an appetite for war (7.460–1). When Allecto causes Ascanius' dogs to rouse to flight the pet stag of Silvia, the sister of King Latinus' herdsman, Ascanius wounds the stag, abruptly ending the treaty. Though Latinus refuses to open the gates of war, Juno intervenes herself; dismayed at the Latins' bloodlust, the king secludes himself.

Taking Homer's catalogue of ships (*Il.* 2.485–760) as his model, Virgil lays out the *dramatis personae* of warriors, including Mezentius, "despiser of the gods," and his son Lausus (7.647–54). The magnitude of the war can be seen in the distance from Latium that soldiers report; Oebalus, Teleon's son, comes from as far away as the island of Capri (735–9), not far from Cumae, where Aeneas' journey in Italy had begun. On the one hand, this catalogue serves as a classical reference to Homer. On the other hand, Virgil's list suggests something further: Virgil's list suggests that there exists a lack of unity and perhaps even a latent furor in the seemingly peaceful land of Italy, to which the arriving band of Trojans will bring a unifying civilization.

As book 7 closes, the last of the warriors mentioned is the princess Camilla, whose bravery is described in some detail. She is skilled in battle (805) and her comportment and status evoke a memory of Dido. This book has thus introduced the motivation for battle, the principal characters, and some of the second half of the *Aeneid*'s most important themes, especially that of Aeneas' *nostos*, which will restore order to Italy as Odysseus' does to Ithaca. The images of Turnus and Camilla, in particular, linger with the reader as Virgil now moves to another moment of future encountering past, this time not through his father's exposition of a *Heldenschau* but through his mother's gift, which bears images of future history.

Book 8: Triplets and Triumph

The eighth book gives form to Rome's future. Virgil effects that form through two devices: he repeatedly develops tripartite patterns throughout the book and, at the book's close, crafts the most extensive ecphrasis in the poem. The former device commences immediately, for the book opens with three subordinate concessive clauses all focused on Turnus' martial activity (1–6). While the repetition of such threefold patterns serves as a structural device to unify a diverse book, the thematic significance of Virgil's repetition of triplets emerges only at the book's close.

The book begins with Aeneas encountering an apparition of the river god Tiber, who explains that a white sow will mark the foundation of Alba Longa (48). Father Tiber also tells Aeneas of Evander and his people, the Arcadians, who have settled on the future site of Rome. These men, already Turnus' enemies, will provide Aeneas with troops necessary for victory. Meanwhile, the Latins also seek additional troops, sending an embassy to the Homeric hero Diomedes, who has settled in southern Italy.

Aeneas promptly sails up river, where he encounters Evander's son Pallas amidst a religious festival to Hercules (103f.). Evander, whose Greek name means "good man," dismisses their former opposition in the Trojan War, invoking their connection through a shared enemy and their blood kinship (132). He thrice repeats their common forebear Atlas' name (135, 140, 141). The vignette is marked by a dualistic variation between friendship and respect, father and son, guest and host, Greek and Italian. Such dualistic variation befits Aeneas' conversation with an

Arcadian, whose native land is also that of Virgil's *Eclogues*, where dualism, as we saw earlier, is a prevalent theme.

Evander tells the story of Hercules' vengeance on the monster Cacus for his theft of cattle, calling attention to the hero's threefold attempt to assail Cacus' den:

> Three times, hot with anger, he scans the whole ridge of the Aventine hill, three times he tries to take the rocky threshold in vain, three times, weary, he sits back down in the vale. (230–2)

Hercules' victory comes once he makes the light shine in on the monster's dark lair (240–46). The struggle between darkness and light is an assertion of the triumph of vision, affirmed by Hercules' gouging of Cacus' eyes (261). The vanquished beast becomes a spectacle, as Hercules stands triumphant over him, depicted in a well-known medallion (Figure 5.3) in a manner similar to Theseus triumphing over the Minotaur.

Figure 5.3. A medallion from the Antonine period (AD 138–160). Monnaies Médailles et Antiques. Med. Cercle No. 18-revers, Image numérique 1.8.50 Mo. Used by permission of Bibliothèque nationale de France. Drawing by Mary Claire Russell.

After Evander's description of this triumph of good over evil – Cacus' name is a virtual transliteration of the Greek word for evil, *kakos* – the rites of the festival are carried out and the banquet renewed, as a chorus sings of Hercules' heroic struggles against Juno's wrath. As deliverer of proto-Rome, Hercules parallels Aeneas, Troy's deliverer and re-founder; both anticipate Augustus.

During a walking tour of the future site of Rome, Aeneas learns the region's connection with Saturn, the god who had once hidden in Latium (*latuisset*, 323), an act that gave the region its "Latin" name. This tour, the topographical equivalent of the *Heldenschau* of book 6, continues with various *regions célèbres* such as the Lupercal, the Tarpeian rock, and the Argiletum, closing with the forum filled with lowing cattle. The threshold to which Evander refers (362) would seem to be at the top of the Palatine's *scala Caci* (steps of Cacus), an incline that rose to Augustus' house. The description of Evander's house, too, Fordyce notes, suggests Augustus' residence. As Gransden points out in his commentary, Virgil "contrasts Rome's pastoral beginnings with her Augustan grandeur" (ad 360–1).

Leaving Aeneas with his welcoming host, Virgil shifts to the actions of the gods, where Venus requests new weapons from Vulcan for Aeneas. Ignited by the flames of love, the fire god acquiesces. In the description of the forging of the arms the repetition of threes is sustained: the Cyclopean craftsmen forge three shafts of hail, three of storm clouds, and three of flame (429f.), only then turning to Aeneas' weapons.

The next day, Evander and Aeneas formalize their alliance, which encompasses Etruscans, the neighboring civilization that had expelled its former king, Mezentius, for engaging in barbaric practices. Evander recognizes Aeneas, a non-Italian, to be the foreign ruler predicted by the Etruscan *haruspex* (soothsayer). In an emotional farewell (imitative of Apollonius, *Arg.* 2.799–805), Evander adds Pallas to Aeneas' company. Donning a lion's pelt in the manner of Hercules, Aeneas accepts his new companion, who is confirmed by a sign from Venus.

Evander's prayer to Jupiter harks back to that of Nestor in *Iliad* 7:

> Father Zeus, Athena and Apollo, would that I were still youthful as when the men of Pylos were gathering and the spear-eager Arcadians engaged in battle by the swift Celadon River before Pheia's walls by the streams of the Iardanus. (132–5)

Nestor here mentions the Arcadians by name; in the *Aeneid*, this is the very people Evander leads, transferred to Italy. Nestor's words suggest

that he was "present" at the battle mentioned here. Like Nestor, Virgil's
Evander recounts his own exploits (*aristeia*):

> By this right hand I sent Erulus, Praeneste's king, to Tartarus below, to
> whom, when he was born, his mother, Feronia, had given three spirits
> (horrible to speak of!), three weapons, to be plied; so did he have to be
> laid low three times. Then did this right hand despoil him of all of his lives
> and just so many times strip him of his weapons. (*Aen.* 8.563–7)

Evander appropriates the role of Nestor in the *Iliad*. In this imitation of
Nestorian storytelling, Virgil includes, yet again, clusters of three. This
threefold repetition of triplets is repeated in the triple protasis of the
condition ("if" clauses) in Evander's prayer for his son that follows:

> If your divine will keeps Pallas safe for me, if the fates preserve him, if I
> live to see him, my only child, to come to him again, I pray for life, I am
> patient to endure any labor. (574–7)

These three conditional sentiments are followed by a similar repetition
of clauses beginning with "while" (*dum*). Such tripartite replication
emphasizes the uncertainty of the future (580–83) and abides by this
book's often repeated pattern of triplets.

Inspired by Evander, Aeneas retreats to a grove where he encounters
his mother who presents him with new weapons. Aeneas beholds and
touches them piece-by-piece (618–19) until he comes to the shield,
which bears tales of Roman identity, beginning with Romulus and Remus
(630–34), continuing with other stories, from the rape of the Sabine
women to Lars Porsenna's attempts to restore the exiled Tarquinius
Superbus (646–8). Its mixture of Roman victories and losses includes the
description of the *dies ater* (dark day) of 390 BC, when Gauls sacked
Rome (655–62), with further negative images of renegade Romans.
Chief among these figures is Catiline facing the eternal punishment that
Cicero had predicted for him at the end of the first Catilinarian oration
(*In Cat.* 1.13.33). In the center lies the victory at Actium that preserved
Roman identity: Augustus and Agrippa stand against Antony and his
"Egyptian wife," Cleopatra (8.688). The conflict of the gods depicted
in this battle gives the shield epic dimensions on a par with Aeneas' own
account of Troy's fall, when Aeneas was permitted to see the divine
conflict that lay behind human events (2.602–23).

The repetition of threes that we have seen throughout the book now
comes to a climax. While the replication of this pattern may reflect the

book's basic tripartite division or the back-and-forth movement necessary for Rome's "new" origins – Italy, to Troy, and then back to Italy – or even suggest the ubiquitous tension between past, present, and future, a further possibility now presents itself:

> But Caesar, having been transported within the walls of Rome in triple triumph, was consecrating three hundred supremely grand shrines through the entire city, his everlasting vow to Italian gods. (8.714–16)

Augustus is depicted on the shield coming home in a triumphal parade, specifically a triple triumph. Book 8's threefold repetitions had been harbingers of this signal event, itself characterized with three hundred altars. The emphasis here is not just on the details of Rome's past but on its fulfillment in this event. Thus, just as all the clusters of three in this book have looked ahead to this moment, so all of Roman history had pointed toward the celebration of Caesar's victory at Actium, which was hailed in 29 BC by the triple triumph, a description "obviously intended to excite the reader … not to inform Aeneas."[18]

As the reader's perception becomes clearer, that of Aeneas, by comparison, remains clouded. The final lines of the book reveal Aeneas' incapacity to understand the events recorded on the shield, although he delights in their image (730). Despite his lack of understanding, it is significant that when he dons his new armor, his burden will not be the past, but the future, which he will carry with him.

Book 9: Raiding Party and "City" Siege

Book 9 opens with Turnus in a grove, where he is visited by Iris. The goddess urges action, and Turnus responds swiftly to her directive by marching against the Trojan camp that has become a virtual city with "walls" (39). Turnus and his troops storm this city-camp, a reversal of the theme of the invading army besieging the established city. Thus Virgil reverses the typical roles in a siege, transforming Turnus and the Rutulians into the invaders.

With his first javelin cast, Turnus unleashes a torrent of battlefield fury. The focus soon shifts, however, to describe the transformation of the Trojan ships into sea-nymphs. Turnus interprets this transformation to mean that any prospect of retreat is lost, comparing this conflict to the *Iliad*'s war. Nisus and Euryalus, two of the besieged Trojans whom the reader recalls were comrades in the footrace of book 5, volunteer for a mission to recall Aeneas from Pallanteum. For this account, which is the book's centerpiece, Virgil echoes the exploits of Odysseus and Diomedes recorded in the Doloneia of *Iliad* 10.

The adventure opens with Nisus positing a theological conundrum: "Do the gods, Euryalus, put ardor into our minds, or does each man's terrible desire become a god for him?" (9.184–5). Nisus desires glory from the proposed expedition that Euryalus joins. When the two come upon drunken and sleeping Rutulians, Nisus tries to restrain Euryalus' carnage, calling him to return to the task of retrieving Aeneas (355f.). A gleaming helmet, however, taken from the sleeping Messapus, betrays Euryalus, who dies like a flower cut down by a passing plowshare, an image evocative of Catullus describing his lost love (11.21–2). This theme is relevant to the Virgilian context, given the close relationship of the two youths and their union in death, as Nisus perishes by falling pathetically upon his dead comrade (445).

Virgil's poetic voice pronounces a rare *makarismos* (declaration of blessedness) over the pair. Although he calls the pair "lucky" because their memory will never fade so long as "the Roman father will hold sway,"[19] the *makarismos* heightens the level of pathos as it comes just before a description of their impaled heads. Soon the report of their death comes to Euryalus' mother, whose soliloquy is one of the most memorable moments of pathos in the poem (481–96). Her words, modeled on those of Andromache (*Il.* 22.448–9), involve a poignant arrangement of pronouns, in accordance with the feature that Otis labeled Virgil's subjective style.

Well into this book Virgil evokes Calliope, the epic Muse, who befits the heroic scenes that follow. These include a fresh attack on the Trojan camp, described as a watchtower holding men. During the siege, Turnus' ruthlessness is emphasized; other clashes are mentioned, such as Ascanius with Numanus Remulus, Turnus' brother-in-law. Ascanius responds to Remulus' taunts about Trojan effeminacy by shooting an arrow through his head, adding that the Rutulians face "Phrygian *men*" (635).

At the gate of the Trojan camp/city, two brothers, Bitias and Pandarus, confront Turnus; Bitias soon falls to Turnus, who then decapitates Pandarus. Though inside the gates, Turnus fails to open them for the Rutulians. Instead, he merely enlarges the body count. Mnestheus and Sergestus rally the Trojans, causing Turnus to step back like a lion unwilling to run. To save Turnus, Jupiter directs Juno to desist from helping Turnus; Turnus thus withdraws, plunging into the Tiber (815–19).

Appearances of the goddess Iris frame the book; she addresses Turnus at the opening and plays a part in his deliverance at its close. In the course of the book's action, we learn that Turnus is a self-proclaimed second Achilles (742). Two episodes in the book are deftly interlaced with Turnus' exploits, namely the daring raid of Nisus and Euryalus and the brief *aristeia* of Ascanius. This book blends the Homeric themes of a night raid with that of a "city" siege, with much attention paid to Turnus' personal victories, his impetuous character, and especially his adherence to the Homeric value of glory (*kleos*) of individual exploits rather than pursuit of the common good.

Book 10: Balance of Powers: *Pietas* in Action

The tenth book lays the foundation for the action of the remainder of the poem. That foundation is intimately connected with Pallas' death and Aeneas' brutal response to it. Turnus has a major role in evoking that response, as he dons Pallas' sword belt, which, later in the epic, will prompt Aeneas' memory of his *pietas* (sense of devotion) to Evander and his son. That sword belt's artwork portrays the fifty daughters of Danaus, all but one of whom kill their newly-wed husband/cousins. The story of a failed betrothal is eerily appropriate for Turnus' plunder, since, contrary to Aeneas' status as rightful suitor, Turnus is a failed bridegroom. Such tension between Turnus and Aeneas for the hand of Lavinia corresponds to the book's action, which is often characterized as a balance between two opposite forces, whether fighter against fighter, army against army, or god against god.

With regard to the last of these, book 10 opens with tension in the gods' assembly on Olympus. Venus addresses the current conflict, disavowing, if disingenuously, her hope of empire (42). In her sarcastic rebuttal, Juno casts Venus' words back at her, resuming the theme of the previous book, calling the Trojan camp a new Troy, and affirming Turnus' claim to the land. Jupiter's terse and not entirely honest response only temporarily stays the goddesses' feud (110–15). Such struggles among the gods form an important secondary theme in this book, in which there is an emphasis on balance.

Against this mythological backdrop, Aeneas makes pacts with the Etruscans, who harbor a virulent hatred of Mezentius (150). Other forces come together, for the introduction of which Virgil invokes the Muses. The catalogue of these forces comes to a climax with the mention of the poet's hometown, Mantua (198–207).

Sailing back to his men, Aeneas encounters the nymph Cymodocea, who explains the earlier transformation of his ships into nymphs, encouraging Aeneas with a prediction of victory (245), itself confirmed by harmless flames shooting from his helmet and armor. This image forms a *mis-en-abime* (an image placed within another similar image) with the portrayal of Augustus depicted on the shield, which Aeneas now carries. To rally his men, Turnus turns to quasi-Iliadic dicta – one recalls he had done so when he encountered Allecto disguised as Calybe – such as "Mars himself is in men's hands" (280) and "Fortune helps the daring" (284).

The battle is portrayed in terms of a scale's balance, "man-to-man, foot-to-foot" (361). If the number three had been an important way of prefiguring the triple triumph of book 8's close, in book 10, the number two is now important, for Virgil frequently compares and contrasts two possible outcomes. We shall see, too, that two young men, Lausus and Pallas, die noble deaths; there are numerous pairs of friends and brothers mentioned throughout the book, e.g., Cydon and Clytius (325), Evandrius and Thymbirus (394), Lucagus and Liger (575f.).

Urged by his sister-nymph Juturna, Turnus pursues Pallas, savagely wishing that Evander could witness the outcome. The battle between the younger man and the experienced warrior is indebted to that of Hector and Patroclus in the *Iliad*. A simile, in which Turnus is likened to a lion and Pallas to a bull, is also Homeric (*Il.* 16.823–4); in the *Iliad* Hector is compared to a lion, Patroclus, to a boar. Virgil's simile is briefer: the lion merely sees the bull at a distance and pounces.

Pallas' prayer to Hercules, the patron divinity of the Arcadians, represents a theological aside. His inability to grant Pallas' prayer grieves Hercules, though Jupiter comforts him: "for each man there stands a day, for all men the time of life is brief and irretrievable; but to further one's fame by deeds, this is the work of valor" (10.467–9). If Virgil's grappling with life-and-death issues does not always bring about a sanguine outcome, he nevertheless shows a degree of sympathy and humanity not previously seen in ancient epic.[20]

After Pallas' failed prayer, Turnus vaunts boldly, "behold how much more penetrating my lance is" (481). Having thus killed Pallas and stripped his corpse, Turnus calls upon the Arcadians to return the body to Evander. Aeneas' devotion to Evander's household leads him to stark actions: he brutally sacrifices eight youths to the shades and then uncompromisingly annihilates various opponents in battle, at no point showing mercy. Even appeals of suppliants, such as Magus, Tarquitus or Liger, are of no avail; the verb employed for such appeals is *orare*, also used in Turnus' final petition (12.933).

An interchange between Jupiter and Juno breaks up this description of carnage. Jupiter tersely states that Venus has facilitated the Trojan advances. In response, Juno asks for the right "to keep Turnus safe from harm for his father, Daunus" (10.615–16), the very argument that Turnus will make to Aeneas at the poem's close (12.932–4). For the moment, Jupiter concedes, permitting Juno to preserve her hero using a false image of Aeneas that leads Turnus away to a nearby ship.

Mezentius becomes the Italic forces' principal warrior and achieves numerous victories in battle. He is likened to a boar, a description comparable to *Iliad* 11.414–15, where Odysseus engages Trojans. A further comparison blends as many as five Homeric lion similes, endowing Mezentius' character with epic authority.

When Aeneas encounters him, Mezentius prays to his own right hand, invoking its help, perverting the normal invocation of a divinity. The intervention of Mezentius' son, Lausus, to prevent Aeneas from killing his father, provokes an apostrophic tribute on the part of the poet (10.791–93). Aeneas sorrowfully returns Lausus' body to Mezentius, who in his anger falls to him. Pinned beneath his own horse, Mezentius asks Aeneas only to be buried with his son (906). Aeneas, however, coldly dispatches Mezentius, anticipating his action when similarly confronted by Turnus.

Throughout this book, Aeneas' devotion to Evander drives him to a level of ferocity; he recalls first meeting with Pallas and Evander, which is a different kind of stimulus than Homeric *kleos*. If the tone has become more brutal – though, as Coffee has suggested, Aeneas seems driven more by social obligation than mere ferocity – the mission remains the same, and the foundation of a new nation depends on Aeneas' victory.[21]

Book 10 emphasizes such a balance of power, while providing the hero with the motivation of *pietas* necessary to make sense of the epic's powerful final scene. The position of the book, too, in the poem's second half, is comparable to that of book 4 in the first half. Book 4 focused on the love affair that would rival Aeneas' true love, Italy, and ended with the cutting of Dido's lock, anticipating her appearance in the Underworld. *Aeneid* 10's mêlée prefigures that of *Aeneid* 12, particularly the final scene of that book and the poem. The emphasis on dualism – hand-to-hand, goddess-to-goddess (Venus and Juno), hero-to-hero (Aeneas and Mezentius) – prepares the reader for the poem's ultimate duel, the final scene between Aeneas and Turnus.

Book 11: Effete Prattle and Dexterous Battle

The eleventh book emphasizes the grimness of war and the power of the right arm in battle, with features that anticipate the poem's conclusion in two ways. First, Virgil sets out the inadequacy of rhetoric and debate in a martial context, going well beyond book 10's failure of suppliants. In book 11, embassies fail, public debate falls short, and the more a character spews forth word upon word, the less persuasive he becomes. Secondly, the book presents Camilla as a character who both resumes the nobility of Dido and, in being distracted, contrasts with Turnus, who is overly focused on one prize.

Book 11 opens with Aeneas grimly affixing Mezentius' arms to a tree trunk as a trophy to Mars. Pallas' funeral takes center stage (39), with a eulogy by Aeneas, who envisions Evander heaping altars with gifts, a gesture that signifies the vanity of religious observance in such a situation. As had Mezentius, Evander laments deeply his son's loss as Virgil assesses the heavy toll of war.

Aeneas accepts responsibility for Pallas' death, and his eulogy recalls Anchises' description of Marcellus in book 6. Such a sense of responsibility leads Aeneas to the extreme response of human sacrifice (11.81), as Achilles had done in the *Iliad* (21.27–8) when reacting emotionally to the death of Patroclus. Aeneas, by contrast, is motivated by devotion to Evander and a sense of duty toward Pallas, in particular, whom he failed to protect.

Thus, when Evander asks for vengeance, specifically for Aeneas' "right hand" (*dextra*) to achieve victory, Aeneas responds willingly. The mention of the right hand is important, for Aeneas had already speculated that either a god or one's own right hand wins life in battle (118). The word for right hand (*dextra*) which occurs most frequently in this book, is used in two distinct ways, for diplomacy or as a conduit of force in battle. The latter characteristic of the right hand is what Evander, relying on Aeneas' sense of *pietas* achieved by earlier diplomacy, asks of him.

The fury driven by such *pietas* is pronounced, albeit Aeneas does at least receive Latin envoys who ask to bury the dead. Among them, Drances, a complex and interesting character, shows deference to the Trojan cause (128f.). In the Latin camp, the negative report of the envoys sent to Diomedes points up the ineffectiveness of verbal persuasion. Diomedes is said to recall having fought Aeneas hand-to-hand and to prefer to offer him gifts (281–3). Aeneas' "hand," he notes a few lines later, kept Troy from falling for a decade (289f.); thus, Diomedes urges that right hands be joined in treaty (292).

When Latinus later calls for peace (320–2), he is supported by Drances, who urges Turnus to meet Aeneas in single combat (370–5). Turnus' response is twice as long as Drances' speech. Dismissing Diomedes' hesitation (428), Turnus predicts a turn of luck. In contrast to Turnus' prolixity, Aeneas takes immediate action against the Rutulians, as a herald reports at the debate's close. Queen Amata is more alarmed than Turnus; with a throng of women she vainly supplicates Athena, evocative of a similar scene in Homer (*Il.* 6.294–311); this further identifies the Rutulians with the losing side in the *Iliad*, as Trojans evermore assume the role and identity of Italians.

As Camilla, a hunter in Diana's retinue, moves to the center of battle, on Olympus Diana tells her attendant, Opis, a touching story of Camilla's childhood. In the battle, however, Camilla wields an ax with her right hand, vaunting over her dying victims. In her furious onslaught, she, like Aeneas, hears no supplication (690–8).

When the colorful outfit of the priest Chlorus draws her attention, Camilla falls victim to Arruns, who had been stalking her (759–67). Camilla's fatal mistake is that she becomes distracted by the splendor of embroidery. As she dies she speaks to Acca, who plays the role of Anna to Dido:

This much, Acca, my sister, could I do. Now a bitter wound brings me down, and round about everything grows dark with shadows. Retreat and bring to Turnus these final commands, that he come into the battle now and repel the Trojans from the city. And now, farewell. (823–7)

Though there is no sexual aspect to the relationship, in some ways Camilla stands to Turnus as Dido had to Aeneas in the poem's first half: each is a victim of a man's mission. A connection to Turnus is also established in the manner in which Camilla's soul departs for the shades below, "with a groan, complaining" (831), identical to the manner of Turnus' soul in the twelfth book.

The book ends with the Latins driven back within their walls, many falling at the gates (890). Turnus gets the bad news, but continues to rage (901), as he heads for the city within sight of Aeneas just before sunset. Thus ends the eleventh book, characterized by debates and the capacity of right hands to make war and peace.

Book 12: Spectacle of Arms

The twelfth book opens with Turnus described as one who sees what is happening and one who is seen by the eyes of all (2–3). When, in his opening speech to King Latinus, he requests the opportunity of single combat with Aeneas, he states that the Latins can sit and watch (15). Spectacle also defines the book's final scene, which brings together the themes of true bridegroom, *pietas*, and vision's dominance over rhetoric.

Related to the theme of spectacle is the importance of weaponry to this book (16), a theme that harks back to the poem's opening word, "arms." This theme is connected with bridegroom and suitors, emphasized when Latinus addresses Turnus:

> It was not right that I unite my daughter with any of the previous suitors; so all the gods and men were foretelling. Yet overcome by my affection for you, overcome by my blood tie and the tears of my grieving wife, I snatched his betrothed from my son-in-law and took up impious weapons. (27–31)

The bride herself is introduced in the lines that follow, as Lavinia blushes when she overhears the possibility of her being betrothed to Aeneas. Interpreting the blush to indicate her love for him, Turnus decides upon single combat with Aeneas and proceeds to arm himself. His sword, we learn, is made by Vulcan, and is thus a match for Aeneas' own (107).

Latinus sets the parameters of single combat with Aeneas, an act that recalls the Homeric duel of Paris and Menelaus for Helen (*Il.* 3.259–309). Like that one, this contest fails to be conclusive, as Juturna, appearing as the warrior Camertus, interrupts it, causing the truce to be broken. She then assesses Turnus, echoing a famous epitaph:

> That man [Turnus] will certainly, by his fame, approach the gods, on whose altars he vows himself, and, alive, be borne on the lips of men. (234–5)

These words, which echo Ennius' epitaph "I will fly, alive, upon the lips of men," ominously presage Turnus' death. Such epitaphs are normally attached to tombs or adopted by poets (cf. *G.* 3.9). Thus, if the application of this epitaph to Turnus extols him, it is also predictive of his death.

When Virgil resumes his description of the fighting, he includes several accounts of Turnus killing Trojans. whose stories Virgil individualizes. Turnus also pursues the wounded Aeneas, a scene modeled on Achilles fighting Hector. Though Aeneas seeks the remedy of being cut (389f.), the physician Iapyx acts cautiously until Venus, intervening, provides the miraculous cure of Cretan *dictamnum* (dittany).

Virgil also describes the war's harsh side effects: Amata, dismayed, commits suicide; Lavinia, grieving her mother, rends her hair and gouges her cheeks. Disguised now as Metiscus, Juturna encourages Turnus, who claims earlier to have known Metiscus' divine identity, as well as that of Camertus.

As Rutulians and Trojans watch closely (705), the two protagonists, like bulls, engage in a conflict that encompasses several features of Roman ritual. While, in epic fashion, Jupiter weighs out their destinies, Turnus discovers that he had taken the wrong sword, which breaks when it strikes Aeneas' divinely made armor. A further simile now defines the two warriors. Aeneas, described as a gaping Umbrian hound, pursues Turnus. While Grattius' later *Cynegetica* will subsequently evidence amply the quality of Umbrian hunting dogs (*Cyn.* 172), Virgil's use of the topographic adjective Umbrian may suggest Aeneas' new local identity as well as present an etymological paranomasia with *umbra* ("shade," a pun attested already in Plautus' *Mostellaria* 769), a metonym for Hades as the final word of book 12.[22]

Though Faunus, Turnus' divine forebear, helps his progeny by retaining Aeneas' spear in a tree trunk, he can only delay the inevitable, for Jupiter and Juno make a final settlement allowing Aeneas to triumph. Though personally barred from further involvement, Juno gains concessions: Trojan designations are to be replaced with those of the conquered – Latium, Alban kings, Rome, Italy and the Latin tongue – in fulfillment of the poem's prologue.

In the final duel Aeneas brandishes his spear, calling on Turnus to confront him. Undaunted, Turnus takes up a boundary stone to hurl at Aeneas (12.897). The notion of a hero picking up a rock to hurl is derived from *Iliad* 12.445–50, where Hector smashes a gate. Yet here a different kind of stone is used. The informed reader of Virgil's text knows that the concept of a boundary stone was particularly significant in Lucretius, Virgil's immediate epic predecessor. We saw earlier that Lucretius had used the image of the "deeply clinging boundary stone," to suggest the intractable quality of natural law (e.g., *DRN* 1.78, 6.66). By taking up such a stone, Turnus is countervening the "natural" right of Aeneas to fulfill his destiny.

The image of the boundary stone also functions as a symbol of territorial division. Turnus seeks to keep Aeneas out of his land, away from Turnus' territorial claim. In uprooting a boundary stone, which should not be disturbed, as we know also from Lucretius' description of such boundary stones, Turnus is violating old human law that parallels natural law.[23] Turnus' attempt to hurl the stone at Aeneas thus appropriately falls short of the mark (12.907).

Before this returning hero, Turnus' rhetorical ploys prove as futile as those of the *Odyssey*'s suitors. Turnus' reliance on rhetoric is explained in a simile describing a man in a dream whose words fail. Turnus' bodily functions now begin to shut down – or rather seem to do so – as he confronts Aeneas. All of this is satisfying, if we regard Aeneas as an Odysseus figure, the rightful husband who has returned home. Yet, the fit is not quite perfect: Lavinia was not Aeneas' wife and Turnus had been more than merely a suitor of Lavinia, for he was betrothed to her.

The actions of Aeneas – and so often, with regard to Virgil's presentation of Aeneas and Turnus, actions simply speak louder than words – settle the score, even if the reader's sympathies are not drawn unequivocally to the victor. In contrast to Turnus' failed hurling of the rock, Aeneas hurls his spear and strikes. The poem's final simile describes the spear's movement: like a whirlwind, it brings black death (924). Knocked to the ground, Turnus turns to rhetoric: "the Ausonians have seen me, conquered, reaching out my hands to you" (936–7). Turnus then appeals to the father–son bond as the basis for his plea for mercy (933–4), an entreaty that temporarily gives Aeneas pause as the four items with which this book opened – weapons, vision, father–son relationship, and wrongful betrothal – all come together.

As Putnam has shown, the thoughtful reader can see that some of the characteristics of Juno's wrath from the poem's prologue are now property of Aeneas:

> Aeneas, after he drank in the reminders of this savage grief, lit up with fury and terrible in his wrath, said: you, bedecked with the spoils of my own people, would you escape me? Pallas sacrifices you with this wound, Pallas exacts the penalty from your wicked blood. (945–9)

Turning his gaze (939), Aeneas comes to look upon the weapons that Turnus took as spoils from Pallas. Now Aeneas is reminded of a different father–son relationship, that of Evander and Pallas. Pallas, Aeneas says, is the one who immolates Turnus (948). The act of the right hand of battle and the recollection of the value of the right hand of loyalty come together for Aeneas' final act in the poem.

The situation with which the poem opened was caused by "the mindful wrath of savage Juno" (1.4). Pallas' belt provides Aeneas with reminders of savage grief, leading to his fury and wrath. By heeding these signals, has Aeneas become the very thing he set out to defeat?[24] Were Aeneas not to hesitate, were there not to be a further stimulus for action, such an argument might prevail. Yet, if Aeneas has taken on some of the characteristics of a wrathful goddess, he has not become the very evil he set out to defeat.

Although Aeneas' wrath is linguistically comparable to Juno's, and as such is admittedly an emotional response to the vision of the sword belt, killing Turnus is not simply an irrational act. Its logic resides not in Aeneas' desire for epic *kleos* – which Turnus seems to think Aeneas wants when he speaks of Ausonians having seen him submitting to Aeneas – but in Aeneas' social obligation (*pietas*) to Evander. In the context of the Augustan milieu, in which Octavian had exacted vengeance for Caesar at Philippi and had saved Rome at Actium, a transferred vengeance ("Pallas sacrifices you with this wound") gives a rational basis for this kill, even if it is a basis that has not always sat well with Virgil's readers.

Anderson noted many years ago that the fact that Aeneas hesitates at all suggests a level of sympathy. That hesitation is connected with the most pronounced aspect of the *Aeneid*'s depth: it is a poem rich in pathos. As such, Conte has shown, it carefully balances the positive aspects of Aeneas' character with the dark forces that he battles within and without. Thus, the line between the Harvard school and the European school turns out to be somewhat fluid.[25]

The content of the artwork on Pallas' sword belt is that of wrongful betrothal, a prominent theme in this book and the poem. Aeneas' eyes drink in a story, the details of which include the question of the proper bridegroom, a story that can be metonymically associated with that of Odysseus. Beyond that metaphor, Aeneas also fulfils the prologue's prescient *dum conderet urbem* ("until he could found the city," 1.5), for in rendering justice on Pallas' behalf, Aeneas gives a "founding" blow, burying the blade – the Latin verb *condere* means both "to bury" and "to found" – to establish a nation.[26] Thus Rome is born, as the proper suitor fulfils his *nostos*, which in this case brings him to a new land and a new life for Troy, achieved through the death of Turnus, whose soul, like that of Camilla, departs to the Underworld indignantly.

Conclusion

Let us now try to make sense of this stream of psychological portraits, epic battle sequences, and carefully crafted plot execution. I have argued that the *Aeneid* shares with the *Eclogues* moments of dualistic ebb and flow and, with the *Georgics*, the purveyance of wisdom, insofar as Virgil addresses the depth of human pathos. The same can be said of the way that Virgil infuses this poem with dualistic features: such dualism does not simply provide the narrative with a balancing effect but also offers a critical ingredient for understanding how this epic reconciles some of these oppositions: east becomes west, Trojan becomes Italian, and the foreign Aeneas turns out to be the proper husband come home. Likewise, what appeared at first to be an epic in the Homeric vein proves to be, in the final analysis, thoroughly Alexandrian.

Without doubt, however, the *Aeneid*'s central idea is mission, a theme very much in step with the tone of the Augustan age. Augustus had reinvigorated Rome, restoring her sense of destiny on an increasingly complex international stage. The political settlement known as the *pax Augusta* (Augustan peace) produced for Virgil and other poets of his age an optimistic moment for "literary peace" (*otium*). After years of civil strife, the poets Virgil, Horace, and Propertius had reason to believe that things have come round right, that Rome could possibly achieve a kind of transcendent greatness both politically and artistically. If tempered by the bloody cost of victory, this was nonetheless a moment of hope. In the relatively optimistic period of the 20s, Virgil folded the features of the dualistic ebb and flow of the *Eclogues'* and the wisdom of the *Georgics'* into the *Aeneid*'s central feature of mission, the *telos* of which is Rome.

As a character, Aeneas is indebted to a number of epic exemplars beyond his former Iliadic self, whom he acknowledges in a telling moment of self-discovery (*Aen.* 1.488). These exemplars include the fierce Achilles, the courageous Hector, the questing Jason, the caddish Theseus, and the itinerant Odysseus. Aeneas is not merely a composite of these heroes, nor is he merely their successor: he is their fulfillment. Virgil has taken qualities of each of them, and added something else: a deep sense of humanity, a characteristic never before attributed to such a degree to an epic hero. Thus Virgil's taciturn hero, who has learned from his travels and travails, reveals himself to be both a real human being and a superior leader.

The *Aeneid* is a masterpiece, for the sum of its many parts brings epic to a new level of pathos. To give prominence to that characteristic of his poetry, Virgil had to redefine the epic code. We have come to understand his code not only through its situation within its ancient context or through the numerous literary interpretations of it but also, quite specifically, through the codex that preserved it. Now we shall turn our attention to several of the codices that have contributed to the preservation of the text we know as Virgil.

Notes

1   On the Greek concept of *telos*, Z. Philip Ambrose, "The Homeric and Early Epic *Telos*," *DA* 24 (1964), 20–2. Further on the distinction between Homer and Virgil, see C. S. Lewis, "Virgil and the Subject of Secondary Epic," in Steele Commager (ed.), *Virgil: A Collection of Critical Essays* (Englewood Cliffs, NJ, 1966), 62–7.

2   The title *Ab Urbe Condita* is often rendered "From the City's (i.e., Rome's) Founding." On Augustus' interest in foundation legends via Apollo, see Heinze, *Virgil's Epic Technique* (London, 1993), 70, 382.

3   Augustus' admiral and confidant, Agrippa, also functioned as the imperial aedile (builder) in the 30s and 20s. Cf. Frederick W. Shipley, *Agrippa's Building Activities in Rome* (St Louis, 1933), 19–34, 61–4; also Stefan Grundmann, *The Architecture of Rome* (Fellbach, 1998), 49. The ground level of the piazza is over a meter higher than the ancient forecourt. Cf. also Kjeld de Fine Licht, *The Rotunda in Rome: A Study of Hadrian's Pantheon* (Copenhagen, 1968), 26–32. John W. Stamper, *The Architecture of Roman Temples: The Republic to the Middle Empire* (Cambridge, 2007), 186, suggests that Agrippa's building had a circular cella.

4   On memory of past trials in Aristotle, see, e.g., *An. Post.* 99b38–100a9; further on memory, cf. Martin Jay, *Songs of Experience: Modern American and European Variations on a Universal Theme* (Berkeley, CA, 2005), 16f.

5   Juan Luis de la Cerda, *P. Virgilii Maronis Priores Sex Libri Aeneidos Argumentis, Explicationibus et Notis Illustrati* (Lyon, 1612), ad loc. See James J. O'Hara, *True Names: Vergil and the Alexandrian Tradition of Etymological Wordplay* (Ann Arbor, MI, 1996), 132; Bernard M. W. Knox, "The Serpent and the Flame," *AJP* 71 (1950), 390; cf. W. S. Anderson, *The Art of the* Aeneid (1969; rpt. Wauconda, IL, 1989), 33f.

6   Cf. Rebekah M. Smith, "Deception and Sacrifice in *Aeneid* 2.1–249," *AJP* 120 (1999), 503–23.

7   For one such Greek vase, cf. *LIMC* "Aineias," 89. On an amphora from Nola, ca. 500 BC (Naples Museum), Aeneas transports Achates followed by a child (Ascanius) and an archer; they are preceded by an attendant and a woman (Creusa). Cf. Fulvio Canciani, *LIMC* s.v. "Aineias," 79. Canciani (395f.) notes that the form of the story of Aeneas' flight does not take its fullest shape before Virgil; cf. Nicholas Horsfall, s.v. "Enea," *Enciclopedia*

Virgiliana, vol. 2 (Rome, 1996), 227; Canciani, *LIMC* 1 "Aineias," no. 395; for Antonine coins, cf. Canciani, *LIMC* 1, "Aineias," no. 132, 136.

8   C.F. Saylor, "Toy Troy: The New Perspective of the Backward Glance," *Vergilius* 16 (1970), 26–8. Cf. also M. Di Cesare, *The Altar and the City: A Reading of Vergil's* Aeneid (New York, 1974), 67–8; R. E. Grimm, "Aeneas and Andromache in *Aeneid* III," *AJP* 88 (1967), 151–62. Brooks Otis, *Virgil: A Study in Civilized Poetry* (Oxford, 1964), 260–1. Buthrotum (modern Butrint) is located near the border of Albania and Greece.

9   George Sanderlin, "Aeneas as Apprentice: Point of View in the Third 'Aeneid,'" *CJ* 71 (1975), 53–6; cf. Eve Adler, *Vergil's Empire: Political Thought in the* Aeneid (Lanham, MD, 2003), 291–9.

10 On Epicurianism, cf. Julia T. Dyson, "Dido the Epicurean," *ClAnt* 15 (1996), 203–21.

11 Denis C. Feeney, "The Taciturnity of Aeneas," *CQ* 33 (1983), 205. For a different view, see Gordon Williams, *Tradition and Originality in Roman Poetry* (Oxford, 1968), 378–83; also R. C. Monti, *The Dido Episode and the* Aeneid: *Roman Social and Political Values in the Epic*, Mnemosyne Suppl. 66 (Leiden, 1981), 45–8.

12 Williams (1972), 4.601–3; cf. Cicero, *De lege Manilia* 22.5–7; Ovid, *Met.* 6.424–674.

13 Gian Biagio Conte, *The Poetry of Pathos: Studies in Vergilian Epic*, ed. S. J. Harrison (Oxford, 2007), 34.

14 Eve D'Ambra, *Roman Women* (Cambridge, 2007), 37; cf. Amy Rose, "Vergil's Ship-Snake Simile (*Aeneid* 5.270–81)," *CJ* 78 (1983), 115.

15 Servius, ad 117.3 says the *gens* Gegania claimed Gyas.

16 Williams (1960), ad 759f. states that "Virgil may have chosen the epithet *Idalia* simply as one of the most famous of the places associated with Venus." Virgil's designation of this temple as that of Venus of Mt Idalia reflects the blending of cultures central to book 5 achieved through nominal connections: Idalia, as a homophone, is close to Italia and as such might hint at the geographically proximate Italian future for Venus' other son, Aeneas.

17 Virgil's account of the death of Palinurus is complicated; further, see ch. 8, Further Reading.

18 Agnes K. Michels, "The *insomnium* of Aeneas," *CQ* 31 (1981), 146 n. 18.

19 Hardie (1994), ad 448–9: "Commentators worry over the precise reference of … *pater Romanus* (Augustus, the *princeps* of the day, father Jupiter, the senate?); it may be preferable not to confine the resonance." Cf. Gordon Williams, *Technique and Ideas in the* Aeneid (New Haven, CT, 1983), 205.

20 Cf. Julia Hejduk, "Jupiter's *Aeneid*: *Fama* and *Imperium*," *CA* (2009), 298–302, who taking a far less optimistic view of this passage qualifies the exchange between Jupiter and Hercules.

21 Cf. Neil Coffee, *The Commerce of War: Exchange and Social Order in Latin Epic* (Chicago, 2009), 98–111. For a different view of Jupiter and Juno's reconciliation, see Hejduk (2009). On Jupiter's sway, cf. Philip Hardie, *Virgil's* Aeneid: *Cosmos and Imperium* (Oxford, 1986), 314 *et passim*.
22 Aeneas could thus even be viewed as the hound of Hades (cf. the suggestively ominous name of Atrius Umber in Livy 28.28.4).
23 G. Williams (1983), 173, notes that Virgil's tone is didactic. Further on Virgil's use of Lucretian boundary stones, cf. Dyson (1996), 203–21.
24 Michael C. J. Putnam, "The Hesitation of Aeneas," in Putnam (1995), 165f. Two important contributions on this topic are those of M.C.J. Putnam, "Anger Blindness and Insight in Virgil's *Aeneid*," in Putnam (1995), 172–200 and Karl Galinsky, "The Anger of Aeneas," *AJPh* 109 (1988), 321–48.
25 Anderson (rpt. 1989), 98f.; Conte (2007), 150–69.
26 M. C. J. Putnam, "*Aeneid* 12: Unity and Closure," in *Reading Vergil's* Aeneid: *An Interpretive Guide* (Norman, OK, 1999), 226.

6

Virgilian Manuscripts: Codex to Critical Edition

The method of textual criticism which has been generally
practised by editors of classical Greek and Latin texts involves two main
processes, recension and emendation. Recension is the selection, after
examination of all available material, of the most trustworthy evidence
on which to base a text. Emendation is the attempt to eliminate the
errors which are found even in the best manuscripts.

Bruce Metzger (*The Text of the New Testament*, 156)

Earlier in this book we considered Virgil's life and the survival of
his poetry, positing the notion of two "Virgils": the historical Publius
Vergilius Maro and the Virgil who survives as his text. These two aspects
of Virgilian tradition are reflected in the variant spellings of the poet's
name: the historical name is Vergil (Vergilius), while the spelling with an
"i" involves a story about Virgil's reputation.

The fifteenth-century humanist Angelo Poliziano explained the vowel
softening as stemming from the poet's growing popularity in late antiquity. Among many stories told about him, a widely circulated tale reported
that Virgil's mother had dreamt that she would give birth to a bough
(*uirga*), which would grow to cover the entire world. Thus, as a play on
the word *uirga*, the spelling of Vergilius was changed to reflect Virgil's
popularity.

That a bough should have an obvious association with Virgil requires
no detailed explanation here. The significance of the story about the
spelling of Virgil's name, however, well suits the manuscript tradition,
which consists not merely of one bough but of many limbs on a thickly
branched tree. This tree bears a name connected with genealogy: *stemma*,
the Greek word for the "wreath" placed on ancestral busts and metonymically associated with the Roman family tree.[1]

Establishing the stemma of an author such as Virgil is an extraordinarily complicated project, through which the paleographer seeks to approximate the ancient author's original document, known as the autograph. The stemma encompasses all of the major codices, branch by branch. By their abbreviations, some of which are given below, these codices are compiled in an apparatus criticus, an exegetical addendum consisting of short-hand notes at the bottom of each page in a critical edition.

To prepare an apparatus criticus, the editor must scrutinize every jot and tittle of each manuscript. A newly discovered scrap of papyrus can cause an editor to rethink an entire passage, while an innovative idea may inspire a fresh explanation of an extreme point of difficulty in the text, known as a *crux* (pl. *cruces*). Some *cruces*, because of insufficient evidence, cannot be resolved and are therefore marked with an "obelus" (or "dagger"). In the case of Virgil, no line is obelized (sometimes referred to as "daggered") but there are, nonetheless, several questionable readings. In this chapter we shall review some samples of such readings.

In addition, I shall consider briefly how the textual Virgil has survived, particularly as the text branched out to form a broad manuscript tradition. Consideration of some examples of variant readings will help to demonstrate how a critical edition is established. Before we address these examples, however, let us consider how the codex itself took shape.

Books and Manuscripts

Virgil could not have envisioned any of his poetic works appearing in the modern book form of the codex. The book of the Augustan age was the unwieldy scroll. The Latin word for such a book, *liber*, first meant "tree bark," the original material used for a scroll.

As papyrus began to be imported from Egypt, books made of bark disappeared, though the designation *liber* obtained. The rolled papyrus formed a *uolumen* (cf. Latin *uoluo*, "roll"), twisted around a dowel called an *umbilicus*. Such a roll was often kept in a box (*capsa*) or bound with other scrolls by a leather band. A *vellum* (calf skin) label was attached along the edge of each *uolumen* bearing the *titulus* (title) of the work (cf. Figure 6.1; interestingly, the man depicted holds a codex in his hands, tangibly representing the shift from the scroll.). Scrolls, like books in the western world today, were read from left to right; as scroll gave way to codex, the *liber* changed yet again.[2]

Figure 6.1. Stele of Timocrates (second century AD). Though Timocrates holds a codex, a bundle of *uolumina* lie at his feet. Drawing by Mary Claire Russell.

For the codex, vellum, though expensive, was preferred, since both sides of each "leaf" could be folded to form distinguishable front-and-back pages (known as "folios") and was far more durable than papyrus. Though both the transition in the Roman legal world from scroll to codex (ca. AD 300) and the desirability of traveling editions of authors such as Virgil or Homer played a role, the chief reason for the transition to the codex was its preference among Christians, evidence of which can be seen already in Paul's second letter to Timothy.[3]

Thus the movement from the bulky *uolumen* to the easily thumbed codex was a paradigm shift not experienced again until the birth of the printing press in the fifteenth century. Between late antiquity and the Renaissance, the fate of Virgil's text rested in the hands of copyists who transmitted the codices of Virgil by painstakingly inscribing vellum manuscripts one line at a time. It is not hard to imagine how errors could be introduced into this laborious process.

If the transition from roll to codex was relatively sudden, the movement from codex to critical edition is, by contrast, a long and arduous journey, which begins with some very old codices. There is no firm agreement among scholars as to which Virgilian manuscript is most reliable. The Virgilian stemma is robust, for we have an "ancient copse" of manuscripts, as Mynors has quipped, using an image from the description of Aeneas' descent into the Underworld (*Aen.* 6.559). Taking up Mynors' analogy, Reynolds refers to the more than 750 medieval witnesses that form the "vast forest" that Virgil describes a few lines later (6.185).

Let us begin our review of the manuscripts with the Codex **Mediceus** (*M*). The Mediceus is vital for reconstructing the text of Virgil, as it is quite old and relatively complete, having lost only its first *quaternio* and a single page, preserved separately in the Codex Vaticanus (3225). Housed in the Biblioteca Medicea-Laurenziana in Florence, the Mediceus includes a subscription by the consul Turcius Rufius Apronianus Asterius, discussed in the first chapter. The date there given (April 21, 494) offers an important *terminus ante quem* (i.e., a date before which the manuscript must have existed). Compiled earlier in that same century in Italy with rustic capital letter forms (the most ancient type of Latin majuscule writing, as can be seen in Figure 6.2), this manuscript found its way to the Bobbio monastery near Piacenza before it was transported to Rome by the abbot. Pomponius Leto used it for his commentary, annotating the manuscript itself.[4]

Just as important for establishing Virgil's text is the **Codex Palatinus** (*P*), which is virtually complete, written in large and ornate rustic capitals in Italy, probably around the turn of the fifth to sixth century.[5] Though it is now housed in the library of the Vatican, this manuscript takes its designation from the time it resided in Heidelberg's Palatine Library. Already in antiquity, three editors, now known simply as P^1, P^2, and P^3, inserted corrections to the manuscript; their editorial remarks are cited with these superscriptions in modern editions to distinguish them from the readings of the manuscript proper.

Marichal proposes for the Palatinus a very old model, written in a semi-cursive script, traces of which may be preserved in some of *P*'s paleographical features.[6] In particular, this manuscript preserves antiquated forms such as *olli* for *illi*, *gnatus* for *natus*, *quoi* for *cui*, and other similar archaisms. Geymonat cautiously suggests that *P* could share a common source with *R* (Vat. Lat. 3867).

That manuscript, the **Codex Romanus (R)**, is also valuable for its antiquity and accuracy, though its original editor would seem to have inserted certain glosses as if they were the words of the poet: e.g., *agricola* replaces *rusticus* (*G.* 2.406), as *colores* does *rubores* (*G.* 3.307), and *honorat* does *instaurat* (*Aen.* 4.94). A slender but important piece of evidence for dating the manuscript rests on certain abbreviations that do not show up before the sixth century (e.g., *deus* shortened to *DS*) and a single line inserted after *Aen.* 6.241, which seems to be an adaptation of a verse from Priscian's translation of the African grammarian Dionysius Periegetes (ca. AD 500). *R* can thus likely be dated to some point in the late fifth or early sixth century.[7]

The Romanus' rustic capitals are similar to those of the Palatinus, possibly even produced in the same workshop. Though incomplete, fortunately *R* preserves the end of the third eclogue and most of the fourth (1–51), lines not found in most ancient manuscripts. The loss of certain pages suggests that the codex was heavily used. The Romanus features nineteen illustrations stylistically different from those of the fragmentary Vatican manuscript.[8]

The Vatican manuscript, known as *schedae Vaticanae* (*F*), is the oldest (perhaps fourth century) of four crucial, if only partial, witnesses. Written in rustic capitals, it preserves sections of the *Georgics* and the *Aeneid* in approximately seventy-five "sheets" or "leaves" preserving twenty-one verses each; it also includes a series of fifty beautiful ancient miniatures. These valuable illustrations have certain stylistic features that may suggest they are based on originals dating to the Severan dynasty (AD 193–211). While little is known of this manuscript's earlier history, in the fifteenth century it was in the possession of the Renaissance poet Giovanni Pontano (d. 1503). By 1579 Torquato Bembo, the son of the illustrious Cardinal Pietro Bembo, had acquired it, passing it to the papal library in 1602.[9]

Another partially preserved manuscript (*V*) in rustic capitals is the fifth-century **Codex Veronensis XL**, known as *Schedae Rescriptae Veronenses*, housed in Verona's Biblioteca Capitolare. The appellation "rescriptae" indicates that these leaves were rewritten; i.e., they were erased by the scraping of ink off the parchment and were then reused. Such a document, known as a palimpsest, has double value, for each page bears both the writing of the more recent manuscript and traces of the original. Modern scholars use magnifying glasses, ultraviolet light, and other means to decipher the writing beneath.[10]

In the case of the Veronensis, the later document is Gregory the Great's *Moralia in Job*, written in a script known as Luxeuil minuscules. According to Geymonat's most recent hypothesis (developed in consultation with Fabio Troncarelli), the rustic script of the original Virgilian document was written at Bobbio by a French abbot before coming to Verona about a century later; it may even have been corrected by Boethius (ca. 480–ca. 525). The surviving fragments are chiefly from the *Aeneid*, though twelve folios preserve sections of the *Eclogues* and *Georgics*. Unfortunately a strong chemical reagent used in the nineteenth century has made parts of this palimpsest very difficult to read. The Virgilian text was not ornate: each page had ample margins for annotation and originally contained only thirteen verses with very few abbreviations – features suggestive of a school edition.[11]

Another important but fragmentary manuscript is the sixth-century **Vergilius Sangalliensis** (*G*, Figure 6.2). Housed in the Stiftsbibliothek of St Gallen, this manuscript likely originated in Italy. At some point this codex was dismantled and used for binding, with only twelve leaves remaining. An explicit ("here ends a book") is preserved. Though it once likely contained the entire Virgilian corpus, now less than four hundred verses are preserved.[12] Its ornate script, known as square capitals (Latin majuscules more precise and box-like than rustic capitals) suggest it was a "coffee-table" edition. We know that the surviving fragments were already in the St Gall Monastery by the twelfth century, when some of its leaves came to be used in a copy of the Vulgate.

The fourth elegant fragmentary codex, **Augusteus** (*A*), also consists of square capitals. Only seven pages, all from the *Georgics*, are preserved: four in the Vatican and three in Berlin. The Augusteus is the oldest manuscript with ornamental initials (i.e., decorative letters that begin new sections in the text). The first page preserves the superscription "Claudius Puteanus [Claude DuPuy] gave this as a gift to Fulvius Ursinus [Fulvio Orsini]"; the latter's handwriting, recognizable because he served as librarian to the Farnese family, appears to have been preserved in the margins.[13]

This manuscript, perhaps sixth century, originally would have included the *Aeneid*, as four verses in an eighth leaf reveal. The eighth leaf is now lost but was reproduced by Jean Mabillon, a famous early paleographer.[14] The Augusteus has been housed in the Vatican's Biblioteca Apostolica since being acquired from the German state library in the nineteenth century (Vat. Lat. 3256).

There are also two eighth-century manuscripts (designated with lowercase letters because they are not as old as those discussed above) that

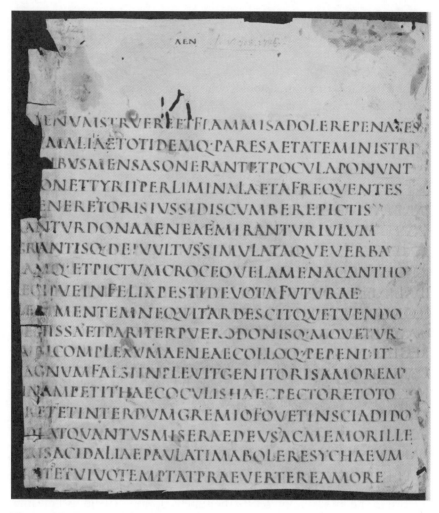

Figure 6.2. Excerpt of G Codex of Virgil (Cod. Sang. 1394). Used by permission of the Stiftsbilbliothek, St Gallen, Switzerland.

are fragmentary. The first of these, *m* (CLA ix 1327), recovered from twelfth-century bindings, is housed in **Munich** and preserves thirty-three lines of late antique capitals per page; it was probably intended only for private use and is not of deluxe status. This manuscript's earliest known whereabouts is the monastery at Tegernsee; it may have originated in northern Italy.[15]

The second important eighth-century fragment is the **Paris** manuscript (*p*). Copied in Germany, *p* was written in two columns with about thirty-five lines per page in a very small script. One fragment, containing the opening of the *Aeneid*, was discovered at Basel. The most important variant readings are found in *p*'s preservation of the fourth book of the *Aeneid*.[16]

There are several other important manuscripts dating from the ninth through the tenth centuries, the consensus of which is referred to as ω. The most significant codex from the ninth century is the Gudianus Lat. 2° 70, known as the **Guelferbytanus** (Wolfenbüttel γ). This manuscript deserves special attention here, for it bears witness to some readings unclear in Palatinus, of which γ may be an indirect descendant.

As the seeds of the Italian Renaissance began to take root in the ninth century, attention to the texts of antiquity grew and Virgilian manuscripts became widely disseminated. By sheer numbers, these manuscripts demonstrate the popularity of Virgil with the intellectual elite in late medieval culture.

Variant Readings

Just as the historian must consider whatever historical evidence survives to evaluate Virgil's life, so the paleographer reconstructs the textual Virgil by practicing the recension of the manuscripts; fortunately, the breadth and quality of paleographical evidence is, if complex, generally speaking more robust than that pertaining to Virgil's life. In many cases, however, recension is inadequate, and a fresh reading must be established through emendation; the reappraisal of a single word can often garner new ways of understanding the text.

Oddly, the best reading can sometimes be the least likely. Karl Lachmann, the great nineteenth-century editor of Lucretius' *De Rerum Natura*, was among the first to employ the editorial principle of the *lectio difficilior, potior* (i.e., the paradoxical preference for the more difficult reading), which assumes such a reading to be correct because copyists are likely to have attempted to make such a reading easier. While this is by no means a comprehensive methodology, especially for poetry, in which metrical constraints can play a large role, it is an important editorial principle. Another like it is *lectio breuior, potior* ("the shorter the reading, the better") but, again, such a *bon mot* is a guideline, not a rule. Let us now turn to some examples for which these guidelines may (or may not) be applicable.[17]

Eclogue 4.62–3

Eclogue 4, a poem preserved in its entirety in *R* and partially in *P*, describes the birth of a child who is to bring peace to the world; there has been little peace, however, for commentators considering line 62. Indeed, West cites this verse in particular as a case of early textual corruption, while Norden speaks of its complexity, which he unfolds in a lengthy footnote.[18] Mynors' Oxford Classical Text reads:

> *qui* non risere *parenti*,
> nec deus hunc mensa, dea nec dignata cubili est. (4.62–3)
> (Those who have not smiled upon their parent, neither has a god deemed this one worthy of his table nor has a goddess deemed him worthy of her bed.)

Manuscripts *P* and *R* read *parentes* (i.e., two parents) instead of the singular *parenti* that Mynors prints. The reading given above represents the current *opinio communis* (at least among Anglophone scholars) and overrides the two manuscripts in favor of the easier and sensible dative *parenti*. Nevertheless, before Mynors, Otto Ribbeck had favored *qui non risere parentes*, although this involves adjusting the normal sense of the verb *rideo*. Remigio Sabbadini did the same, with a long note in his critical apparatus.

One might simply accept this reading were it not for certain testimony beyond the manuscripts. Referring to this passage, the ancient grammarian Quintilian cites it as an example of *figura et in numero*, a rhetorical device whereby a plural noun follows a singular antecedent (*Inst.* 9.3.8.1–5). Quintilian clearly takes *qui* ("those who") as the nominative plural subject of the verb (*risere*), regarding it as an irregular plural following the singular addressee, "little boy" (*parue puer*).

Mynors, Norden, and others, ignoring Quintilian's citation of the text but accepting his explanation of the change from singular to plural, emend *parentes* to *parenti*. Yet if one regards *parentes* as the object of the verb *risere*, one must sidestep the lexicographical tradition that supposes this verb to suggest derision rather than smiling when it governs the accusative case. Williams advances the argument for the emendation of *parentes* to the dative singular *parenti* by connecting the verb *risere* with the notion of the child smiling at his mother in verse 60 (*incipe, parue puer, risu cognoscere matrem* ["Begin, little boy, to recognize your mother with a smile"]). While this is plausible, an obvious objection is that Quintilian's text must also be emended. Add to this that Quintilian's *figura et in numero* seems uncomfortable: a singular boy (*parue puer*) suddenly becomes a group of children (*qui risere*) who smile at one parent. All such deduction is based on the notion that Quintilian is secure in his reading of the passage and right about his interpretation of it.[19]

Another possibility, however, supported by the manuscript tradition, is the prospect of *qui* being the equivalent of the dative *cui*, with *parentes* serving as the subject of *risere*. The manuscripts *P*, *R*, and γ all introduce the line with *qui*, except Quintilian, who reads *cui*. It is possible that Virgil, in the mode of Lucretius, who deliberately archaized, wrote *quoi*; the fact that *R* includes numerous archaisms could well be explained by the tendency of the poet to engage in this practice. Indeed, Geymonat concludes this in his critical edition of 1973, for he follows Sabbadini and Perret in preserving *parentes* and introducing the archaic form of *quoi* for *cui*. The objection to this possibility is chiefly that to regard *qui* as a dative requires the reader to view the parents as smiling at the child, a scenario that seems to some scholars too obvious for Virgil to have stated.[20]

The possibility of *qui* as a dative responds nicely to the child's smile of line 60 and, more importantly, requires no major emendation, for to regard *qui* as the equivalent of *quoi* is not a far stretch. The γ manuscript, whose readings are often wiser than its relatively late date, reads *cui*. One branch of the manuscript tradition, therefore, supports this reading, while another branch, admittedly earlier, has *qui*, which Sabbadini and Geymonat presume to represent *quoi*, the archaic variant of *cui*. If this is accepted, we assume that Virgil wrote the archaic form of *cui*, namely *quoi*, which the copyists changed to *qui*. In its favor is the early testimony of Servius, who preserves this reading.

What of Quintilian's uncomfortable *figura et in numero*? Quintilian either read the line wrong – which is possible if the transition from *quoi* to *cui* went on roughly a century before Quintilian – or he was confused about his singulars and plurals. Even grammarians can make mistakes.[21]

Allowing for an error on Quintilian's part, therefore, the best reading of this line permits the manuscripts' *qui* to stand for the supposed autograph *quoi* (i.e., *cui*) following *rideo*, a verb that, according to Clausen (ad loc.), calls for the dative case when it denotes "smiling at" rather

than "deriding." Such an interpretation offers the added benefit of allowing a single family to be involved here (two parents and one child, rather
than multiple children), a configuration that would resonate better in the
context of this poem, which is about the unique birth of a particular
child.

Georgic 4.415

In *Georgic* 4, the nymph Cyrene seeks to comfort her son, Aristaeus,
after giving him instructions about grasping Proteus to learn from
him how to regenerate his lost bees. She drenches him with the scent of
ambrosia:

> haec ait et liquidum ambrosiae <u>defundit</u> odorem,
> quo totum nati corpus perduxit; at illi
> dulcis compositis spirauit crinibus aura
> atque habilis membris uenit uigor. (415–18)

(These things she spoke and pours down on him the liquid scent of
ambrosia, with which she covered the entire body of her son: But a sweet
aura infused his well-kempt hair, and nimble strength came to his limbs.)

Neither of the two main verbs, *defundit* and *perduxit*, has suited all the
manuscripts' copyists or editors. For example, the late manuscripts *d*, *e*,
h, and *v* and the earlier St. Gall codex read *defundit*, the present tense,
but other ninth- and tenth-century witnesses (*a* and *t*) read *defudit* (the
perfect tense), while the Oxford manuscript (*f*) reads a different verb's
present tense, *defendit*. Manuscripts *M*, *b*, *c*, *r*, and *γ* have *diffundit*, while
P has *perfundit*. Add to this that *M* has the final noun in the ablative
case (*honore*). The Codex Romanus goes in an entirely different direction,
reading *depromit*, and alters the verb of line 406, *perduxit*, to *perfudit*.
One can see immediately that these lines present a thorny problem.

The meaning of the verbs differ significantly – "pour," "defend,"
"conduct," etc. – and thus it is is important to determine which Virgil
actually employed. Mynors takes the *lectior difficilior* to be *defundit*,
which does not coordinate well with the perfect tense of the next line,
perduxit. The reading of the Romanus manuscript reveals the copyist's
struggle to make sense of the line's infelicitous coordination of verb
tenses. Ultimately, though Mynors' choice of the *lectio difficilior* seems
to be the best solution, we must in this case remain less than certain
about Virgil's autograph.

Aeneid 8.223

In the eighth book of the *Aeneid*, Evander describes the monster Cacus as he looks on Hercules in terror. In this scene Cacus' vision shows how disturbed he is:

> tum primum nostri Cacum uidere timentem
> turbatumque *oculis*, fugit ilicet ocior Euro
> speluncamque petit, pedibus timor addidit alas. (8.222–4)
> (Then for the first time our people saw Cacus afraid and disturbed in his eyes; he flees swifter than the East wind and seeks his cave, as fear has given his feet wings.)

In *M* the -*is* termination of *oculis* is barely legible, occurring as it does on one of the worst preserved folios of the manuscript. The γ manuscript alone preserves an alternative reading: *oculos*.

If the reading *oculi*, which Servius attests "others" preserve, were to be accepted (as it is by Sabbadini), then whose eyes are referred to here would be at issue, as in that case *oculi* would be taken to agree with *nostri*. Thus Servius writes, "Others read 'oculi' and accept [the reading] from those who came before them, '[our] eyes saw him, disturbed'" (Servius, ad 8.223). The accusative *oculos* cannot be entirely dismissed, though only the γ manuscript preserves this reading. All other relevant manuscripts read *oculis*, which is either ablative of specification or dative of reference. My own autopsy of the Mediceus seems to substantiate *oculis* in that manuscript.

After weighing all the evidence, one comes to a point of decision. Inasmuch as the spectacle of Hercules and Cacus prefigures the final clash of Aeneas and Turnus, the reading *oculi* (referring to the audience's gaze) seems to me most palatable. Still, the *lectio difficilior* – *oculos* – as well as the reading *oculis*, preserved in the majority of manuscripts including the Mediceus, cannot be ruled out.

Aeneid 10.558

Aeneid 10.558 is a particularly interesting case. This line, which has two key textual variants, reads in the editions of Sabbadini, Geymonat, Perret, and Mynors as follows:

istic nunc, metuende, iace. non te optima mater
condet humi <u>patrioque</u> <u>onerabit</u> membra sepulcro:
alitibus linquere feris, aut gurgite mersum
unda feret piscesque impasti uulnera lambent. (10.557–60)
(Now lie there, once a man worthy to be feared.
No noble mother will bury you in the earth and burden
your limbs with an ancestral tomb: you will be left for the
birds of the wild or, pulled under in a whirlpool, a wave
will hoist you and hungry fish lick at your wounds.)

Aeneas vaunts over the corpse of Tarquitus, who, like so many victims
of his fury in book 10, had appealed to him in vain. Aeneas tells Tarquitus
that his mother will not bury him in the earth and then adds something
else, which is the part of the line in question. As it stands now, Tarquitus'
noble mother is said to wish to "burden [his] limbs with an ancestral
tomb," which only makes sense if we assume that the entire phrase is to
be viewed as virtually tautological with *condet humi* ("bury [him] in the
earth").

To arrive at this reading, the editors must accept the reading of the
manuscripts *M* and *f*, which have the adjective *patrio* ("ancestral") modi-
fying *sepulchro* ("tomb"). *P¹* reads *patrique*, while the editors of *P²* and
several codices, among which are *R* and γ, read *patrioue*. Both of these
keep *mater* as the subject of the verb *onerabit*. Based on the *P* reading,
Gent once suggested the reading *patria atque* be added to *P*'s verb
onerauit. Leaving the tense of the verb aside for the moment, this reading
either indicates a change of subject or assumes that *patria* is an appositive
with *mater*. Yet if taking "mother" as the "mother land" works gram-
matically, it is less than satisfying for the sense of the text. The power of
Aeneas' vaunt is significantly diminished if he tells Tarquitus' corpse that
his mother country will not bury (or has not buried) him. Surely the
passage's profundity comes from his mother being denied the right to
offer proper burial.

The unity of the three major editions on the portion of the line
that begins with *patrioque* offers little consolation in light of the diversity among other manuscripts. There is also trouble with the verb, as
the *P* reading just cited indicates and as Geymonat's extensive apparatus
shows. The Wolfenbüttel manuscript reads *honerauit*, corrected by
a later editor (γ¹) to *honorauit*, while a fragment from the D'Orville
collection offers a more sensible future tense of that same verb,
honorabit.

Consideration of the Homeric Achilles speaking to the dying Hector may shed some light on Virgil's line. Hector pleads for his life by suggesting to Achilles that his body would be worthy of ransom:

> I ask you, by your life, your knees, and your parents,
> do not allow me to be dinner for the
> dogs by the ships of the Achaeans,
> but accept both bronze and abundant gold
> gifts that *my father and mother* will offer you,
> and grant my body be taken back home, that
> the *Trojans and their wives* may cast me, dead,
> upon the pyre. (*Il.* 22.338–43)

Hector's appeal is based on the interest of both of his parents in his body's return. Achilles retorts angrily, including both parents in his response:

> Dog, do not supplicate me by knees or *parents*,
> …
> Not even if they bring a ten- or twenty-fold ransom
> and weigh it out and even promise more hereafter,
> nor even if *Priam son of Dardanus should offer me your weight in gold!*
> *Nor will the lady your mother, thus laying you out*
> *on the funereal bed, make lament over the son she bore,*
> but dogs and birds will eat you completely. (*Il.* 22.345, 349–54)

Achilles' interest is in the vantage point of both parents – the recompensing father and the lamenting mother – which heightens the pathos of Hector's situation. Further, his mention of mother and father separately presents a contrast to the dogs and vultures that will replace them in the mutilation of Hector's corpse. In light of the Homeric model, it would be satisfying, though not necessary, to find in Virgil's text the involvement of both parents.

In his apparatus, Geymonat notes that the state of the Codex Veronensis for this text is dubious. My own close inspection of this codex with ultraviolet light – though admittedly the parchment may have degenerated since Geymonat performed his study in the mid-1960s – suggests that there is at least a possibility that the reading of lines 557–8 could be reconstructed as follows:

> non te optima mater
> condet humi *paterue honorabit* membra sepulcro.

(Your noble mother will not bury you in the earth
or your father dignify your limbs with a tomb.)

Though autopsy of *V* is admittedly inconclusive, this reconstruction
seems preferable, for it better reflects the Homeric model by mentioning
both parents. On this reconstruction we find both the "best mother"
(557), who would wish to bury her son but cannot, and the father, who
could have honored his son with a tomb but will be prevented from
doing so.

This emendation demands not only paleographical analysis but critical
and comparative investigation of the context. The scholar confronted
with such a textual challenge engages in a different sort of code breaking
than that of the general reader. Nevertheless, the work of the paleographer does ultimately concern even the casual reader

Conclusion

In the first chapter of this book, we saw that Virgil appropriated and
personalized the epic code he inherited. Virgil's great contribution to the
epic code is his expansion of it, his combination of the constancy of classical models with Alexandrian flair. Within three hundred years of Virgil's
death, his seventeen volumes of poetry were transferred to codices, the
collation of which produces the critical editions on which we rely for
appreciation of the "original" Latin and from which translations are
rendered.

Such a translation is, in one sense, obviously at a far remove from the
autograph of Virgil; yet this gap can be bridged if the reader approximates
the Model Reader, developing an appreciation of the epic code, the late
antique codex, the preservation and proliferation of medieval manuscripts, the complexity required for crafting a critical edition, the interpretation of the critical edition by literary critics, and, finally, the work
of the modern translator.

The reader who would seek to know better the Virgil that is his text,
therefore, has embarked on an odyssey far wilder than Aeneas' voyages.
We have now come to the last portion of this journey, namely the way
that Virgil's work has been received and reinterpreted at various points
throughout this process. German scholars refer to this aspect of an
author's influence as *Nachleben*, to a brief consideration of which we may
now turn.

Notes

1 Edmund Thomas, *Monumentality and the Roman Empire: Architecture in the Antonine Age* (Oxford, 2007), 169.

2 E. M. Thompson, *A Handbook of Greek and Latin Palaeography* (London, 1901; rpt. Chicago, 1980), 54–61; Fabrizio Pesando, *Libri e Biblioteche* (Rome, 1994), 17–22; Anthony Grafton and Megan Williams, *Christianity and the Transformation of the Book: Origen, Eusebius, and the Library of Caesarea* (Cambridge, MA, 2006), 10.

3 L. D. Reynolds and N. G. Wilson, *Scribes and Scholars: A Guide to the Transmission of Greek and Latin Literature* (Oxford, 1968; 3rd edn., 1991), 22–34. 2 Timothy 4:13. Cf. Colin H. Roberts and T. C. Skeet, *The Birth of the Codex* (Oxford, 1983), 35.

4 The manuscript begins at *E.* 6.48. Cf. H. R. Fairclough, "Observations on Sabbadini's *Variorum* Edition of Virgil," *TAPA* 63 (1932), 216. Mario Geymonat, "Codici," *EV* 1 (1984), 833. L. D. Reynolds, "Virgil," in Reynolds (ed.), *Texts and Transmission: A Survey of the Latin Classics* (Oxford, 1984), 433–6. Regarding *M* as based on Virgil's autograph, cf. Geymonat (1984), 833. Fabio Stok and Giancarlo Abbamonte, "Intuizioni esegetiche di Pomponio Leto nel suo commento alle *georgiche* e all'*Eneide* di Virgilio," in *Esegesi dimenticate di autori classici*, ed. Carlo Santini and Fabio Stok (Pisa, 2008), 135–210, treat thoroughly Leto's redaction of Virgilian texts.

5 Cf. Armando Petrucci, "Virgilio nella cultura scritta Romana," in *Virgilio e noi*, ed. Franceso Della Corte (Genova, 1981), 65–9.

6 Robert Marichal, "Quelques apports à la tradition ancienne du texte de Virgile," *REL* 35 (1957), 81–4.

7 Geymonat (1984), 834f.; cf. Guglielmo Cavallo, "La cultura a Ravenna tra Corte e Chiesa, in Le sedi della cultura nell'Emilia Romagna," *L'alto medioevo* 1 (1983), 29–51. Cf. also Geymonat (2000), 306.

8 Most extensively, Erwin Rosenthal *The Illuminations of the Vergilius Romanus (Cod. Vat. Lat. 3867): A Stylistic and Iconographic Analysis* (Zürich, 1972), 43–88; cf. Geymonat (1984), 834.

9 Geymonat (1984), 835f.; further, Pierre de Nolhac, "Les peintures des manuscrits de Virgile," *MEFR* 4 (1884), 305–33. Carolus Zagemeister and Guilemus Wattenbach, *Exempla Codicum Latinorum Litteris Maiusculis Scriptorum* (Heidelberg, 1876), 3. On Pontano, see Letizia Panizza, "The Quattrocento," in Peter Brand and Lino Pertile, *The Cambridge History of Italian Literature* (Cambridge, 1996), 150. On Bembo, see Carol Kidwell, *Pietro Bembo: Linguist, Lover, Cardinal* (Montreal, 2004), 257. Bembo also acquired some of Pontano's art collection; cf. Beatrice Cacciotti, "La tradizione degli '*Uomini Illustri*' nella collezione di Don Diego Hurtado de Mendoza ambasciatore tra Venezia e Roma (1539–1553)," in *De*

Martino: Occidente e alterità, ed. M. Massenzio and A. Alessandri (Rome, 2005), 232 n. 97.

10   Cf. Mario Geymonat, *I Codici G e V di Virgilio in Memorie dell'Istituto Lombardo* 29.3 (Milan, 1966), which reproduces the manuscript's readings. I have examined this manuscript under ultraviolet light; I thank Mons. Piazzi for his courtesy.

11   For the precise citations, see Geymonat (1984), 834–5. E. A. Lowe, *Codices Latini antiquiores* IV, Italy: Perugia–Verona (Oxford, 1947), no. 498, xxv and 27. Mario Geymonat, *"Arithmetic and Geometry in Ancient Rome: Surgeons, Intellectuals, and Poets,"* forthcoming; cf. Fabio Troncarelli, "Thrice-born Boethius: The Last of the Romans from Late Antiquity to Renaissance," in *Thrice-born Latinity*, ed. Brian P. Copenhaver (Turnhout, forthcoming).

12   Geymonat (2000), 307; Reynolds (1984), 436. The original Latin phrase was *explicitus est liber or explicitum est uolumen*, meaning, "the book (or roll) has been unwound" (Anthony Grafton, "On the Scholarship of Politian and Its Context," *Journal of the Warburg and Courtauld Insitutes* 40 [1977], 151; Thompson [1980], 59). Qua conjugated verb, *explicit* does not exist, for the *explicare* is an -a- stem; therefore "here ends" should have been *explicat* but was written as *explicit* by analogy with *incipit liber*, the designation of a book's beginning. Regarding the contents of the Sangalliensis, one finds *G*. 4.345–419, with the exception of lines 363, 382, and 401. Other parts preserved include *G*. 4.535–66, *Aen*. 1.381–418, 685–722; 3.191–227 (less line 209), 457–531, less lines 475, 494, and 513; *Aen*. 4.1–37, less line 19; *Aen*. 6. 655–9, 674–724, less lines 685–7.

13   Geymonat (1984), 836; Reynolds (1984), 436. Further, see A. Pratesi, "Osservazione paleografiche (e non) sui Codices Vergiliani antiquiores," in *Atti del convegno mondiale scientifico su Virgilio, 19–24 sett. 1981* (Milan, 1984), 223.

14   Carl Nordenfalk, *Vergilius Augusteus* (Graz, 1976). Geymonat (1984), 836, suggests an early sixth-century date; cf. also Geymonat (1984), 836.

15   See Geymonat (1984), 836 and Geymonat (2000), 310; cf. also B. Bischoff, *Die alten Namen in lateinischen Schriftarten*, in *Mittelalterliche Studein I* (Stuttgart, 1966), 1–5.

16   Geymonat (2000), 310; also Geymonat (1984), 837.

17   For an example beyond those given here, cf. Gian Biagio Conte, *Poetry of Pathos: Studies in Virgilian Epic*, ed. S. J. Harrison, tr. Elaine Fantham and Glenn Most (Oxford, 2007), 212–18.

18   Martin L. West, *Textual Criticism and Editorial Technique Applicable to Greek and Latin Texts* (Stuttgart, 1973) 11; Eduard Norden, *Die Geburt des Kindes: Geschichte einer religiösen Idee* (Leipzig/Berlin, 1924), 62 n. 2. Cf. Chiara Guadagno, "Riflessioni su Virg. *Ecl.* 4.60–63," *Vichiana* 9 (2007), 41–53.

19 Norden (1924), 62–3; Cf. Ethel Mary Stuart, "Qui non risere parenti," *CR* 40 (1926), 156. R. D. Williams, "Virgil *Eclogues* 4.60–63," *CP* 71 (1976), 119–21. See Clausen, ad 62, 144. E. Coleiro, *An Introduction to Vergil's Bucolics with a Critical Edition of the Text* (Amsterdam, 1979), 321, accepts *parentes* as accusative. Williams (1976), 119–20; Reynolds and Wilson (1991), 219.

20 These possibilities are neatly explained in Williams (1976), 119–21; cf. Clausen, ad 62, and Coleiro (1979), 321–2; cf. also Clausen, ad 62; J. P. Postgate, "An Early Corruption in Virgil," *CR* 16 (1902), 36–7.

21 Cf. C. J. Fordyce, *Catullus* (Oxford, 1961), ad 1.1 and D. F. S. Thomson, *Catullus* (Toronto, 1997), ad 1.1. Fordyce (1961), 84 discusses the change from *quoi* to *cui*. Sabbadini, ad loc. seems surprised that Quintilian forgets that he had seen *quoi* written as *cui* (cf. Quintilian 1.7.27).

7

The Virgilian Legacy

If we approach a poet without this prejudice we shall often
find that not only the best, but the most individual parts of
his work may be those in which the dead poets, his ancestors,
assert their immortality most vigorously.
T. S. Eliot (*Tradition and the Individual Talent*, 74)

Virgil's Nachleben is Western literature.
Gian Biagio Conte (*Latin Literature:*
A History, 284)

In the first chapter of this book, we considered the importance of Turcius
Rufius Apronianus Asterius to the Virgilian tradition. He painstakingly
punctuated and edited the Virgilian manuscript known as the Codex
Mediceus. His labor contributed to Virgil's legacy in a number of ways,
from the preservation of this text to the advancement of classical studies
in the late antique period, when a pagan author such as Virgil could easily
have been overshadowed by Christian texts. But Apronianus, we recall,
was interested in Rome's past and appreciated the richness and beauty
of Virgilian poetry. Though Apronianus is not the first person with whom
we associate the preservation of Virgil's legacy, his name should not be
forgotten.

Numerous books have been written on the Virgilian tradition, prominent among which is the recent tome of Ziolkowski and Putnam. Large
as it is, this contribution covers only the first fifteen hundred years of
Virgil's influence; earlier work on this topic had already treated various
aspects of Virgilian *Nachleben* after the Renaissance. This chapter will not
go beyond these detailed discussions but rather will simply touch upon
the breadth of Virgil's influence with select examples of how Virgil's
legacy has expressed itself in the various fields of art and literature.

Caldwell has recently argued that Virgil's popularity has often depended on the appropriateness of his poetry's message to the events of a given age. Accordingly, inasmuch as the *Aeneid* is a foundational epic with nationalistic values that focuses on a single hero, it spoke to the values and politics of those living in eighteenth-century England. In nineteenth-century American society, democratic and egalitarian, Virgil did not fare as well.[1]

At first blush, Kallendorf's important contribution on Virgil in Venice of the cinquecento might be cited to support Caldwell.[2] Certainly sixteenth-century Venetian culture did fancy itself the new Rome, and Kallendorf has deftly shown that Virgil's *Aeneid* was appropriated by the ruling authorities to advance Venice's political and social agenda. Its widespread popularity reveals that the ruling elite in Venice saw that the poem could be employed to this end; even school notes and manuscript marginalia demonstrate that such an interpretation worked its way into the Venetian educational curriculum. Yet while Kallendorf details how the Venetians were able to appropriate the text, he nowhere suggests that such appropriation is a necessary precondition of the reception of Virgilian texts.

The quality of a work such as the *Aeneid* does not rest upon its political, communal, or even aesthetic appeal, but upon the reader's sense that the text points toward universal truths. As Conte's *Poetry of Pathos* demonstrates, Virgil's poetry conveys insight about the depth of the human experience. Thus, Conte argues, Virgil alone of ancient poets could give rise to two coexistent scholarly interpretations as divergent as the Harvard and European schools.

T. S. Eliot's famous essay, "What Is a Classic?" addresses this transcendent quality, and the quotation of Eliot cited at the outset of this chapter points toward Virgil's open-ended legacy, which this chapter will, if only very selectively, address.

Virgil in Antiquity

It is no understatement to say that every epic poet of the imperial period composed his poetry in the shadow of the *Aeneid*. No other poem left so large a mark on the Roman poetic landscape, nor was the impact of Virgil's poetry, particularly the *Aeneid*, gradual. Within a quarter century Ovid's *Metamorphoses* responded not simply to the *Aeneid* but to all of Virgil.

It would require several books, not merely a subsection of a chapter, to consider fully Virgil's impact on the *Metamorphoses*. Put simply, the *Metamorphoses* responds to Virgil in three significant ways. First, like the song of Silenus in the sixth *Eclogue*, the *Metamorphoses* is an Alexandrian cosmological epic that consists of multiple levels of narrative, often written as a tale-within-a-tale or via other related compositional techniques. Secondly, Ovid's *Metamorphoses* responds inversely to the *Georgics*. The *Metamorphoses* is also an ostensibly didactic epos, but, unlike the *Georgics*, which consists of several books of didactic instruction followed by an *epyllion*, Ovid's magnum opus presents several books of *epyllia* followed by a long didactic set piece. Ovid treats the epic tale of Aeneas merely as one event in all of history, which he rehearses from its inception. If in the *Aeneid*, Aeneas is synecdochic, representing all Romans, in the *Metamorphoses*, Aeneas is simply another character.[3]

Lucan's *Pharsalia* is also indebted to the *Aeneid*. Lucan crafts a pivotal event in Roman history, Caesar's victory over Pompey at Pharsalus, into an epic. With regard to the events of Roman history, Lucan's poem is seemingly more like the ecphrasis of the shield in *Aeneid* 8 than like the *Aeneid* as a whole. It also resumes and reverses the chief protagonists of the *Aeneid*. Caesar becomes Aeneas' successor, but he does not share all the heroic qualities of his forebear. Rather, he is a new Achilles, as flawed as that character is in Homer. Instead, Pompey is the tragic hero of the poem, a true and noble Roman stoic character, who is indebted to the Homeric and Virgilian representations of Hector, the finest hero of Troy other than Aeneas. Caesar, by contrast, is less compelling. He speaks with pathetic excuses to the goddess Roma about his action in crossing the Rubicon, recalling Aeneas' effete excuses to Dido in *Aeneid* 4.

Statius, too, owes much to Virgil both with regard to his use of Virgilian material for his battle scenes and, more especially, in his development of Theseus in his *Thebaid* as a confident hero based on Aeneas. Yet, as Hardie has shown, whereas Aeneas in his hesitancy and pathos reveals that he is a human hero, Statius' Theseus is poised, so much so that he is "a self-sufficient epic 'man.'"[4] Still, the *Thebaid*'s hero does reflect qualities of Aeneas, from his *pietas* to his bravery.

Valerius Flaccus' *Argonautica*, though obviously indebted to Apollonius Rhodius' work of the same name, also shares much with the *Aeneid*, in part because Valerius emphasizes the historical significance of Jason's quest just as Virgil endows Aeneas' quest with meaning for the future of Rome. Valerius adopts some Virgilian narrative elements, though he ingeniously reworks them by retaining roles of characters from the *Aeneid* but creating entirely different characters for these roles.

Of the imperial epics, Silius Italicus' *Punica* is in a sense the truest "successor" poem to Virgil's. The *Punica* is bound to Virgil's epic through the central theme of the Carthaginian enmity toward Rome, derived from Dido's curse in *Aeneid* 4. Like Lucan's *Pharsalia*, which is a contemporary reassessment through Caesar and Pompey of the *Aeneid's* final conflict between Turnus and Aeneas, the *Punica's* altercation of Scipio and Hannibal has a similar function. Through the connection to Dido's curse, Silius' epic fulfills, and in a sense completes, Virgil's epic more than any other of the imperial poems.

Late Antiquity through the *Aetas Vergiliana*

Even before Virgil's death, Q. Caecilius Epirota, a close friend of Gallus and one of Atticus' freedmen, held seminars on Virgil's works (*Suet. Gramm.* 16). After his death the *Aeneid* was edited by Plotius and Tucca, two of his friends and fellow poets. The *Aeneid* itself immediately became a regular part of the educational system. Gaius Julius Hyginus, a freed-man of Caesar who, Suetonius tells us, was given charge of the Palatine Library by Augustus (*Gramm.* 20), wrote a Virgilian commentary. As Reynolds and Wilson observe, Virgilian scholarship "was thus inaugu-rated by a younger contemporary of the poet himself."[5] Not many years later, the Flavian professor of rhetoric, Quintilian, canonized the *Aeneid* as Rome's epic (*Inst.* 10.85).

In an earlier chapter, we considered the work of the early Virgilian commentator, Servius, noting his reliance on Aelius Donatus, the teacher of St Jerome. Before Servius, imitators of Virgil outside the epic tradition had already emerged. For example, Ausonius (310–394) wrote *Eclogues* and "centos," a genre that he dubbed *opusculum ludicrum de seriis* ("a funny little work based on serious ones"). A cento, which represents "an extreme case of intertextuality,"[6] consists of pastiches of poetic lines from various places with no discernible reasoning behind the imitation. In his recent work on centos, McGill calls attention to this lack of reasoned redeployment of lines of Virgil, pointing up the centonists' stark infusing of "alien signifying properties" into words that were intended otherwise by the poet.[7] In the opening of the *Cento Nupitalis*, Ausonius offers an exposition of how he constructs the Virgilian cento. He states that it is the amusing business of memory to understand and collect the scattered bits of Virgil, the "blame" for which dismemberment Ausonius ascribes to none other than the Emperor Valentinian himself, who is portrayed as a devotee of the cento's form.

Not all imitations of Virgil were as humorous. For example, the fifth-century poet Sedulius closely imitates Virgil in a more traditional manner, appropriating and Christianizing numerous lines of Virgilian poetry. We recall that Apronianus, the early editor of the Codex Mediceus, was intimately involved with the publication of both Sedulius and Virgil, a connection based in part on those poets' close intertextual relationship and his care for both authors. Though few argue that Sedulius' imitations of Virgil are brilliant, they nevertheless well reflect Virgil's abiding poetic authority in Christian Rome during the first half of the fifth century.

Sedulius' near contemporary, Claudian, whose unfinished epic *De raptu Prosperpinae* was written at the end of the fourth century, also draws on Virgil in a similar manner, with imitations ranging from epic invocation to his use of storm imagery.[8] The vast dissemination of Virgilian manuscripts allowed writers from every part of the empire access to him, including Vernance Fortunat (sixth century), whose *Monumenta* includes over one hundred Virgilian echoes, while his contemporary Gregory of Tours has forty imitative lines. Meanwhile, as far away as Ireland, figures as important as Adomnán of Iona were involved with the care of Virgilian poetry through commentary and analysis.[9]

Closer to home, St Augustine shows many debts to Virgil, even if he intimates otherwise when describing how his misplaced devotion in his lament over Dido's death led him at first to fail to understand the gospel message (*Conf.* 1.13.20). Nevertheless, Augustine clearly patterns his peregrinations in the *Confessions* on Aeneas' wanderings, while his mother Monica stands as a kind of Dido figure. As Spence has noted, "Monica plays out the fulfilled Dido, not the foreshortened, frustrated version found in the *Aeneid*."[10]

The eighth and ninth centuries, sometimes called the *aetas Vergiliana*, saw a wide-ranging interest in Virgil, particularly in Alcuin, Ermoldus Nigellus, the Welsh poem *Cad Godden*, the *Carmina Cantabrigiensia*, and Fulbert of Chartres.[11] Epic themes with debt to Virgil appear soon also in French novels (*romans*) such as *Le Roman d'Enéas* (twelfth century). About the same time Dante makes Virgil the obvious inspiration not only for his *Inferno*, but arguably for the entire *Commedia*. As a character in Dante's text, Virgil serves as the later poet's escort just as the Sibyl had for Aeneas' katabasis in *Aeneid* 6. Qua character and author, therefore, Virgil is for Dante the only author fully to transcend temporal and textual boundaries to become a kind of living intertext and literary guide.

Less well known, perhaps, is the impact that Virgil had on the much younger contemporary of Dante, Boccaccio (1313–1375). In many ways, Boccaccio stands in relation to Dante as Ovid had to Virgil. Just as Dante's epic, like Virgil's, is a mission-driven journey of a hero toward a promised land, so Boccaccio's response, albeit in prose, is, like Ovid's, a work with exploding sensuality and a less clearly definable goal. Boccaccio, both in style and content, reacts to Dante and Virgil at once. Chaucer, too, could be mentioned here, as he was influenced by Boccaccio and, of course, was himself indebted to Virgil, particularly Virgil's portrait of Dido.[12]

By the late middle ages, Virgil's influence had spread, in no small part through the general proliferation of codices, and he enjoyed widespread popularity, particularly in England, as numerous English manuscripts reveal. Meanwhile, in a twelfth-century manuscript from Austria, one finds a depiction of Aeneas as a medieval knight with a helmet of the period and protective mail, mounted for a jousting match (Figure 7.1). Not only has Aeneas found a wide readership, it is a readership ready to bring the hero, properly attired, into medieval culture, riding a horse in combat, something for which Aeneas is not known in Virgil.[13]

Virgil and Renaissance/Post-Renaissance Literature

The importance of Virgil to Renaissance literature is rich and various. In Venice, the *Aeneid* became a symbol of renewed statehood, much the way that David became the symbol for Florence in the same period. In the fifteenth century, an interesting and highly literary development occurred. In contrast to the form of the cento, which saw the quixotic stitching together of Virgilian verses, writers such as Maffeo Vegio (1407–1458) went beyond imitation by continuing the *Aeneid* where the poet had left off. Though a contemporary of Vegio also made a beginning on such a project and, after Vegio, other poets attempted the same feat (e.g., Jan van Foreest and Simonet De Villeneuve, both seventeenth century), Vegio's *Supplement* or *Book XIII* of the *Aeneid*, rich in Virgilian emotional power, stands out. Although he wrote it at a very early age – it was published when he was only twenty-one – it is of remarkably high quality. His goal seems to have been to present Aeneas as a hero marked by classical virtue. Though several renaissance writers

Figure 7.1. Depiction of mounted Aeneas, Klosterneuburg manuscript (twelfth century). Codex CCl 742. Used by permission of Stift Klosterneuburg, Kultur und Tourismus, Stiftsmuseum, Austria.

continued other ancient poems (e.g., Ovid's *Fasti*, Lucan's *Pharsalia*, and Valerius Flaccus' *Argonautica*), none achieved the success of Vegio's *Supplement*, which received a commentary, was illustrated, is widely representative in surviving manuscripts, and, not long after it first appeared, was translated into several languages.[14]

The *Aeneid* was not the only work of Virgil's that authors of this period desired to imitate. Another Italian poet, Jocopo Sannazaro, wrote *Eclogues* in the manner of Virgil and, more famously, an *Arcadia*, consisting of a lyrical mixture of prose and poetry (1504).[15] As in Virgil's

Eclogues, this work is characterized by the struggle between urban and rural. This tension is emphasized by Sannazaro's main character, Sincero, journeying back and forth between the city (Naples) and the country-side. The sting of death abounds in this work, a feature not atypical of cinquecento (sixteenth-century) poetry, in which "even in Arcadia" there is an awareness of death.

Torquato Tasso (1544–1595) also draws on Virgil in his account of the First Crusade's siege of the holy city in his epic *Gerusalemme liberata* (*Jerusalem Delivered*, 1574). Tasso's debt to *Aeneid* 7–12 for the martial aspects of his poem is clear, as his character Allecto is modeled on Virgil's fury of the same name. Though, as Nash suggests in the introduction to his 1987 translation of Tasso, not a page of Dante lacks an imitation of Virgil, Tasso by contrast engages Virgilian poetry in a somewhat less programmatic and more eclectic fashion, keeping his primary focus on the *Aeneid*. The hero of the *Gerusalemme*, Godfrey of Bouillon, is clearly indebted to Virgil's Aeneas in his sense of steadfast devotion, though obviously Christianized and, in light of his mission, zealously so.

Writing in the same period as Tasso, Portuguese poet Luís Vaz de Camões (1524–1580) produced the epic *Os Lusíadas* (1572). The content of the *Lusíadas* focuses on the numerous Portuguese exploratory voyages that occurred during the fifteenth and sixteenth centuries. Defining the Portuguese nationalism in part by contrast with the Saracens, Camões lays out the destiny of the Portuguese people in a manner comparable to Virgil's exposition of mission in the *Aeneid*. Camões frequently alludes to the *Aeneid*: Vasco da Gama, one of the poem's chief heroes, is explicitly compared to Aeneas in the prologue (*Canto* 1.12).

Vida of Cremona's *Christiad* (1535) adapts several themes of Virgil's *Aeneid* to Christian understanding. One such example of Vida's allusive dexterity can be seen in his description of the handing over of Christ to Pontius Pilate in *Christiad* 2.965–75:[16] in *Aeneid* 2, Sinon, a captive brought before the Trojans by shepherds secures his release and brings about destruction through lies; in the case of Christ, when the good shepherd is bound and brought before the Roman authority, he is not believed (despite speaking the truth) and incurs personal destruction but effects salvation for humanity.

In *Paradise Lost*, John Milton (1608–1674) invokes the Holy Ghost to help "justifie the wayes of God to men" (*PL* 1.26). As Kallendorf has richly demonstrated in his contribution to the *Classics and the Uses of Reception* (ed. Martindale and Thomas, 2006), Milton's epic is both psychologically and allusively indebted to Virgil. Burrow whose contribution is discussed in the Further Reading, has shown some of the ways in which Milton's allusive program is executed, as has Quint. Two of Quint's examples include how Virgil's Carthage and Rome are both folded into Milton's Pandemonium. Milton uses the storm of *Aeneid* 1, too, for his description of the lake of Hell in *PL* 1 and for Christ's creation of the cosmos in *PL* 7.[17] The compelling depiction of Satan is at least in a general sense influenced by Virgil's sympathy even with characters who are ostensibly not sympathetic, as Brooks Otis once demonstrated. Though his content is thoroughly different from Virgil's, Milton's infusion of mission and pathos into *Paradise Lost* reflects impressively the general outlook of Virgil's magnum opus.

In the post-Renaissance period, numerous other authors drew heavily on Virgil, from Rabelais to Paul Scarron. The early nineteenth century saw the publication of Joel Barlos' *Columbiad*, an epic that casts Columbus in the role of Virgil's hero as a discoverer of a new world.[18] In the twentieth century, Virgil's poetic authority, if less broadly disseminated, has remained undiminished. Near the beginning of the century, widely popular writers, such as Axel Munthe (1857–1949) drew on Virgil allusively to enrich their literary programs. A polymath and personal physician to Sweden's Queen Victoria, Munthe composed his quasi-autobiographical novel entitled *The Story of San Michele* (1929), in which Virgil's Aeneas provides a model for the main character's long journey toward Capri. In it, Munthe, like Aeneas, is the restorer of his home. Whereas Aeneas lays the groundwork for Roman culture in Italy, Munthe brings his own culture to Italy by building his house on top of an ancient imperial villa.

Possibly driven by the political and military events of the 1930s, a shift from delicate allusions such as Munthe's to a strong claim to Virgil as the poet par excellence occurs within fifteen years of the publication of Munthe's work. At the height of the Second World War (1943), the Virgil Society was founded in London by a group that included the American ex-patriot poet T. S. Eliot. Eliot offered an inaugural address to the group, noting Virgil's style as characterized by a gravity and universality that defines and transcends the culture of Rome: "Virgil's maturity of mind, and the maturity of his age, are exhibited in ... awareness of history." In an often-quoted line, Eliot proclaims Virgil to be "our classic, the classic of all Europe."[19]

Writing just at that time, Austrian author Hermann Broch made Virgil the central character of his best-known work, *Der Tod des Vergils*; the English version (*The Death of Virgil*) appeared at the same time as the German version (1945). Composed in a stream-of-consciousness style that mixes poetry and prose, the novel describes the last hours of Virgil's life. Set in Brundisium, the town where the poet died, Broch's Virgil reflects on his life through the lens of pathos, an outlook influenced by Broch's personal history, for he had known suffering. A Jew, Broch had been imprisoned by the Nazi regime in the late 1930s. He thus offers a broad perspective of the role of literature in culture, a perspective that he fancies Virgil to have had, for Virgil was also a figure standing at cultural crossroads that paralleled Broch's own.[20]

A poem from Robert Lowell's collection, *The Mills of the Kavanaughs*, entitled "Falling Asleep over the *Aeneid*," appeared just after Broch's novel and Eliot's treatise. Lowell constructs the poem around the funeral of Pallas from *Aeneid* 11, a passage with which his character's sleepiness and the ubiquitous sense of death dovetail. Lowell's poem in many ways anticipates the later "two voices" argument (sometimes referred to as the Harvard school). Ralph Johnson's thoughtful analysis points up Lowell's struggle with the heavy toll of war and his personal concerns about American "imperialism" that echo Virgil's dualistic quality.[21]

It would be a long process to flesh out the numerous works since the middle of the last century that are in some way indebted to Virgil's poetry. A few recent works stand out: Wendell Berry, who is a modern-day Virgil in terms of agricultural poetry, certainly is indebted to the wisdom of Virgil's *Georgics* for his own work of wisdom, *The Farm* (1995). Virgil's characters, too, have enjoyed a life beyond his own text. Recently, Jo Graham released a novel entitled *Black Ships* (2008) that retells Aeneas' wanderings from Troy, while Ursula LeGuin's *Lavinia* (2007) tells the story of that quiet character and her courage to become Aeneas' wife. Beyond such adaptations, Virgil has maintained a place on vendors' bookshelves through several fresh translations of each of his works, and Colin Burrow has devoted an entire essay to the importance of English translations in the dissemination and preservation of Virgil.[22] David Ferry's translation (1999) of the *Eclogues* is lively and engaging, and John Van Sickle's new volume of translated and annotated *Eclogues* (forthcoming) will also be a major contribution. Janet Lembke's *Virgil's Georgics* (Yale, 2005) is a graceful rendering of the poem, and Christina Chew has also recently published a lively translation (2002), as has Peter Fallon (2006). Among all modern translators of Virgil, however, the name of the late Robert Fagles stands out: his version of the *Aeneid* is truly remarkable, supplanting even the fine editions of Mandelbaum (1961) and Fitzgerald (1981). Fagles' poetic range will allow his work to stand for many years as the *Aeneid* translation for our time.

Finally, I will offer an observation on just how far Virgil's cultural influence has spread. In his discussion of ideological treatments of Virgil, Ziolkowski demonstrates that Virgil has been appropriated by mystics, ideologues, fascists, and Christians; in the Gigante collection, Kobayashi has also considered how Virgil has been received in Japan.[23] More recently, in a startling piece entitled, "Comrade Aeneas," Tsao proclaims, "how China's recent history resembled the miserable plight of the Trojans! Troy was besieged by the Greeks, the old China by imperialist forces."[24] Such descriptions amply demonstrate the remarkable flexibility of the Virgilian legacy.

Virgil in Art

Like all sections in this chapter, a book could be written on Virgil in art; and, as in other cases, this is already the case. I refer to the now somewhat outdated study of Tervarent, which work, with others like it, offers but a glimpse of Virgil's vast impact.[25]

Were one to consider only the *Eclogues* and the *Georgics*, that vastness would not be as daunting. The *Eclogues* were illustrated in the manuscript tradition, and the content of the particular poems illustrated suits the artist's imagination, with numerous pleasant vistas populated by livestock and singing goatherds. Among later Renaissance and post-Renaissance artists one thinks of Poussin's portrayal of shepherds in Arcadia (1638) in the Louvre or Guercino's famous *Et in Arcadia Ego* (1546), now housed in Rome's Galleria Borghese. In that painting, two young shepherds stare at a skull, under which is inscribed "Et in Arcadia Ego," meaning death is to be found even in Arcadia. This gloomy theme that goes back to the pathos present in Virgil's *Eclogues* is preserved by Evelyn Waugh in the Latin title (*Et in Arcadia Ego*) of the first chapter of his twentieth-century English novel *Brideshead Revisited* (1945).

The *Georgics* are best represented through illustrations of the episode in them that is ostensibly the least didactic, namely the story of Orpheus and Eurydice found in the Aristaeus epyllion of *Georgic* 4. In the eighteenth century, Antonio Cavona created a superb statue of Eurydice being pulled into the Underworld as she speaks words of farewell, her left hand with palm up extended in a pathetic gesture (Museo Correr, Venice). In the fifthteenth century, Giovanni Bellini had already made Orpheus the subject of one of his paintings, a theme also taken up about a century later by Rubens (1636) and Savery (1628).

The *Aeneid*, rich in episodes that invite illustration, has received the most attention by artists. We have seen in the previous chapter that several major manuscripts preserve illustrations, the prototypes of which can in some cases be traced to the Severan period (193–211). Best known among these is Aeneas in the storm making his opening speech; another famous one is that of Dido on her pyre.

In the Renaissance, characters and scenes from the *Aeneid* were widely illustrated. Michelangelo (1475–1564) included a Sibyl of Cumae in the painting of the Sistine Chapel's ceiling, thereby connecting the Christian present with classical models. The Sibyl remained a subject of illustration for other artists, though the way she was depicted varied widely. Domenichino, for example, painting about a century after Michaelangelo, portrays a much younger Sibyl who gazes quizzically, holding in her hands a scroll with musical notation and her book of oracles. Further illustrations of the Sibyl include Maffei's portrait of her with Aeneas in the Underworld (1650), as well as that of Joseph Turner, who portrays Aeneas and the Sibyl by Lake Avernus (ca. 1800).

Aeneas, too, has frequently been the central subject of paintings, from Federico Barocci's *La fuga di Enea da Troia* (1598; Figure 7.2) to

Figure 7.2. Flight of Aeneas from Troy by Federico Barocci (1526–1612). Galleria Borghese, Rome, Italy. Photo Credit: Scala/Art Resource, New York.

Raphael's depiction of the same in his "Incendio del Borgo" (Vatican Palace, 1514); in the next century Simon Vouet also produced a similar painting.

Dido, of course, is another central character in numerous paintings of Renaissance and post-Renaissance art. In the fifteenth century, Francesco di Giorgio, for example, portrays the meeting of Dido and Aeneas, and few subjects were as popular as Dido in the two centuries following, in part because she became a central character in numerous operas. Artists such as Rubens depict her dismounting after the hunt, while nineteenth-century artist John Atkinson Grimshaw painted a haunting portrait of Dido standing alone before an altar, scantily clad, against the backdrop of gloomily overcast Carthage. In the first half of the twentieth century, German artist César Klein painted a portrait of Dido, as well.

Other topics from the *Aeneid* are also widely represented. While the Hellenistic Belvedere Laocoon (portrayed somewhat similarly in a seventeenth-century painting of El Greco) may be the most well known, further topics range from Aeolus loosing the winds to the portrait of Aeneas hanging up Turnus' armor (French school) to the Trojan horse to the death of Turnus, a linocut of which Swedish artist Jan Thunholm rendered as recently as 2005.

Themes from the *Aeneid* are not uncommon in sculpture, as well. In seventeenth-century baroque art, one thinks of Bernini's famous statue of Aeneas, Anchises, and Ascanius, housed in Rome's Galleria Borghese, and at the beginning of the next century Augustin Cayot's poignantly rendered suicidal Dido (Figure 7.3), his reception piece among the French artistic academy in 1711. Now housed in the Louvre, this baroque and emotive piece befits the contemporary dramatic interest in Dido.[26]

Virgil in Music

Virtually every musical reference work reminds the reader that, beyond his mention of the *fistula* – i.e., syrinx or the pipes of Pan, also referred to as *calami* – Virgil makes no mention of music per se. Nevertheless, Virgilian themes have frequently been the subject of musical scores. The seventeenth century, in particular, saw the production of two important works based on Virgil: Cavalli's *La Didone* (1641) and Purcell's *Dido and Aeneas* (1689). The second half of Berlioz' *Les Troyens* (1859), entitled *Les Troyens à Carthage*, is also modeled on *Aeneid* 4.[27] Two centuries before Berlioz, Cavalli had brought Dido to the stage in his

Figure 7.3. Cayot, Augustin (1667–1722). Death of Dido (La mort de Didon). Marble, MR 1780. Louvre, Paris. Photo Credit: Erich Lessing/Art Resource, New York.

Didone of 1641. Cavalli had his own fondness for classical themes, as his operas treat numerous subjects from classical history or literature. *La Didone* was only Cavalli's third of many operas, his first on a Virgilian theme. Even more than his earlier Ovidian operas, *La Didone* catapulted Cavalli to fame, allowing him to be one of the most productive writers of opera in the seventeenth century.[28]

The British composer Purcell's opera *Dido and Aeneas* (1689) appeared not long after Cavalli's work. Purcell's operatic works, the culmination of a brief but brilliant career, were but a small portion of his musical production. While an important inspiration for *Dido and Aeneas* would seem to have been Busenello's libretto in Cavalli's *La Didone*, Purcell also responds to Virgil's text directly, offering a stimulating alternative to Virgil's steadfast Aeneas. In the closing scene of Purcell's opera, for example, Aeneas returns to Dido, stating plainly that he is willing to stay in Carthage for her. Purcell's rendition of Dido's final lament, too, reinterprets and renders afresh the nobility and misery of Virgil's heroine: Dido will not accept Aeneas' contrition; rather, like Virgil's heroine, she embraces death nobly:

> Thy hand, Belinda, darkness shades me,
> On thy bosom let me rest,
> More I would, but death invades me;
> Death is now a welcome guest.
>
> When I am laid in earth, may my wrongs create
> No trouble in thy breast.
> Remember me, but ah! forget my fate.

The eighteenth century saw the proliferation of similar works, with an impetus coming from the great Italian poet Metastasio's *Didone abbandonata*, set to music by Domenico Sarro (1724). At the end of that century, there were further variations on this theme,[29] including Joseph Martin Kraus' *Aeneas i Cartago*, written specifically for the opening of the Stockholm's Royal Theater in 1799, after which the popularity of the Virgilian theme did not wane.

Berlioz' remarkable *Les Troyens* occurred within a century of Kraus' opera. Berlioz knew Virgil's work well, a result of his diverse education, that ranged from literature to medical studies to music. *Les Troyens* is an opera on an epic scale that, as the *Aeneid* once did, countered the more delicate works of the period, such as Gluck's *Orfeo ed Euridice*, itself inspired by Virgil's account of the tale in the fourth *Georgic*. The return to simpler less baroque diction among the Italian school of the seventeenth century known as the Arcadian Academy, too, contributed to a trend toward a more "Alexandrian" style, to which Berlioz' work, written at the urging of Liszt, stands as a contemporary counterbalance. Still, Berlioz' epic work is not merely imitative of Virgil; he introduces Cassandra as a major character, expanding on Virgil's mere passing reference to her during the fall of Troy.[30]

Even in the current century, Virgil's presence abides. The contemporary pop music singer Dido appears to be responsive to Virgil's legacy.

While Dido's musical persona does not seem to assert any connection with the queen of Carthage beyond what her name alone suggests, nevertheless the fourth song of her album, "No Angel," is interesting. In it she sings the lament of a woman who has lost her lover, which, if generically removed from Purcell's libretto, shares with it epic passion. A portion of the lyrics from the song, fittingly entitled "My Lover's Gone," identifies Dido afresh with that tradition: "Returns no more, I will not watch the ocean, / my lover's gone, no earthly ships will ever / Bring him home again" (5–7).[31]

Virgil in Film

While Virgil's legacy has been preserved remarkably well in art and music, one cannot say as much for the medium of film. Obviously neither the *Eclogues* nor the *Georgics* are easily adapted to the silver screen. More surprising, however, is the fact that there are very few big screen versions of the *Aeneid*. Among the few existing, one finds the poorly executed *The Avenger* (1962), directed by Giorgio Rivalta; this film, also known as *The Last Glory of Troy*, starred the then-famous body-builder Steve Reeves as Aeneas.[32] A better film, though representing only the second book of the *Aeneid*, is the production entitled *Troy* (2004), directed by Wolfgang Peterson, with a screenplay by David Benioff. That film stars Brad Pitt as Achilles and features Frankie Fitzgerald as Aeneas, though admittedly Aeneas has a limited a role.

Only once, some forty years ago, did the *Aeneid* receive adequate attention in film. A six-hour, made-for-television Italian film directed by Franco Rossi entitled *L'Eneide*, starring Giulio Brogi as Aeneas, is the best film version of Virgil's epic. No attempt in English or any other language approximates the quality of Rossi's work.

Virgil in Society and Virgilian Societies

Outside of the arts, Virgil's legacy has been preserved formally in two societies. We have already briefly discussed the Virgil Society, located in England, earlier in this chapter. That group, formed during the Second World War, was founded on the basis of "the love of the poetry of Virgil," who "sought to bring home to the Romans of his day that … a people with a great past is a people with great responsibilities which should look to a great future; and ... he sought to remind his fellow-countrymen of their pristine virtues."[33]

Some six years earlier Virgilophiles in Italy and the United States had formed the Vergilian Society "to promote the study of Vergil by means of lectures, conferences," and the like; its first president was the celebrated archaeologist, Amadeo Maiuri. Based in Cumae, the Vergilian Society has been an important institution for the promotion of educational exchange between American and Italian scholars and has a positive influence in both the scholarly community and local culture of Campania.

Conclusion

Though the *Aeneid*, Virgil's final work, ends with death, the poem looks beyond the grave to the foundation of a new nation, Rome, imbued with purpose and a strong sense of mission, which, together with dialogue and wisdom, are the principal themes of Virgil's poetry. These themes and the style that supports them, rich in sympathy and encoded with innumerable allusions, inform and engender Virgil's great legacy. Restaurants and ships named after a Virgilian heroine are not in and of themselves sufficient evidence of that legacy, nor does Virgil's relevance lie in merely the occasional appropriation of his *Aeneid* by culture or a political leader for imperialistic purposes.[34]

The last words that Martin Luther wrote concisely allude to the profundity of Virgil's legacy: "Don't dare assail this divine *Aeneid*, but, prostrate, adore the tracks it leaves. We are but beggars: this is true."[35] Even a legendary *Aeneid*-toting football coach barely reflects the breadth of Virgil's influence, the power of his legacy or the impact he has had on human thought. Rather, the relevance of all of Virgil's poetry lies in the way his three major themes transcend the text, leaving the reader with an abiding sense of Virgilian pathos and humanity that is not subject to time or place.

Notes

1 Tanya M. Caldwell, *Virgil Made English: The Decline of Classical Authority* (New York, 2008), 216 *et passim*.
2 Craig Kallendorf, *Virgil and the Myth of Venice: Books and Readers in the Italian Renaissance* (Oxford, 1999), esp. 31–8.

3   Philip Hardie, *The Epic Successors of Virgil: A Study in the Dynamics of a Tradition* (Cambridge, 1993), 4–13.

4   Hardie (1993), 48.

5   L. D. Reynolds and N. G. Wilson, *Scribes and Scholars: A Guide to the Transmission of Greek and Latin Literature* (Oxford, 1968; 3rd edn., 1991), 27.

6   Hans Armin Gärtner and Wolf-Lüder Liebermann, *New Pauly* 3, s.v. "Cento," 115.

7   Scott McGill, *Virgil Recomposed: The Mythological and Secular Centos in Antiquity* (Oxford, 2005), 18; on Valentian, 6.8.

8   Cf. Kevin Tsai, "Hellish Love: Genre in Claudian's *De raptu Prosperpinae*," *Helios* 34 (2007), 46–8, 52f.

9   Louis Holtz, "La Survie de Virgile dans le Haut Moyen Âge," in R. Chevallier (ed.), *Présence de Virgile: Actes du Colloque des 9,11, et 12 Décembre 1976* (Paris, 1978), 215–19.

10 Sarah Spence, *Rhetorics of Reason and Desire: Virgil, Augustine, and the Troubadours* (Ithaca, 1988), 59.

11 L. Traube, *Vorlesungen und Abhandlungen II: Einleintung in die lateinische Philologie des Mittelalters*, ed. P. Lehmann (Munich, 1911), 113. Cf. also Jan M. Ziolkowski and Michael C. J. Putnam (eds.), *The Virgilian Tradition: The First Fifteen Hundred Years* (New Haven, CT, 2008), 96–107.

12 Lao Paoletti, "Virgilio e Boccaccio," in R. Chevallier (ed.), *Présence de Virgile: Actes du Colloque des 9, 11, et 12 Décembre 1976* (Paris, 1978), 249–63. Cf. Ziolkowski and Putnam, 418f. and (on Chaucer), 145f.; also Craig Kallendorf, *The Virgilian Tradition: Book History and the History of Reading in Early Modern Europe* (Aldershot, 2007), 40–2.

13 Christopher Baswell, *Virgil in Medieval England: Figuring the* Aeneid *from the Twelfth Century to Chaucer* (Cambridge, 2006), 23, 285–308.

14 M. C. J. Putnam and James Hankins (eds.) *Maffeo Vegio: Short Epics* (Cambridge, MA, 2004). Cf. Craig Kallendorf, "*Maffeo Vegio: Short Epics*, ed. M. C. J. Putnam and J. Hankins (rev.)," *Vergilius* 50 (2004), xix, 216. Woodcuts were first printed in the edition of Brant-Güninger (1502) and were reproduced in the 1529 edition of Crespini, reproduced in Stefano Bonfanti with C. Bo, *Maffeo Vegio: Supplementum: Libro XIII dell'Eneide* (Milan, 1997), *passim*. Cf. also Kallendorf (2004), 217.

15 Giuseppe Gerbino, "The Madrigal and Its Outcasts: Marenzio, Giovannelli, and the Revival of Sannazaro's 'Arcadia,'" *Journal of Musicology* 21 (2004), 17f.

16 Noticed but not explained by Hardie (1993), 28 n. 21.

17 David Quint, "The Virgilian Coordinates of *Paradise Lost*," *MD* 52 (2004), 177–97.

18 Cf. John C. Shields, *The American Aeneas: Classical Origins of the American Self* (Knoxville, TN, 2001), 255–8. Shields' work is important, for beyond

Barlow he teases out numerous points of contact between Virgil's hero and the construction of the American psyche.

19　T. S. Eliot, *What Is a Classic? An Address Delivered before the Virgil Society on the 16th of October 1944* (London, 1945), 20, 31; further, see Ziolkowski (1993), 132–3.

20　Luciano Zagari, "Harmann Broch e l'antimito di Virgilio," in Marcello Gigante (ed.), *La Furtuna di Virgilio* (Naples, 1986), 317–90; M. M. Sarrabezolles, "Hermann Broch, 'Der Tod des Vergil' ou 'L'Éneide' en autriche a l'Époque de l'Anschluss (Une psychanalyse vraisembable du génie de Virgile)," in Chevallier (1978), 443–55; Charles-Marie Ternes, "Le Dialogue entre le Prance et le Poète dans 'Der Tod des Vergil' de Hermann Broch," in Chevallier (1978), 457–68; Fiona Cox, *Aeneas Takes the Metro: The Presence of Virgil in Twentieth-Century French Literature* (Oxford, 1999), 29–56. For a detailed analysis of Broch and Virgil, Theodore Ziolkowski, *Virgil and the Moderns* (Princeton, NJ, 1993), 203–22, esp. 220: "Broch knew little of the historical Virgil, using him merely as a figure upon which to impose his own views and concerns." Cf. also Michèle Lowrie, "Blanchot and the Death of Virgil," *MD* 52 (2004), 211–12, who considers Blanchot's view of Virgil, particularly in response to Broch.

21　W. R. Johnson, "Robert Lowell's American Aeneas," *MD* 52 (2004), 227–39; cf. Ziolkowski (1993), 181.

22　Colin Burrow, "Virgil in English Translation," in Charles Martindale (ed.), *The Cambridge Companion to Virgil* (Cambridge, 1997), 21–37.

23　Kozue H. Kobayashi, "Virgil in Japan," in Marcello Gigante (ed.), *La Fortuna di Virgilio* (Naples, 1986), 507–23. See Ziolkowski (1993), 27–56.

24　Gene C. Tsao, *Aeneas from China* (Bloomington, IN, 2005).

25　Guy de Tervarent, *Présence de Virgile dans l'Art* (Brussels, 1967) focuses primarily on sixteenth- and seventeenth-century French painting, including select bucolic vistas based the *Eclogues* and, more prominently, the paintings of the Palais-Royal's Galerie d'Enée; cf. also Peter Grau and Hans Ludwig-Oertel, Carmina Illustrata: *Zur Veranschlaulichung von* Odysee, *Aeneis und* Metamorphosen (Bamberg, 2004).

26　Michael Levey, *Painting and Sculpture in France, 1700–1789* (New Haven, CT, 1995), 76.

27　For a general discussion, cf. Warren Anderson, T. J. Mathiesen, and Robert Anderson, s.v. "Virgil," in *Oxford Music* (Oxford, 2007, the updated edition of the *Grove Dictionary of Music and Musicians*, New York, 1920). Cf. also the detailed studies of David Cairns, "Berlioz and Virgil," *Proceedings of the Royal Musical Association* 45 (1968–9), 97–110.

28　Simon Towneley Worsthorne, *Venetian Opera in the Seventeenth Century* (Oxford, 1954; rpt. 1984), 152.

29   These composers included Albioni, Galuppi, Porpora, Jommelli, Piccinni, Paisiello, and Rossini. Cf. Anderson, Mathiesen, and Anderson (2007); also, in the nineteenth century the operas of Paer (1810), Mercadante (1823), and Reissiger (1824) continued this tradition.

30   David Cairns, "*Les Troyens* and the *Aeneid*," *Responses: Musical Essays and Reviews* (New York, 1973), 88–110. Cf. also William Fitzgerald, "*Fatalis Machina*: Berlioz's *Les Troyens*," *MD* 52 (2004), 206–7.

31   R. A. Smith, "Dido as Vatic Diva: A New Voice for the Persona of the Lost Lover," *CJ* 98 (2003), 435–6.

32   Jon Solomon, *The Ancient World in the Cinema* (New Haven, CT, 2001), 129.

33   From the preface, "The Virgil Society," H. E. Bulter, T. S. Eliot, J. W. Mackail, A. Moncrieff, R. W. More, V. Sackville-West, and R. Spaeight, in Eliot (1945), 3. Cf. www.virgilsociety.org.uk/. On the Vergilian Society, see www.vergil.clarku.edu/.

34   One such restaurant is "Elyssa Dido," 85 Orchard Street, New York; the ship is the Second World War AA class cruiser HMS *Dido*, Royal Navy, launched 1939 and scrapped 1958. The football coach referred to is Joe Paterno, coach of the Penn State Nittany Lions; Paterno writes about the importance of the *Aeneid* to him in, *Paterno: By the Book* (New York, 1989).

35   "Hanc tu ne divinam Aeneida tenta, sed uestigia pronus adora. Wir sein pettler; hoc est uerum." See Carl P. E. Springer, "Arms and the Theologian: Martin Luther's *Adversus Armatum Virum Cochlaeum*," *IJCT* 10 (2003), 41.

8

Further Reading

This short chapter is meant merely to highlight works of scholarship that have influenced this study and can facilitate further consideration of Virgil. In light of the vast quantity of Virgilian scholarship, these select works are presented section by section rather than en masse.

Virgilian scholarship boasts of more than a few seminal works. Viktor Pöschl's, *The Art of Vergil: Image and Symbol in the* Aeneid (tr. Seligson, 1962), considers individual characters and addresses universal human issues, while Brooks Otis' *Virgil: A Study in Civilized Poetry* (1963) also enlarges on these themes, visiting the topic of structural considerations, as well. Otis' signal contribution is a discussion of Virgil's subjective style. W. S. Anderson's *The Art of the* Aeneid (1969, rpt. 1989) is slight but powerful, while on a grander scale, G. N. Knauer's *Die Aeneis und Homer* (Göttingen, 1964) should be mentioned; Knauer painstakingly traces the various influences of both Homeric epics upon the *Aeneid*. Gordon Williams' *Tradition and Originality in Roman Poetry* (1968) contextualizes the work of Virgil within the Roman poetic tradition. Meanwhile, scholars such as Galinsky (*The Herakles Theme*, 1972) and Monti (*The Dido Episode and the* Aeneid, 1981) concentrate on how individual episodes effect the entire poem.

Near the end of the twentieth century, a slender tome edited by Charles Segal presented to the English-speaking world the research of an Italian scholar named Gian Biagio Conte. *The Rhetoric of Imitation* (1986) proved to be a landmark study with ramifications not just for Virgil but for Latin poetry in general. Conte's student, Alessandro Barchiesi, furthered the Italian influence on Virgilian scholarship, while the British are no less well represented, with contributions from Hardie, Harrison, Horsfall, and Mynors, to name but a few. Two scholars from New Zealand must also be mentioned: Richard Thomas, whose work on the *Georgics*, in particular, is profoundly influential and Denis Feeney. The latter scholar's *Gods in Epic* is of great value for considering the *Aeneid* as is his "The Taciturnity of Aeneas," *CQ* 33 (1983), 204–19, which, as few articles had before, offered new insights about the character of Virgil's hero. Finally, Galinsky's *Augustan Culture* (1996) provided a much needed overview of the cultural milieu of Virgil's life. These are merely a few of the works that have laid the groundwork for this study. I should also mention the bibliographical work of George E. Duckworth, Alexander G. McKay, and Shirley Werner.

Chapter 1

The following works should be considered, in addition to those cited in the footnotes, for my thoughts in the introductory chapter. Generally speaking, Niklas Holzberg's *Vergil* (2006) is a valuable resource and has given me much to think about. Jasper Griffin's *Virgil* (1986) has had similar effect.

On the codices of Virgil, see the discussion of further reading for Chapter 7; for the fate of Virgil in Christian hands, the contributions of Cameron, Shelton, Grafton, and others, cited in the footnotes are valuable.

Homer's importance to Virgil is fundamental. While Lansing's brief analysis of the first forty-eight words of the *Aeneid*'s prologue (*Vergilius* [2008] 3–8) is discussed in the introductory chapter, perhaps of wider importance is the distinction between Homeric primary epic and Virgilian secondary epic, about which one can read in C. S. Lewis' *A Preface to Paradise Lost* (1961). In this regard, Milman Parry's *The Making of Homeric Verse* (1971) remains vital for consideration of Homeric composition.

Regarding various influences on Virgil, the reader would do well to consult Ingo Gildenhard, "Virgil vs. Ennius, or: The Undoing of the Annalist," in Fitzgerald and Gowers, *Ennius Perennis* (2007). According to Porcius Licinius (recorded in Gellius, *Atticae Noctes* 17.21.44), Naevius first claimed to have brought the Greek Muse (sc. Homeric Muse) from Greece to Italy; cf. S. J. Harrison (ed.), *A Companion to Latin Literature* (London, 2005), 23. For later influences on Virgil, Lyne's "The Neoteric Poets" (*CQ* [1978]; rpt. in Gaisser, *Oxford Readings: Catullus* [2007], 109–40), is very useful. On Lucretius and Virgil, there are several important treatments, including Philip Hardie, *Virgil's* Aeneid: *Cosmos and*

Imperium (1986), 157–240, Joseph Farrell, *Vergil's* Georgics *and the Traditions of Ancient Epic* (1991), 169–206, and Monica Gale, *Virgil on the Nature of Things* (2000). On specific Lucretian allusions, see Julia Dyson's "Dido the Epicurean," *ClAnt* 15 (1996), 203–21 and Leah Kronenberg's "Mezentius the Epicurean," *TAPA* 135 (2005), 403–31. On Epicureanism and Virgil generally, cf. the contributions of Delattre and Gigante in the Armstrong/Fish/Johnston/Skinner collection, *Philodemus, Vergil and the Augustans* is important.

On Virgil's influence on Ovid, Hardie's "Ovid's Theban History," *CQ* 40 (1990), 224–35, remains a vital contribution. One could also see my 1997 Michigan monograph and, more recently, Sophia Papaioannou's *Epic Succession and Dissension: Ovid*, Metamorphoses *13.623–14.582 and the Reinvention of the* Aeneid (2005). For the influence of Greek tragedy on Virgil, see the fresh treatment by Vassiliki Panoussi, *Greek Tragedy in Vergil's* Aeneid (Cambridge, 2009).

Regarding the Harvard school, one may begin with Robert A. Brooks, *"Discolor aura*. Reflections on the Golden Bough," *AJPh* 76 (1953): "the *Aeneid* is a web of antithetic symbols, of tensions and oppositions never finally resolved" (276). Parry (1963) advanced this discussion as did Wendell Clausen, in his "An Interpretation of the *Aeneid*," *HSCP* (1964). One should also see M. C. J. Putnam's *The Poetry of the* Aeneid (1965). W. R. Johnson has persuasively argued (*MD* 2004) that the origins of "two voices" can be seen in Robert Lowell's "Falling Asleep over the *Aeneid*" published in 1947. Further, see Ernst Schmidt, "The Meaning of Vergil's *Aeneid:* American and German Approaches," *CW* 94 (2001), 145–71, and especially, Conte, *The Poetry of Pathos: Studies in Virgilian Epic*, ed. S. J. Harrison (Oxford, 2007), 150–69.

For "Model Reader" see Conte (1986), 30–1, and R. A. Smith, *Poetic Allusion and Poetic Embrace in Ovid and Virgil* (1997), 17–24. On the poetic rivalry of the *telchines*, see K. Spanoudakis, "Poets and Telchines in Callimachus' *Aetia*-Prologue," *Mnemosyne* 54 (2001), 425–41. For the importance of the *Argonautica* to the *Aeneid* see the seminal contribution of Damian Nelis, *Vergil's* Aeneid *and the* Argonautica *of Apollonius Rhodius* (2001).

Chapter 2

On the ancient lives of Virgil, the work of Brugnoli and Stok (*Vitae Vergilianae Antiquae* 1997) is fundamental. Horsfall offers a rich discus-

sion in his Brill *Companion to the Study of Virgil* (2000). T. Frank's
Vergil: A Biography (1922) could also be consulted, albeit judiciously.

On the late republican background, see e.g., Marcel Le Glay, Jean-
Louis Voisin, Yann Le Bohec, with D. Cherry and D. G. Kyle, tr. A.
Nevill, *A History of Rome* (3rd edn., 2005). Specifically on the Lex Julia
of 90 BC and the Lex Plautia Papiria of 89 BC, see T. Robert S. Broughton,
The Magistrates of the Roman Republic, vol. 2, *99 B.C.–31 B.C.* (1984).
For dating Virgil's early poetical works, see Kumaniecki's *"Quo ordine
Vergilii eclogae conscriptae sint,"* *Eos* 29 (1926), 69–79, as well as H. J.
Rose, *The* Eclogues *of Vergil* (1942), 251–2. On Sulla's *foedus* and Italian
voting rights, see Edward Bishpam, *From Asculum to Actium: The
Municipalization of Italy from the Social War to Augustus* (Oxford, 2007)
194.

On the confiscations of property in northern Italy, a primary source is
Appian, *Civil Wars* 5.2.12–17; see also Michael Winterbottom, "Virgil
and the Confiscations," *G&R* 23 (1976), 55–9, and Cary and Scullard's
A History of Rome (1975), 290f.

For the relationship of Antony and Cleopatra, Starr's discussion (*The
Emergence of Rome as Ruler of the Western World* [1955] 45–7) remains
useful; cf. also T. R. Holmes, *The Architect of the Roman Empire,* vol. 1
(1928), 227–31. These also touch on Antony's adolescent comportment,
as does my *Vergilius* article (2007), esp. 59–63, where several footnotes
offer further reading.

On Augustus' inscription of his Res Gestae, one should consult P. A.
Brunt and J. M. Moore, *Res Gestae Divi Augusti: The Achievements of
the Divine Augustus* (1967). Also F. W. Shipley, *Velleius Paterculus:
Compendium of Roman History and the Res Gestae Divi Augusti* (1924).

Regarding patronage, in addition to White, cited in the footnotes for
this chapter, Clarke's "Poets and Patrons at Rome," *G&R* 25 (1978),
46–54, remains useful. For Virgil's house on the Esquiline, Witherstine's
"Where the Romans Lived in the First Century B.C.," *CJ* 21 (1926),
566–79, is still relevant. Cf. also Horsfall (2000), 8f. On Virgil's connection with Maecenas and Maecenas' possible fall from grace, Gordon
Williams' "Did Maecenas 'Fall from Favor'? Augustan Literary Patronage,"
in Rauflaab and Toher, *Between Republic and Empire* (1990), 258–75,
is important, as is Peter White, "Maecenas' Retirement," *CP* 86 (1991),
130–8. Cf. also E. S. Lowell Bowditch, "Horace's Poetics of Political
Integrity: *Epistle* 1.18," *AJPh* 115 (1994), 409–26.

The inscription that speaks to Gallus' situation is found in Hermann
Dessau, *Inscriptiones Latinae Selectae* (rpt. 1979), III.2.8995 [= *CIL*

III.14147, 5]. J.-P. Boucher, *Caius Cornelius Gallus* (1966), 45, views the stele as a declaration of Octavian's political agenda. Further discussions of Virgil's relationship to Gallus include W. B. Anderson, "Gallus and the Fourth *Georgic*," *CQ* 27 (1933), 36–45; Robert Coleman, "Gallus, the *Bucolics*, and the Ending of the Fourth *Georgic*," *AJPh* 83 (1962), 55–71; J. Hermes, "C. Cornelius Gallus und Vergil. Das Problem der Umarbeitung des vierten Georgica-Buches" (diss., 1980); Loupiac, Annic, "Orphée-Gallus, figure de l'évolution morale et poétique de Virgile des *Bucoliques* à l'*Énéid*," *REL* 79 (2001), 93–103. Harriet I. Flower, whose work is always worth reading, discusses *damnatio memoriae* which pertains to Gallus' situation in *The Art of Forgetting* (2006).

Chapter 3

Regarding the way that Virgil crafted his collection of *Eclogues*, Van Sickle's thorough study, *The Design of Virgil's* Bucolics (2nd edn., 2004), remains seminal. Holzberg (2006), 87, views the arrangement of the collection to be three groups of three, with the tenth poem as a coda. Other important studies include Michael Putnam's *Virgil's Pastoral Art* (1970), Eleanor Leach's *Vergil's* Eclogues: *Landscapes of Experience* (1974), Paul Alpers' *The Singer of the* Eclogues (1979), David Halperin's *Before Pastoral* (1983), H. Seng's *Vergils Eklogenbuch* (1999), Brian Breed's *Pastoral Inscriptions* (2006), T. Saunders' *Bucolic Ecology* (2008), as well as Conte's classic discussion of *Eclogue* 10 in *The Rhetoric of Imitation* (1986).

On the title *Eclogues*, cf. Nicholas Horsfall, "Some Problems of Titulature in Roman Literary History," *BICS* 28 (1981), 103–14, and M. Geymonat, "Ancora sul titolo delle Bucoliche," *BICS* 29 (1982), 17f.

Regarding the antiquity of dactylic hexameter, see Henry M. Hoenigswald, "*Lipous' adroteta*, Elision, and Prosody," in Farrell and Rosen (eds.), *Nomodeiktes: Greek Studies in Honor of Martin Ostwald* (1993), 459–66. On genre more generally, see E. A. Schmidt, *Poetische Reflexion* (1972), 46, who discusses the amoebean (dialogic) format of the collection.

On the philosophical impulses and the interesting aspect of number(s) to the collection, see the sensible discussion of Van Sickle (2004), 209–13 *et passim*. Earlier interesting but more speculative studies include P. Maury, "Le secret de Virgile et l'architecture des Bucoliques," *Lettres d'Humanité* 3 (1944), 71–147; Jacques Perret, *Virgile* (1965). One could consult also the recent work of Antonio La Penna, *L'impossible giustifiazione della storia* (2005), who cautions against pressing the text too tightly vis-à-vis philosophical associations such as Stoicism, for example (297).

Titles, mentioned briefly in this chapter, that reflect the dualism of the *Eclogues* include the work of T. K. Hubbard, "Intertextual Hermeneutics in Vergil's Fourth and Fifth *Eclogues*," *CJ* 91 (1995/6), 11–23, as well as two articles of Charles Segal: "*Tamen cantabitis, Arcades*: Exile and Arcadia in *Eclogues* 1 and 9," *Arion* 4 (1965), 237–66, and "Pastoral Realism and the Golden Age: Correspondence and Contrast Between Virgil's Third and Fourth *Eclogues*," *Philologus* 121 (1977), 158–63. Others include Schmidt's "Freedom and Ownership: A Contribution to the Discussion of Vergil's First *Eclogue*," *PLLS* 10 (1998), 185–201, Leach's "Nature and Art in Vergil's Second *Eclogue*," *AJPh* 87 (1966), 427–45; MacDonald's "Dueling Contests: Theocritus and Vergil's Third and Seventh *Eclogues*," in Deroux (ed.), *Studies in Latin Literature and Roman History* 11, Collection Latomus 272 (Brussels, 2003), 199–207; Barry Powell, "*Poeta Ludens*: Thrust and Counter-Thrust in *Eclogue* 3," *ICS* 1 (1976), 113–21; Nisbet's "Virgil's Fourth *Eclogue*: Easterners and Westerners," *BICS* 25 (1978), 59–78; Paschalis' "*Semina ignis*: The Interplay of Science and Myth in the Song of Silenus," *AJPh* 122 (2001), 201–22; Sullivan's "*Et eris mihi magnus Apollo*: Divine and Earthly Competition in Vergil's Seventh *Eclogue*," *Vergilius* 48 (2002), 40–54; Baudy's "Hirtenmythos und Hirtenlied: Zu den rituellen Aspekten der bukolischen Dichtung," *Poetica* 25 (1993), 282–318; and Hardy's "Vergil's Epitaph for Pastoral: Remembering and Forgetting in *Eclogue* 9," *Syllecta Classica* 2 (1990), 29–38.

Clausen (ad 40) offers insight regarding Damoetas' knowledge of mathematicians: possibilities include the second-century astronomer Hipparchus, who explained the motions of the moon and the sun; Euctemon, Euclid, and even Hesiod. Also see Edwin L. Brown, "*Numeri Vergiliani*: Studies in 'Eclogues' *and* 'Georgics,'" Collection Latomus (1963), 88–92, and Wormell, "The Riddles in Virgil's Third *Eclogue*," *CQ* 54 (1960), 29–32. On prize cups much like those mentioned in *Eclogue* 3, see Ann L. Kuttner, *Dynasty and Empire in the Age of Augustus: The Case of the Boscoreale Cups* (1995). For a good discussion of the riddles, see Keith Dix, "Vergil in the Grynean Grove: Two Riddles in the Third Eclogue," *CP* 90 (1995), 256–62. On riddles in Roman comedy, see Eduard Fraenkel, *Plautine Elements in Plautus*, tr. Mueke and Drevikosky (Oxford, 2007).

On *Eclogues* 1 and 9, Syme, *The Roman Revolution* (1939), 153–6, offers some background information, as does Karl Galinsky, "Vergil and *Libertas*," *Vergilius* 52 (2006), 3–19. On movement to and from the city, cf. Van Sickle (2004), 184; Putnam (1970), 294; Leach (1974), 205. Cf. also Andrew Becker, "Poetry as Equipment for Living: A Gradual Reading of Vergil's Ninth *Eclogue*," *Classics Ireland* 6 (1999), 1–22, and Solodow, "*Poeta impotens*: The Last Three *Eclogues*," *Latomus* 36 (1977), 757–71, who aptly notes that in *Eclogue* 9 "the country is not merely a refuge from the city: it is a potential victim of it" (764). Also important is Hardy (1990), cited above and Brenk's "War and the Shepherd: The Tomb of Bianor in Vergil's Ninth *Eclogue*," *AJPh* 102 (1981), 427–30, as well as Sophia Papaioannou, "Losing my Mind: Memory Loss as Reflection of Political Insecurity in Vergil's *Eclogues*," *La Parola del Passato* 61 (2006), 11–20.

On Theocritus' seventh *Idyll* as a transition to the new genre of bucolic, see Kathryn Gutzwiller, *A Guide to Hellenistic Literature* (2007), 171. M. Fantuzzi and R. L. Hunter in *Tradition and Innovation in Hellenistic Poetry* (2004), regard the Bourina spring "parallel to Hesiod's Hippocrene" (147), noting how nymphs replace Muses (153–4). Also N. Krevans, "Geography and Literary Tradition in Theocritus 7," *TAPA* 113 (1983), 201–20. Cf. K. Spandouakis, "Callimachus Fr. 1.9–12 Again," *ZPE* 121 (1998), 59–61. A contrast between nymphs and Muses is made by Theocritus' character Simichidas at *Id.* 7.92–5. Nymphs, rather than Muses, are addressed at the close of Theocritus' *Idyll* (7.154). On the Tityran mode, cf. Van Sickle (2004), 187–8.

On *Eclogues* 2 and 8, Breed (2006), Putnam (1970), and Perutelli in Horsfall (2000). Van Sickle (2007), 154; also Clausen (1994), 233–6. Other studies include David Mankin, "The Addressee of Virgil's Eighth *Eclogue*: A Reconsideration," *Hermes* 116 (1988), 63–76, and Glenn W. Bowersock, "The Addressee of the Eighth *Eclogue*: A Response," *HSCPh* 82 (1978), 201–2. Van Sickle (2004), 134–5, sees Virgil progressing in *Eclogue* 8 from pastoral toward epic through tragic modes within the boundaries of the bucolic genre; cf. Van Sickle, 183.

On the name Alexis, cf. Van Sickle (2004), 125, n. 61, and especially James O'Hara, *True Names: Vergil and the Alexandrian Tradition of Etymological Wordplay* (Ann Arbor, 1996), 246; also, DuQuesnay in *Creative Imitation and Latin Literature* (ed. West and Woodman, 1979), 44.

On *Eclogues* 3 and 7, see M. Bettini, "Corydon, Corydon," *Studi classici e orientali* 21 (1972), 261–76. Van Sickle (2004), 177–8, suggests that Corydon's poetics prevail in the remaining *Eclogues*. It seems that the allusion to Theocritus exalts Corydon to the level of Daphnis. See also Hubbard (1998), 101; Putnam (1970), 251–2.

Of the vast bibliography of *Eclogue* 4, one could see Alpers (1979), 183, who connects this *Eclogue* with the *Aeneid*: "If it is not prophetic of the birth of Christ, it at least heralds the *Aeneid* in combining fine, self-conscious artistry." Alpers takes the child generally to symbolize the new age. Eleanor Winsor Leach, *Vergil's* Eclogues: *Landscapes of Experience* (1974) views the child as "an abstraction, a link to bind together the visionary world and the real" (225); see also Andreas Luther, *Historiche Studien zu den* Bucolica *Vergils* (2002), 16–17. On the poem's sense of destiny, see Eduard Norden, *Die Geburt des Kindes: Geschichte einer religiösen Idee* (1924), 61–4. On the age in which the child would be born, cf. Putnam (1970), 153–5; Leach (1974), 222, writes, "the new age brings forth a unique sign of accord between nature and man."

On the connection with the Ara Pacis, see David Castriota, *The Ara Pacis Augustae and the Imagery of Abundance in Later Greek and Early Roman Imperial Art* (1995), 122, 134; Servius notes on *colocasia*, that Virgil "wants this plant, which came to be known in Rome after he [Augustus] had conquered Egypt, to seem to have sprouted to Augustus' honor" (Servius, ad 4.20.2–5). Cf. the discussion of Alpers (1979), 187. Barbette Spaeth, "Ceres in the Ara Pacis and the Carthage Relief," *AJA* (1994), 65–100. Galinsky (1996), 106, sees the figure as "characterized by multiple associations." Further on polysemy in Virgil, see Richard Thomas, "A Trope by Any Other Name: 'Polysemy,' Ambiguity and *Significatio* in Virgil," *HSCP* 100 (2000), 381–407. See also Karl Galinsky's "Reading Roman Poetry in the 1990's," *CJ* 89 (1994), 297–309.

On the relationship of *Eclogues* 4 and 5, cf. Thomas K. Hubbard, "Intertextual Hermeneutics in Vergil's Fourth and Fifth *Eclogues*," *CJ* 91 (1995), 11–23. On the association of Pales with Rome, cf. Vinzenz Buchheit, *Der Anspruch des Dichters in Vergils* Georgika (1972), 90–2.

On *Eclogues* 6 and 10, see G. Williams (1968), 234f. Further on Orpheus, see Gutzwiller (2007), 171, and Conte's classic treatment in *The Rhetoric of Imitation* (1986), 120–3.

Chapter 4

In addition to those mentioned in the footnotes to this chapter, general studies that have shaped my understanding of the *Georgics* include Otis, *Virgil: A Study in Civilized Poetry* (1964); Wilkinson, *The* Georgics *of*

Virgil (1969); Boyle, *The Chaonian Dove: Studies in the* Eclogues, Georgics, *and* Aeneid *of Virgil* (1986); Putnam, *Virgil's Poem of the Earth: Studies in the* Georgics (1979); Miles, *Virgil's* Georgics (1980); Ross, *Virgil's Elements: Physics and Poetry in the* Georgics (1987); Farrell, (1991); Llewelyn Morgan, *Patterns of Redemption in Virgil's* Georgics (1999); Gale (2000); Horsfall (2000); Christopher Nappa, *Reading after Actium* (2005); Holzberg (2006); von Albrecht, *Vergil:* Bucolica, Georgica, Aeneis, *Eine Einführung* (2006).

Virgil alludes to Lucretius in book 1 and throughout the *Georgics*. For the particular allusions to the prologues to *DRN* 3 and 5, see Gale (2000), 26f. For other allusions, such as Virgil's use of Eratosthenes' *Hermes* or his adaptation of Varro's prose, cf. Richard Thomas' "Prose into Poetry: Tradition and Meaning in Virgil's *Georgics*," *HSCP* 91 (1987), 229–60, and his important "Virgil's *Georgics* and the Art of Reference," *HSCP* 90 (1986), 171–98.

A portion of the section title, "*Georgic 2: In uino, ciuitas*," is taken with permission of the editor, Patricia Johnston, from my "*In uino ciuitas:* The Rehabilitation of Bacchus in Virgil's *Georgics*," *Vergilius* 53 (2007), 53–87. On the ambiguous nature of human progress discussed in this section, cf. C. G. Perkell, "A Reading of Virgil's Fourth *Georgic*," *Phoenix* 32 (1978), 211–21. On the scolding of the vines, see Ross (1987), 128–30.

In my analysis of *Georgic 3*, I follow several scholars from Ross (1987), who made similar observations, to Heinz Hofmann, "Ovid's *Metamorphoses: Carmen Perpetuum, Carmen Deductum*," *Papers of the Liverpool Latin Seminar* 5 (1985), 223–42, for the use of the verb *deducere* as a coded expression. See also Stephen Hinds, *The Metamorphosis of Persephone: Ovid and the Self-Conscious Muse* (1987), 126f.

On book 3's prologue as a whole, see Thomas (1988), ad 3.1–48. Callimachus is of particular importance to this section, as Thomas shows in "Callimachus, the *Victoria Berenices*, and Roman Poetry," *CQ* 33 (1983), 92–113. This contribution and other important articles by Thomas can be found in *Reading Virgil and His Texts* (Ann Arbor, 1999). For the phrase "Caesar ... in the middle," see Kytzler, " 'In medio mihi Caesar erit' III: zu den Zentren der Eclogen Vergils," *Journal of Ancient Civilization* 9 (1994), 75–81, Thomas (1988), ad 3.7–8, Wilkinson (1969), 170f., and Kofler, *Aeneas und Vergil* (Heidelberg, 2004), 47–9. For the breaking down of the boundary between man and animal in book 3, see Thomas (1988), ad 215–16. Holzberg (2007), 113–15, also has a rich analysis of animals in the third book; on their death, G. Williams (1968), 676–9, and David West, "Two Plagues: Virgil, *Georgics* 3.478–566 and Lucretius 6.1090–1286," in West and Woodman, *Creative Imitation and Latin Literature* (1974), 71–88.

For book 4, important contributions include Christine Perkell's 1978 article, cited above, and her "On the Corycian Gardener of Vergil's Fourth *Georgic*," *TAPA* 111 (1981), 167–77, as well as Thomas' "The Old Man Revisited," *MD* 29 (1992), 35–70. Further on Orpheus as nightingale, Emily Katz Anhalt, "A Matter of Perspective: Penelope and the Nightingale in *Odyssey* 19.512–534," *CJ* 97 (2001), 145–59.

Regarding the unlikelihood that the Aristeus section of *G.* 4 was originally dedicated to Gallus, cf. G. P. Goold, "Servius and the Helen Episode," *HSCP* 74 (1970), 137. On the term window reference, see Thomas (1986). I owe the observation about the four windows of *G.* 4's epilogue being a "literal" window reference to Sophia Papaiouannou.

Chapter 5

There are numerous outstanding studies of the *Aeneid*. Among general contributions, Holzberg's recent brief but solid treatment stands out, as does that of Horsfall (2000) and the Perkell collection, *Reading Virgil's Aeneid: An Interpretive Guide* (1999). Beyond these there is a vast sea of scholarship, a small sample of which is discussed below or in the chapter's endnotes.

I open my discussion by touching upon how the *Aeneid* begins with the end in mind; on the poem's teleology, see Klingner, *Virgil: Bucolica, Georgica, Aeneis* (Stuttgart, 1967), 383; cf. Heinze (1993), 384f. As I consider the notion of Aeneas as a suffering hero, I have in mind the ideas of L. R. Lind, *Vergil's Aeneid* (1963), xv; Francis Sullivan, "Virgil and the Mystery of Suffering," *AJPh* 90 (1969), 161–77, as well as the contribution of Philip Hardie, "The *Aeneid* and the *Oresteia*," *PVS* 20 (1991), 29–45.

For Aeneas' emotional state and character, cf. Viktor Pöschl, *The Art of Vergil: Image and Symbol in the* Aeneid (1962), 40f., 93; Anderson (rpt. 1989), 21; Galinsky, "The Anger of Aeneas," *AJPh* 109 (1988), 321–48; R. O. A. M. Lyne, "Vergil and the Politics of War," *CQ* 33 (1983), 188–203; and Eve Adler, *Vergil's Empire: Political Thought in the* Aeneid (2003), 77–101.

Book 1's ecphrasis of the Juno temple rehearses much epic background. On this topic see Putnam, *Virgil's Epic Designs: Ekphrasis in the*

Aeneid (1998) and Fowler's often-cited article "Narrate and Describe: The Problem of Ekphrasis," *JRS* 81 (1991), 25–35; cf., too, Fowler's "Deviant Focalization in Vergil's *Aeneid*," *PCPS* 216 (1990), 42–63; also Putnam, "Daedalus, Virgil, and the End of Art," *AJPh* 108 (1987), 173–98, as well as my thoughts about ecphrasis in my 1997 monograph, 26–43.

On the banquet scene in Dido's palace and the gift exchange therein, cf. Roy K. Gibson, "Aeneas as *Hospes* in Vergil, *Aeneid* 1 and 4," *CQ* 49 (1999), 184–202; on the significance of exchange in the *Aeneid* generally, see the excellent new study by Neil Coffee, *The Commerce of War: Exchange and Social Order in Latin Epic* (2009), 39–114.

In book 2, Virgil evokes the description of Troy from the *Iliad*; cf. Erik Wistrand, "Virgil's Palaces in the *Aeneid*," *Klio* 38 (1960), 146–54. The description of Priam as paralleling Pompey's fate, cf. Servius, who suggests (ad *Aen.* 2.557.2f.) that *ingens* (huge) is a pun on *Pompeius Magnus* (Pompey "the Great"). Cf. O'Hara (1996), 134 and Williams (1983), 196.

On the authenticity of book 2's Helen episode, cf. Heinze (1993), 25f.; Gian Biagio Conte, *The Rhetoric of Imitation*, ed. Ch. Segal (1986), 196–207; Jeffrey Fish, "Anger, Philodemus' Good King, and the Helen Episode of *Aeneid* 2.567–89," in D. Armstrong, J. Fish, P. A. Johnston, and M. B. Skinner, *Vergil, Philodemus and the Augustans* (Austin, 2004), 110–38.

For book 3, Horsfall's commentary (2006) is invaluable. Regarding the power of past memories in the book, see David Quint's "Painful Memories: *Aeneid* III and the Problem of the Past," *CJ* 78 (1982), 30–8; also, his *Epic and Empire: Politics and Generic Form from Virgil to Milton* (1993), 53–65; also Grace Starry West, "Andromache and Dido," *AJPh* 104 (1983), 257–67. For the name games in this book, cf. H. Mørland, "Zu den Namen in der Aeneis," *SO* 36 (1960), 21–9, and O'Hara (1996), 142. On the first omen in Italy (i.e., that of the four white horses), see Neil Coffee, *The Commerce of War: Exchange and Social Order in Latin Epic*, (2009), 39–41, as well as Sarah Spence, "The Polyvalence of Pallas in the *Aeneid*," *Arethusa* 32 (1999), 149–63.

The disjunctive partitioning of book 4 was noted over a century ago by A. J. Bell, "Virgil and The Drama," *The School Review* 13 (1905), 458–74. More recently, cf. Niklas Holzberg, *Vergil: Der Dichter und Sein Werk* (2006), 65, 150f.; Lee Fratantuono, *Madness Unchained: A Reading of Virgil's Aeneid* (2007), 99. A brilliant article treats the flames of books 2 and 4, namely Bernard Knox, "The Serpent and the Flame: The Imagery of the Second Book of the *Aeneid*," *AJPh* 71 (1950), 379–400. On Anna's intervention and the interruption of Aeneas' mission, a useful contribution is that of Steven Farron, "The Aeneas–Dido Episode as an Attack on Aeneas' Mission and Rome," *G&R* 27 (1980), 34–47. On the possibility that Aeneas could have granted Dido's request for more time, see Sergio Casali, "Staring at the Pun: 'Aeneid' 4.435–6 Reconsidered," *CJ* 95 (2000), 103–18.

On Aeneas' national identity as it pertains to his movement toward Latium, see the fine contribution of Joël Thomas, *Structures de l'imaginaire dans l'*Enéide (Paris, 1981), 270f. On the names and the families of book 5, see O'Hara (1996), 159f.; also Kevin Muse, "Sergesthus and Tarchon in the *Aeneid*," *CQ* 57 (2007), 586–605, who connects Virgil's naming in book 5 with Varro's *De familiis Troianis* (591f.); cf. W. Nicoll, "Chasing Chimeras," *CQ* 35 (1985), 134–9, and Wilhelm Schultze, *Zur Geschichte lateinischer Eigennamen* (1904), 424. Servius, ad 117.3 says the gens Gegania claimed Gyas. Nicoll (1985), 138f., suggests a connection with Antony. On the lack of national origin in the final competitions in Sicily, cf. Williams (1972), ad 492. Jay Reed, *Virgil's Gaze* (2007), discusses the blending of ethnic identity, while Michael Paschalis' contribution about proper names is also valuable (*Virgil's* Aeneid: *Semantic Relations and Proper Names*, 1997), esp. 197–201. Further studies include C. Weber, "Some Double Entendres in Ovid and Vergil," *CP* 85 (1990), 209–14; James J. O'Hara, "Etymological Wordplay in Apollonius of Rhodes, *Aeneid* 3 and *Georgics* 1," *Phoenix* (1990), 370–6. On general etymological notions, cf. O'Hara (1996), 71–3. Georgia Nugent, "Vergil's Voice of the Women in *Aeneid* V," *Arethusa* 25 (1992), 255–92, sees women as the "quintessential other" misunderstood by males. Regarding Virgil's debt to Euripides' *Troades*, cf. the now very old contribution of May Johnson, "Vergil's Debt to the *Hecuba* and *Troades* of Euripides," *CW* 3 (1909), 50–2. The presentation of Palinurus' death in the *Aeneid* is problematical; cf. Aldo Setaioli, "Palinuro: genesi di un personaggio poetico," *BStudLat* 27 (1997), 56–81; Frederick Brenk, "*Unum pro multis caput*: Myth, History, and Symbolic Imagery in Vergil's Palinurus Incident," *Latomus* 43 (1984), 776–801. On Palinurus' name, cf. Philip Ambrose, "The Etymology and Genealogy of Palinurus," *AJPh* 101 (1980), 449–57.

From the many works of scholarship on book 6, I mention here but a few. J. E. G. Zetzel's contribution, "Romane Memento: Justice and judgment in *Aeneid* 6," *TAPA* 119 (1989), 263–84, is important for the entire katabasis. On the strangely allusive words of Aeneas when he encounters Dido in the Underworld, see my 1993 article, esp. 310–13; Susan Skulsky, "'Inuitus, Regina ...': Aeneas and the Love of Rome," *AJPh* 106 (1985), 447–55; Suzanna Braund, "Speech, Silence and Personality: The Case of Aeneas and Dido," *PVS* 23 (1998), 129–47. It should go well beyond the scope of the study to seek to disentangle the many philosophical and theological strands that Virgil has woven together to form his unique version of reincarnation. Some studies include J. Bews, "Philosophical Relevation and Its Function in *Aeneid* 6," in Bonanno and Vella (ed.), *Laurea Corona: Studies in Honour of Edward Coleiro* (1989), 91–8; Susanna Morton Braund, "Virgil and the Cosmos: Religious and Philosophical Ideas," in Martindale (ed.), *The Cambridge Companion to Vergil* (1997), 204–21; John Ferguson, "Vergil and Philosophy," *PVS* 19 (1988), 17–29; Thomas Habinek, "Science and Tradition in *Aeneid* 6," *HSCP* 92 (1989), 223–55; Joseph Kivuila-Kiaku, "Poésie, prophétie et rêve dans l'*Énéide* VI ou La 'philosophie du destin romain' dans l'imaginaire virgilien," *LEC* 65 (1997), 49–64. On the precedent of monarchy for Roman rule, cf. Francis Cairns, *Virgil's Augustan Epic* (Cambridge, 1989), 61f. For the question about the gate through which Aeneas departs the Underworld, cf. Williams (1972), ad 893–94; also, Robert Brooks' article in *AJPh* (1953), 260–80, cited above. Anderson's *The Art of the* Aeneid (1969; rpt. 1989), remains insightful (cf. 62).

Scholarship on book 7 is less prolific than that of the sixth book. Holzberg's recent book (2006) is important, for he deemphasizes the division of the poem into Odyssean and Iliadic halves, emphasizing instead Aeneas as an Odysseus figure throughout the poem. With regard to Virgil's choice of inspiration for the second half, Servius (ad 7.37) quips on Erato, "pro Calliope"; see Sara Mack, "The Birth of War: A Reading of *Aeneid* 7," in Perkell (1999), 129. On Celaeno, cf. O'Hara, *Death and Optimistic Prophecy in Vergil's* Aeneid (1990), 25.

The ecphrasis of book 8 and the Hercules' saga have each spawned much scholarship. On the story of Hercules and Cacus, see Galinsky, "The Hercules–Cacus Episode in *Aeneid* VIII," *AJPh* 87 (1966), 18–51. On the Homeric model for the shield, see Knauer (1964).

The focus of scholarship for book 9 tends toward the Nisus and Euryalus episode; for its Homeric echoes as interpreted by Hellenistic commentators, cf. Robin Schlunk, *The Homeric Scholia and the* Aeneid: *A Study of the Influence of Ancient Literary Criticism on Vergil* (Ann

Arbor, 1974), 59–81. Cf. also, Alessandro Barchiesi, *La traccia del modello* (1984), 43–52, and Steven Farron, *Vergil's* Aeneid: *A Poem of Grief and Love* (Leiden, 1993), 19–24.

The key work of scholarship on book 10 is Stephen Harrison's remarkable commentary (1991). On Juno and Jupiter (and the latter's concern for power and reputation), see Julia Hejduk, "Jupiter's *Aeneid*: *Fama* and *Imperium*," *CA* 28 (2009), 279–327; on Turnus' pursuit of Pallas, cf. Barchiesi (1984), 11–16. The five Homeric lion similes that describe Mezentius are drawn from *Iliad* 3.23–28, 12.299–301, 17.61f., *Odyssey* 6.130–40, 22.402–8; on which, see Harrison (1991), ad 723–9.

The best general piece on book 11 is that of W. S. Anderson, "*Aeneid* 11: The Saddest Book," in Perkell (1999), 195–209. Other treatments of various incidents in the book include that of Dennis Pausch, "*hi nostri reditus exspectatique triumphi?* Die Heimkehr des Pallas zwischen pompa funebris und pompa triumphalis (Verg. *Aen.* 11.1–99)," in Helmut Krasser, Dennis Pausch, Ivana Petrovic (ed.), *Triplici invectus triumpho: Der roemische Triumph in augusteischer Zeit* (2008), 239–64. Cf. Conte (2007), 45. On the speeches in the book, cf. Elaine Fantham, "Fighting Words: Turnus at Bay in the Latin Council (*Aeneid* 11.234–446)," *AJPh* 120 (1999), 259–80, Anderson (rpt. 1989), 89f. and my own 2005 monograph, 135f. On Camilla's fatal mistake, Hardie (1994), 26; cf. Valeria Viparelli, "Camilla: A Queen Undefeated, Even in Death," *Vergilius* 54 (2008), 9–23, esp. 22f.

Despite Virgil's sympathetic portrayal of Turnus and the sometimes brutal nature of Aeneas' battlefield deportment, book 12 ultimately reaches the *telos* layed out in *Aeneid* 1's prologue, providing Rome with a clear inception in Turnus' death. On these themes, see Hardie, *Virgil's* Aeneid: *Cosmos and Imperium* (1986), 154, and Smith (2005), 128–75. On Lavinia's appearance, see R. Todd, "Lavinia Blushed," *Vergilus* 26 (1980), 27–33; Julia Dyson, "Lilies and Violence: Lavinia's Blush in the Song of Orpheus," *CP* 94 (1999), 281–8; R. O. A. M. Lyne, "Lavinia's Blush: Virgil *Aeneid* 12.64–70," *G&R* 30 (1983), 55–64; Dorothea Woodworth, "Lavinia: An Interpretation," *TAPA* 61 (1930), 175–94. On Turnus' pursuit of the wounded Aeneas, see Barchiesi (1984), 91–122. For an insightful treatment of ritual aspects of the battle between Aeneas and Turnus, see Dyson (2001), 196f. *et passim.*

On the term *Kollectivgedict* cf. Edgar Martini, "Ovid und seine Bedeutung für die römische Poesie," 165–94, in *Epitymbion Heinrich Swoboda dargebracht* (1927), 167–8 and Brooks Otis, "Ovid and the Augustans," *TAPA* 69 (1938), 188–229.

Chapter 6

The best discussion of manuscripts in English remains that of L. D. Reynolds and N. G. Wilson, *Scribes and Scholars: A Guide to the Transmission of Greek and Latin Literature* (3rd edn., 1991). See also Colin H. Roberts and T. C. Skeet, *The Birth of the Codex* (1983).

On the spelling of Virgil's name, one should begin with Poliziano, *Miscellenea* 1.77. Scholarly discussion includes Pedro Martín Baños, "De Virgilius a Vergilius: Poliziano y la Bibliografía de Antonio de Nebrija," *Revista de Filología Española* 87 (2007), 79–102; Manlio P. Stocchi, "Polizano," in *Virgilio: Enciclopedia Virgiliana,* ed. Francesco della Corte (1984), 172. Anthony Grafton, "On the Scholarship of Politian and Its Context," *Journal of the Warburg and Courtauld Institutes* 40 (1977), 150–88. See also Holzberg (2006), 12f.

On the transition from scroll to codex, see Reynolds and Wilson (1991), 22–34, who call attention to the apparent Pauline reference to the codex in 2 Timothy 4:13. Also, see Roberts and Skeet (1983), 35. On manuscript pages, cf. C. R. Gregory, "The Quires in Greek Manuscripts" *AJPh* 7 (1886), 27–32. The best Latin editions of Virgil are those of R. A. B. Mynors, *P. Vergili Maronis Opera* (1969) and that of Geymonat (1973), who offers an extensive critical apparatus. Other important editions are those of Ribbeck, *Prolegomena critica ad P. Vergili Maronis opera maiora* (1866), Sabbadini (1930–1), and E. Saint-Denis and R. Lesueur, *Virgile:* Bucoliques (1999); idem, *Virgile:* Géorgiques (1995); and Jacques Perret and R. Lesueur, *Virgile:* Énéide (2002, in three volumes). On emendation and recension, see Fredrick Hall, *A Companion to Classical Texts* (rpt. 1988), 108–98.

On the revival of classical texts among Renaissance intellectual élite, cf. Julia Haig Gaisser, *Catullus and his Renaissance Readers* (1993); Craig Kallendorf, *Virgil and the Myth of Venice: Books and Readers in the Italian Renaissance* (1999), and his *In Praise of Aeneas: Virgil and Epideictic Rhetoric in the Early Italian Renaissance* (1989).

On the familiar pose of Theseus in Pompeian painting, cf. Smith (2005), 152f. Cf. A. Van Buren, "A Medallion of Antoninus Pius," *JRS* 1 (1911), 187–95.

Chapter 7

For Virgil's *Nachleben,* the recent contribution of M. C. J. Putnam and Jan M. Ziolkowski, *The Virgilian Tradition: the First Fifteen Hundred*

Years (2008) is of the utmost importance. One should also see the valuable contribution of Theodore Ziolkowski, *Virgil and the Moderns* (1993).

For Virgil in antiquity, see Siegmar Döpp, "Vergilrezeption in der ovidischen 'Aeneis'," *RhM* 134 (1991), 327–46; idem, *Virgilischer Einfluß im Werk Ovids* (1968); Sophia Papaioannou, *Redesigning Achilles: "Recycling" the Epic Cycle in the "Little Iliad" (Ovid,* Metamorphoses *12.1–13.622)* (2007); Smith, *Poetic Allusion and Poetic Embrace in Ovid and Virgil* (1997). Also Hardie, *The Epic Successors of Virgil* (1993).

For how certain characters in later epics are based on Virgilian originals, such as Theseus and Aeneas, cf. J. Burgess, *"Pietas* in Virgil and Statius," *PVS* 11 (1971–2), 48–61. Further on the cento, see Hans Armin Gärtner and Wolf-Lüder Liebermann, "Cento," *New Pauly* 3 (2008), and Scott McGill, *Virgil Recomposed* (2005) *passim.*

On Sedulius and Virgil, see Antonino Grillo, "La presenza di Virgilio in Sedulio, poeta parafrastico," in R. Chevallier (ed.), *Présence de Virgile: Actes du Colloque des 9, 11, et 12 Décembre 1976* (1978), 185–94. For St. Augustine's debt to Virgil, see Carol Ramage, "The Confessions of St. Augustine: The *Aeneid* Revisited," *PCPh* 5 (1970), 54–60; Sabine MacCormack, *The Shadows of Poetry: Vergil in the Mind of Augustine* (1998), 97–9; James J. O'Donnell, *Augustine: A New Biography* (2005); also idem, *The Confessions* (1992), ad V.8.15, 307f. On Tasso's allusion to Virgil, Torquato Tasso, *Jerusalem Delivered: An English Prose Version*, tr. and ed. Ralph Nash (1987), xii. See also Vladimiro Zabughin, *Vergilio nel Rinascimento Italiano da Dante a Torquato Tasso: Fortuna, Studi, Imitazione, Traduzione e Parodie, Iconographia*, 2 vols. (2000). For Spencer's debt to Virgil, one can consult John Watkins, *The Specter of Dido: Spenser and Virgilian Epic* (1995). On Milton and Virgil, see David Quint's *Epic and Empire: Politics and Generic Form from Virgil to Milton* (1993) and Colin Burrow's *Epic Romance: Homer to Milton* (1993), as well as Burrow's "Virgils, from Dante to Milton," in Martindale (1997), 79–90; further, see the superb contribution of Kallendorf, "Allusion as Reception: Virgil, Milton, and the Modern Reader," in Martindale and Thomas (eds.), *Classics and the Uses of Reception* (London, 2006), 67–79.

On Virgil and Rabelais Lucienne Deschamps, "Virgilio nell'opera di Rabelais," in Marcello Gigante (ed.), *La Fortuna di Virgilio* (1986), 195–206. For Virgil and Paul Scarron, see Luigi de Nardis, "Virgilio 'deriso' in Francie nel xvii secolo," in Gigante (1986), 196f. On the neuming of Virgil's text in the middle ages, see Jan Ziolkowski, *Nota bene: Reading Classics and Writing Melodies in the Early Middle Ages* (Turnhout, 2007).

For Virgil in art, one should consult the useful work of Jane Reid, *The Oxford Guide to Classical Mythology in the Arts, 1300–1990s* (Oxford, 1993).

Index